WITH H.M. 9TH LANCERS.

Dedicated to the Memory

OF THE GALLANT

OFFICERS AND MEN OF H.M. 9TH LANCERS,

WHO

PROVED THEMSELVES HEROES DURING

THE INDIAN MUTINY.

WITH H.M. 9TH LANCERS

DURING THE

INDIAN MUTINY

THE LETTERS OF
BREVET-MAJOR O. H. S. G. ANSON

EDITED BY HIS SON,
HARCOURT S. ANSON

The Naval & Military Press Ltd

published in association with

FIREPOWER
The Royal Artillery Museum
Woolwich

Published by
The Naval & Military Press Ltd
Unit 10 Ridgewood Industrial Park,
Uckfield, East Sussex,
TN22 5QE England
Tel: +44 (0) 1825 749494
Fax: +44 (0) 1825 765701
www.naval-military-press.com

in association with

FIREPOWER
The Royal Artillery Museum, Woolwich
www.firepower.org.uk

The Naval & Military Press

MILITARY HISTORY AT YOUR FINGERTIPS

... a unique and expanding series of reference works

Working in collaboration with the foremost regiments and institutions, as well as acknowledged experts in their field, N&MP have assembled a formidable array of titles including technologically advanced CD-ROMs and facsimile reprints of impossible-to-find rarities.

PREFACE.

THE writer of the letters herein set forth was Brev.-
Major O. H. S. G. Anson, H.M. 9th Lancers. They
were written to his wife, who was at Kussowlee. At
the commencement of the Mutiny he was in command of a squadron of that regiment, and, during
subsequent operations, he was at intervals in command of the regiment itself. When the Mutiny
broke out he had already seen some twenty years'
service in India, and had fought at the battle of Pun-
niar, and at Sobraon, in the Sutlej campaign, and at
Goojerat and Chilianwallah in 1849. It is perhaps
needless to say that the letters were not intended
for publication ; it has, however, been thought that
the extracts given would be acceptable to a wider
circle than that of the family, and that some incidents
necessarily omitted from works dealing with the campaign in general, but here related, would not be without interest to the relatives and friends of those concerned.

It cannot be supposed that letters written under
the trying circumstances of those days of trouble

should in every case say all that might have been
said, or even be always accurate in statement. It
has been the compiler's endeavour to avoid printing
anything that might seem to be unwarranted in
criticism ; at the same time, many of the facts in
connection with the Indian Mutiny were ugly facts
and as such have been described.

Major Anson's last day's work was twelve hours
on horseback in front of Lucknow, on 6th March,
1858, which, in his own words, strained him all over,
and made him feel something like a wreck. Although
he was able soon after to take rest, he never really
recovered from the illness brought on by the wear
and tear of the campaign. He died at Dehra Doon,
on 14th January, 1859, aged forty-one years.

H. S. A.

WITH H.M. 9TH LANCERS DURING THE INDIAN MUTINY.

CAMP PANIPUT,
June 1st, 1857.

I am sitting on my charpoy under a canopy rigged up by the bearer, and a very effective one it is ; but writing is rather difficult in the posture I am obliged to assume. Three days ago it was 112 degrees in my shuldaree, and yesterday it must have been some degrees more. After our short nine and a half miles' march this morning I went to see Colonel Herbert, and found him quite well and looking an old veteran all over, with plenty of grey whisker. He marches about 7 p.m. every march day, arrives between 10 and 11 at his next encamping ground ; no tents are pitched—the men just unload their bedding and lie upon it all night. I hardly know what to say of the practice. It compels an early dinner at $3\frac{1}{2}$, when it is too hot to eat and drink with any relish, but as far as the men are concerned it is, I daresay, a comfortable plan, but I have strong doubts. Some rascals looted my buggy and servants about two miles out of Kurnal. I lost a bridle, blanket, and other trifles.

B

The servants lost money, and the syce's wife her jewels. The servants are very attentive, and I have nothing to complain of. I have promised Jones a cup of tea of a morning till his things come up. Hope* and Hamilton left us at 6 p.m. yesterday for a ride of forty-two miles to the place where our three squadrons, some guns and Irregulars are protecting a bridge some twenty miles from Delhi, where the Meerut force are expected to cross and join us. Soon after leaving Meerut, they had an engagement with the enemy, who wanted to stop their progress. The Carabineers had again warm work to do against the Sappers, who, it is said, fought well against us. I should not wonder if Hope's force had a skirmish with the rogues. Yesterday evening, while Martin (75th) and Fagan were destroying a bridge over the Jumna, some two or three miles from camp, they were attacked by between two and three hundred, who fired three volleys into them without touching either. A small Infantry force from camp was sent against them, and they ran away. All but two or three wells at Delhi have been poisoned by dead bodies having been thrown into them, and fears are entertained lest we may be sadly incommoded for want of water. Poor House was obliged to leave mess yesterday evening, he felt so ill. I drink a good bottle of beer mixed with water at dinner and a glass of sherry and soda-water during the day, besides oceans of tea and toast-and-water. One must keep up the system this hot weather but it is fatal to overdo it, especially with brandy.

* Sir Hope Grant,

CAMP SIRSOWLEE,
June 2nd.

It is about 12 noon, and having had some sleep and received yours of Sunday, I will just write you a few lines while I can. Pen and ink are out of the question. You have no idea what an awful day this is in camp in a shuldaree; cool and pleasant enough, I dare say, in a double-pole tent, with tatties and punkahs. There is a furious hot wind blowing, raising up clouds of dust on the hard, dusty plain we are encamped on. Everything inside is a mass of dirt and dust. I cannot bear being always at mess, much prefer my company to the society of those I care little about. Young G—— and J—— are not of the most agreeable disposition, Evans* and Smith are much nicer fellows. I am so glad Mrs. Grant sent me back "Christian Retirement." It is the greatest possible comfort to me; I do not know of any book that I am fonder of. These double marches are very trying for the servants, who have done their duty hitherto exceedingly well. Norman was dining with young Grant yesterday evening, and told us that Colonel C—— was fast becoming useless, and was thinking of returning to Kurnal, where will be our most important sick depôt and magazine during this fearful campaign. The general's horse is the grandest catch possible for me: he steps out nobly, carries me handsomely, and has made the march, such as it is, endurable. A low caste people, going by the name of Goojurs, have been very cruel and mischievous.

* Lieut.-Colonel Evans, V.C.

Reed with his Deyra Regiment, is giving a handsome account of them with sword and fire. House is rather better, but very shaky.

CAMP SIRSOWLEE (three marches from Delhi),
June 2nd, 1857.

We made a forced march here this morning from Paniput, distance twenty-two miles. Having been unable to have a good sleep for three days, I felt very much fatigued. Besides, we missed our mess tea half way, and I had only a small cup given me by the Artillery. We marched all night, *i.e.*, from 10 p.m. till 5½ a.m. A hot wind was blowing for some hours, parching our throats and expending our strength pretty considerably. To-morrow we join Hope's force at Raee, where we have to punish a village for harbouring mutineers, and disgraceful conduct to one of our poor ladies. There was a tremendous fire in the Meerut direction, raging all night. The Meerut force have completely defeated the mutineers, who came out to meet them on the banks of the Hindan, and taken four heavy guns and one 24-pounder howitzer. We hope soon to be at them. It is much feared that some European lives have been sacrificed at Hansi and Hissar. Poor Mowatt is dead.

CAMP RAEE (about twenty-two miles from Delhi),
Wednesday, June 3rd, 1857.

Here we came this morning, eleven miles from Serrowlee, and here we found our three squadrons and all pretty well, thank God, but Goldie, who is but just convalescent from a formidable liver attack, which has reduced him two or three stones. Upton looks very well, but very thin. Martin gave me a cup of tea, and made me a polite speech about all your kindness to his wife. What a nice thing it is to be able to be kind to people.

Close to camp this morning we met the force of our ally, the Rajah of Jheend Bahadoor, infantry, cavalry, and artillery, on their march to burn a village said to harbour some plunder. I gave Evans, Jones, and Smith leave to go and see the fun, which turned out poor after all, the place being full of grain. The five men who abused and stripped some of our women who were escaping from Delhi were hung upon a tree here yesterday. I have little doubt but that our Jemadar of Syces will, when tried, share the same fate. Brigadier Halifax died at Kurnal, and Showers has joined in his place. Poor Mrs. Mowatt and Mrs. Halifax! how completely have their husbands been sacrificed by these troublous times. I do not know whether we halt here or not to-day, most probably we shall, so as to enable the Meerut force to join us. They have had another and more serious fight, which lasted five hours. Lieutenant Perkins, Artillery, and Captain Andrews, H.M. 60th, were killed ; 500 of the mutineers were killed. Six thousand Sepoys and 4,000 Loswallas turned out against Wilson, who gave them a handsome licking. Hope and Hamilton got over their long ride wonderfully well, and the former will not take less than 500 (rupees?) for his Heratee

horse. Hope is very thin. He works like a Trojan.
I hope he will not knock up. We are pitched in a
dense jungle. We cannot remain in it with any
safety, so I have no doubt we shall move ten miles
on to-night.

CAMP ALIPORE (eleven miles from Delhi),
June 4th, 1857.

We marched here this morning, and will probably
halt here two or three days to admit of the joining
of the Meerut force and the siege-train. We are
protecting the flanks of the army, and the 1st and
4th Squadrons and Headquarters are on the left, the
2nd in advance protecting a bridge, and the 3rd is
on the right flank. We cluster round the mess-tent
like bees round a hive. There were eleven more
villagers hung yesterday, to the great delight of
Fawcett, Blair, and Evans, who nearly forfeited their
dinner for the butchery. Hope had to approve of
their sentence, and gave directions about a strong
enough rope just before he sat down. The Jemadar of Syces is to be tried to-day, and will most
probably be hung before sunset. All this is very
horrid work, preceding as it does the blood-stained
horrors of the battle-field. We are living in critical
times, and must never depend on natives again. I
am very sorry to say that the bearer met with a bad
accident this morning. I can ill bear the loss of his
valuable and attentive services. I thought Martin
was going to be very ill last night. He called up the
doctor (Smith), C—— having refused to go, because
Smith was so much nearer him.

CAMP ALIPORE,
June 7th, 1857.

I do hope and trust this will find you well again. I cannot bear to think of your being ill, and with so much to do as you have. You are sensible and religious enough, I know, not to feel unwarrantable anxiety about me. I have the liveliest joy and trust in my precious Saviour, and pray to Him daily to give me grace and strength not to fear what man may do unto me. What a sweet, precious bond is community of religious principle and sentiment. I do find the greatest comfort and consolation in my Bible. I am reading Job, Gospel of St. John, and Hebrews, and drink in grace, mercy, and peace every morning. I find that, away from the softening influence of female society, I am naturally of a proud, fierce, rebellious spirit, which requires constant curbing. The Umballa siege-train arrived this morning with a squadron of the 4th Lancers. Brigadier Wilson, who is much prized as a gallant, clear-headed officer, is in camp. His force joins us to-morrow. The general idea seems to be that, after defeating the enemy, who have strongly entrenched themselves outside Delhi, Delhi itself will be razed to the ground, a fate which it has well long deserved, having long been the focus of intrigue and rebellion. Lord Canning says that the mutineers have but little to do with this affair, that they are only a kind of scape-goat, but that it is a regular Mussulman plot to oust India from us. Yule joined us this morning, and has relieved me, I am thankful to say, of the responsibilities of command. He had got as far as Poonah, when he met

some Artillerymen, who gave him the news which
induced his immediate return by forced marches and
mail-cart from Jullundur to this.   There was another
breeze at mess last night between F——, M——, and
B——, and I got well scolded for not interfering to
shut up the disputants, who quarrelled vehemently
after leaving mess, and were all taken to Hope's tent
to have the matter settled.   There are supposed to be
thirty-seven lacs in Delhi, and we have a number of
friends in the place who mean to afford us every
assistance in their power.   A canal sergeant and his
wife and family were the only people murdered at
Hansi, and a quartermaster-sergeant's wife, of the
name of Stafford, at Hissar; but the fate of the
Wedderburns and others, who shut themselves up in
the fort, is very uncertain.   I was in Hope's tent
the day before yesterday.   I found it very cool and
pleasant, and he was as happy and well as possible,
saying that he found it cooler out here than in
Cantonments.

CAMP ALIPORE,
Sunday, June 7th.

Here I am on main picquet, without Irregulars to
assist me, and some of the enemy within sight; a
ticklish position.   To-morrow the whole army (for
the Meerut force came in this morning) moves forward in battle array to drive the enemy from their
position in front of Delhi, and take up our position
in front of the place.   The accounts from down
country are bad.   Fletcher Hayes has been murdered
at Lucknow, and Rohilcund is in a state of revolt.

Camp Delhi,
Tuesday, June 9th.

We had a hard day's fighting yesterday. The first shot was fired by the enemy at 4½ a.m., and the last by one or other of us about 11½ a.m. The enemy had taken up a very strong position about four miles in our front ; indeed, I never saw a stronger country than that which we passed through. Strong serais, old buildings, woods, swamps, canal cuts, and walled villages defied our efforts for some time, particularly, too, as the enemy fought most determinedly. We have taken up a splendid position on Hindoo Rao's hill for bombarding Delhi, and hope to be in it in less than a week. There were more casualties in my squadron than in any other. We had twelve men killed, amongst them poor Sergeant Lindsay. I got hit by a spent ball on my left side behind, and it seemed to me perfectly wonderful how I escaped. What a providential mercy it was my having the general's horse ! He carried me nobly through a hard day's work. I should have been left behind and cut up had I been on the old Cape. Upton had his chestnut killed under him by a round shot, and both the doctors lost their horses. Poor Colonel Chester and a Mr. Russell were killed early in the fight by the same round shot. Delamain has also lost his life. Jones, with a small party, captured one of the enemy's guns, and it was fired four times against them with success. The enemy fired all day from Delhi, and their shot command the hill. Soon after we arrived a shot of theirs blew up one of our tumbrils, and grievously wounded by the explosion was young Davis. Another shot disabled one of Light's guns, and killed four of his men, and another shot carried off two Carabineers. Light got wounded in the head, and was covered with blood. Hope's flank movement was not quite so successful as he wished, owing to the very difficult country poor Turner* had to drag his guns through. At one time they were left unprotected, and were in great danger of falling into the enemy's hands, our squadrons being too eager and impetuous for the charge to stand patiently by to protect them. Turner is well. I must finish.

CAMP DELHI CANTONMENT,
June 10*th*, 1857.

We were turned out yesterday about 2 p.m., for a couple of hours, the enemy having threatened our left flank. Yule being on duty I was in command, but there was nothing to do. There was a good deal of fighting at the picquets on the right, and the Guide Corps, which only came in this morning, highly distinguished themselves in the afternoon, getting three officers wounded—one, poor Battye, mortally, I fear —shot through the stomach. I saw him on his bed just now a little easier, but in great pain. The Guide Corps is a sight to see. Their dress is highly peculiar, and the men are chiefly of two sorts, viz., the tall, powerful, swarthy Afghan, and the short, muscular, olive-skinned Goorkha. They are the admiration of the camp, having marched 580 miles in twenty-two days — a feat unparalleled in the records of Indian marching. Poor Yule came late into mess yesterday

* Major-General Turner, .A., C.B.

evening, dreadfully tired from F.O. duty at the main picquet, where he has been under cannon and rifle fire all day long. The general opinion seems to be that we cannot afford to go on playing at long balls much longer. In the 1,000 yards that intervene between the ridge our batteries are on and the walls of Delhi, there is all sorts of superb cover for the enemy's skirmishers, and what between their fire and disease in camp, some thirty Europeans were disabled yesterday. Hope, always eager and impetuous, is for an immediate advance of the whole force to within 300 yards of the walls, knocking them down, and walking at once into the place. I am disposed to think that his opinion is, in this instance, sound and good. If it be not adopted, I see no chance of our taking the place for the next ten or twelve days. It is of enormous extent, and one might keep firing into it at 1,000 yards for ever. Both the surgeon and assistant-surgeon of the 75th—Coglan and Whylock—are dying, or dead, of cholera. We had one case yesterday. We are pitched in the hollow on the parade-ground, close to the canal, and if it comes on to rain, which it promises to do soon, we may be sure that we shall suffer severely from sickness. The poor Carabineers look dreadfully heavy and oppressed in their blue clothing and overalls. They envy us much our comfortable white clothing. Gifford is looking uncommonly well. Ellis is in camp, but I have not seen him. The day after tomorrow I come on main picquet duty. I was under my bed nearly all day yesterday, and found it very cool and pleasant.

CAMP DELHI CANTONMENT,
Thursday, June 11*th*, 1857.

I received yours of 7th and 8th yesterday, and am glad to find that you get my letters somewhat more regularly. I do hope that Mrs. Grant has had good accounts from Bijnore. Our friends, the 60th, have bolted from Rohtuck, having previously fired their officers' tents, shot at them, and wounded the sergeant-major in the leg. They have gone to Delhi. Our chiefs are getting tired of playing at long balls, and are meditating a closer advance. An attempt will be made in a few days to take the place by a *coup-de-main.* What we are doing now is all nonsense. We had two alarms last night. Once the whole line turned out, and the second time the picquet behind us began to fire. General Reed arrived yesterday, and assumed command. I was out this morning watching the practice of the batteries. To-morrow I shall be doing so all day. On my way home I fell in with poor Battye's funeral, and joined the party. He was buried by Mr. Rotton, in the Cantonment burial ground. It will be easy, comfortable work destroying Delhi after we have taken it. I hear that there are a number of killed and wounded in the place. Colonel Custance, of the Carabineers, dined with Hope last night. I was much amused with the natural way in which he said that he never expected to see so soon such hard times in India, and to find himself on service in June before the regiment was anything like formed. He anticipated enjoying great arām (rest) at Meerut, and was walking leisurely in his compound, on peaceful thoughts intent, when a panic-stricken individual rode in to order him to turn out immediately, as the troops were in arms, murdering every Christian they met. All my poor men's kits (five of them) were sold this morning. How some of the purchasers will be able to carry what they bought I do not know. It is curious enough looking down on Metcalfe's house and the racket-court. Fawcett looted a cow at Raee, and sent us a bottle of milk each yesterday evening.

CAMP DELHI CANTONMENT,
June 12th, 1857.

I could not write yesterday, having had a very busy, hazardous day of it, under fire the whole time ; and in the morning, when the picquets were attacked, and Captain Knox and eight men killed under my nose, it is perfectly marvellous how I escaped unhurt. During the day I frequently visited the batteries, and the 24-pound shot came whistling over them in fine style. Up to yesterday 400 of them had been picked up, and re-fired against the enemy. They tried to turn our right flank, but caught it handsomely over the face and eyes. Their loss altogether is estimated at 500 killed. We were going to take advantage of the defeat they sustained yesterday, and were going to attack Delhi this morning early, but for some reason or other the orders were countermanded, and we are in *statu quo*, with the exception of having pushed on somewhat in advance. I saw Geneste yesterday ; he gave me some tea. I also made the acquaintance of young Lambert, Mrs. Montgomery's brother, a nice gentlemanly young fellow. I saw a lot of people under the portico of Hindoo Rao's house—Mr. Walker, Mr. Warde, Fagan, Chesney, Morris, Fisher, Kennedy, St. George, fat Thomson, Turner, Dirom, Light, and many others. One of the men of the 75th found twenty-six gold mohurs, besides a lump of gold, on one of the men that he killed. I saw some of the gold mohurs, fine large ones; he made his bheesty a present of one of them. Poor General Reed has hardly been able to lift his head up since his arrival. I made the acquaintance of Brigadier Graves yesterday. Poor old gentleman! he will never be able to stand the heat and worry of camp life. My Syce, Baluk, and the grass-cutter and the coolie, Lechman, behaved very well yesterday. Mind that all the servants with me have a present; they richly deserve one. Our poor Kitmutgar lost his leg from a round shot two or three days ago while bringing up his master's victuals. The big guns and mortars were firing fiercely all night on the enemy, who were very slack in returning the fire, and now every minute our mortars or 24-pounders are sending them a pill; but we are too far off, and Delhi will never be taken in this way.

CAMP DELHI CANTONMENT,
June 12th, 3½ *p.m.*

Up to this we have had a quiet day of it. I wanted it after the hard work of yesterday, and it is lucky, too, for my troop, being on inlying picquet, would be the first to be called out in the event of any alarm. I went to see Hope this morning when I came in, and found him in bed fairly knocked up with hard work. He commands the whole Cavalry, and has harassing outpost duties to attend to. How very apposite‚ some of the psalms of 11th and 12th days of the month are to our present position. The whole of the 56th suits our condition. So does the 57th. The 59th, most of it, finds an echo in our hearts. The 60th is very appropriate. There is something very comforting in the 61st and 62nd and 63rd, and very significant in the 64th. There is no doubt that the rod of God is upon us, that men's hearts are failing them for fear, that God is proving us, bringing us into the snare, and laying trouble upon our loins. Most sincerely do I join in the devout prayers and wishes of the 67th, and three first verses of the 68th.

A tattee seems to make a wonderful difference in the coolness of a tent when a good strong hot wind is blowing. I have been under my bed for five hours to-day, lying on such a hot mattress and breathing such hot air, but I suppose I am getting fairly used to the heat, for I do not feel it as much as I did. Yesterday I walked in the sun all day long, just as one would in England, but I felt at one time uncommonly queer, and one had to watch and dodge the cannon-balls so, that doubtless doing so diverted one's attention from the heat.

An awful responsibility attaches itself to the command of this force just now. It is not strong enough to cope with the present exigency without running a great risk. Only fancy how disastrous just now anything like a check or failure would be. Delhi is eight miles in circumference, with a high wall and deep ditch all round it. The wall is no protection, but the size of the place is. We want at least four more European regiments to be sure of success. Hope, Wilson, and Showers are at present our three best Brigadiers. Poor Chester is a great loss to the army. I am going on picquet, so no more to-day. We were all turned out yesterday at 5 p.m. The Oude force came to look at us. Kennedy, of the Guide Corps, was wounded yesterday.

CAMP DELHI CANTONMENT,
Monday, June 15th, 1857.

I do hope that this Delhi business will soon be over, and that we may have the exceedingly great happiness of meeting again. I hear that they are fighting hard amongst themselves in the town, and that frightful anarchy and disorder prevail, which will probably end in their opening the gates and entreating us to come in and put an end to their misery. There is too much *couleur de rose* for us, however, in this report. My own impression is that directly Johnstone joins with the 8th Regiment we shall attack them and make ourselves masters of the place. I had a very quiet day on picquet yesterday though I was much exposed to the sun. It was very pleasant, and a great treat indeed meeting Hunter there. I shared his shuldaree, and we read the morning and evening lessons and psalms together. He reads so nicely, and seems to have such a fervent spirit of Christianity about him, fostered much by the letters of a very pious brother at Bombay, that I enjoyed his company very much. He was very nearly badly wounded on the 8th, a shot going through his boot about two inches above the heel and just grazing the skin off. The tendon is such a strong and important one, that if the shot had torn it, he would probably have been lame for life, and then he got his leg, the calf of it, crushed a bit by a gun. He is getting quite grey, and attributes it to the many bad accidents he has had during his life, having twice seriously injured his spine, besides breaking his arm. I got my " Friend of India " and two " Examiners " the other day, quite a literary treat, though it is hard work reading in the glare and heat, which is so damaging to one's energy. Hope continues very well, and is never better than when he has lots to do. Mrs. U. will be glad to hear that Upton has got a squadron at last. Fawcett and Hutchinson have been pronounced too green to have one, and have consequently been put under me in the 3rd Squadron. Upton has the 1st with Martin, Head has the 2nd with Blair, and Jones the 4th with Goldie. I am to be a sort of acting-Major, and to be exempted from doing orderly-officer's work, which the other captains have been ordered to do. The officering of the squadrons is the grand puzzle of the day. I saw Showers yesterday afternoon looking very spruce and well. He led his brigade splendidly on the 8th. I became acquainted with two more officers yesterday, Captain Campbell and Lieutenant Sandford, of the 9th Irregulars. One makes new acquaintances every day in camp. Turner has revived again, and is feeling quite himself.

C

CAMP DELHI CANTONMENT,
June 16*th*, 1857.

The outposts had a smart affair with the enemy yesterday. Eight men of the 75th were killed, and one of ours, Corporal Whitehead, had a very narrow escape ; a musket-ball striking him in the middle of his stomach, was only prevented going through him by the brass plate of his waist-belt. The 60th N.I. mutineers attacked the picquet on the right, and were vigorously repulsed by the Goorkhas, who, knowing that they, the 60th, were conversant with our bugle sounds, sounded the retreat, which made the mutineers come on fiercely. The Ghoorkhas had hidden themselves behind the crest of the hill, and when the 60th came close, poured a most damaging volley into them. I have seen Hay and Brabazon of the 60th. All the officers had a most narrow escape from Rohtuck, especially poor Drought, who fairly blown with running, would have been taken had not Shebbeare, in the noblest way, come up and said to him, " Here, Colonel, take my horse ; I can run faster than you can." Whereupon Drought mounted, but, being a very bad rider, he had not gone more than a hundred yards, clinging by his eyelids, when he was thrown heavily on the road, and lay insensible to the numerous shots that were fired at him in that predicament. The officers lost nearly everything belonging to them. They had no time to look after their arms even, the friendly Sepoys bundling them neck and crop away. We are expecting Neville Chamberlain in a day or so. He has been appointed Adjutant-General, and will virtually command the army. The Headquarters people seem to have lost their senses altogether. Johnstone, with the Jullundur force, is within three days of us, and Havelock is expected shortly in camp. He is a good soldier, and will be gladly welcomed in camp, where we have so much need of good sterling stuff. We had a quiet night last night, and I slept like a top for six hours. I am on a court-martial to-day, and a flogging must be the result, for we have no other means of punishment. The men want an example; they seem to have an idea that they can do just as they please on service. Sergeant-Major Thonger has got his cornetcy. Frank Grant thought of it, proposed it to Yule, who spoke to Hope, and Hope, flying to Headquarters, clenched the business at once. Sergeant Allan Deane is to be the new Regimental Sergeant-Major. We are getting anxious about our mess supplies. We are running short of beer, and have no good brandy.

CAMP DELHI,
June 17th, 1857.

I was very sorry to think you felt so low and wretched on the 14th. Keep up your spirits, dearest. The Lord being your helper, do not fear what man may do unto you or yours. Jesus has said, "I will not leave you comfortless, I will come to you. Peace I leave with you, *my* peace I give unto you, not as the world giveth give I unto you. Let not your heart be troubled, neither let it be afraid." Whatever happens to me you may be sure will be the best for me. Our times are in His hand. I have every confidence myself in my merciful God and Saviour We had a quiet night again last night. I was vexed with Upton for waking me out of a deep sleep to look at a tremendous blaze in Delhi. What do I care for a fire in comparison with a good sleep? You should have seen how quickly the servants made themselves comfortable yesterday in the shuldaree (tent). The bearer's child is constantly crying, but he finds his wife a great comfort in preparing his meals. General Johnstone was at Umballa on the 14th, and will probably be here about the 21st. They are waiting, I believe, only for his accession of force to act decisively. Captain Daly,* the Commandant of the Guide Corps, dined with Hope yesterday, and a fine, sharp, spirited, good-looking fellow he is. Poor Kennedy, the Adjutant, has been severely wounded in the groin ; one hairsbreadth more either way and the wound must have been fatal. Daly gave such a noble description of Battye, his perfect horsemanship and heroic valour. Young Chalmers is doing duty with the corps. Shebbeare is likely to prove a useful man. He is the acting Adjutant. The Guides require the best of officers, for they are always fighting away in front. Daly himself has been wounded in the head and leg slightly each time. Major Martin came to Hope yesterday evening, terribly disgusted with the distrustful way in which they were treating his Irregulars, and not answering for the consequences if they sent away his headquarters from this. We are all dreadfully

* General Daly, C.B.

disgusted with the vile untruthfulness of the General's despatch about the battle. I fear there is no doubt of Delamain's death. We are short of Artillerymen. Our men are obliged to work in the batteries. Most of the H.A. troops were, at the beginning, short of their proper complement of men, some of whom, too, were raw recruits. The heavy guns at the battle were worked under great difficulties. Sawyer is not in camp ; he is commanding the Headquarters at Meerut. Both Hope and Frank are in a most flourishing condition. I saw Colonel Thomson and Tretton yesterday evening.

CAMP DELHI,
Friday, June 19th, 1857.

We had another quiet day yesterday, but one of our men who was working in the battery was grievously wounded by a shell, and died early this morning. His name was Rudland, a fat, chubby, handsome young fellow, in the band, who had a superb bass voice and used to sing in the choir. I suppose you have heard of the murder of our people at Shahjehanpore while they were at church. Most earnestly do I trust that our friends, the Sneyds and Lysaghts, have escaped. Only fancy dear old Mrs Sneyd placed in such horrible circumstances. It is reported now that Dr. Hay managed to escape, wounded, to Nynee Tal. I hope this is true. Jones was out reconnoitring yesterday with twenty men, and came across one solitary old man who was nearly the death of him, for he fought vigorously and succeeded in wounding Jones' horse, when he was run through by a lance and killed. Three of

our men have died of the wounds they received on
the 8th, so that eighteen men have gone from us;
the bandsman makes nineteen. Turner had a fall
from his horse yesterday; no bones broken, but he
was much shaken. Pat Grant will be here in about
ten days. My turn for picquet comes round about
once a week. Yesterday evening one of the Carabineers was slightly wounded on picquet, while standing as a vedette, by a shell bursting close to him and
a piece of it striking him in the face. To-day our
new subaltern, Thonger, is on, and I have lent him
my shuldaree, which the servants were too lazy to
pitch yesterday after Upton came in, and, as their
comfort was chiefly concerned in pitching it, I allowed them to do as they pleased about it. General
Johnstone left Umballa on the 16th. Yes, indeed,
if you only had Dr. Procknow (a German missionary)
amongst you, what a comfort he would be; but
young Grant tells me that his hands are full, for
disease is raging in the interior of the hills. Yes, it
would be most cruel to think that God was not on
our side. We have His own covenant and promise
to guide and protect us eventually; but knowing
India and our people in India as well as I do, I am
not in the least surprised at His sending this severe
judgment upon us. I look upon this business in the
light of a heavy punishment for the ungodly, infidel
lives the greater part of us have lived in India. Such
utter and intense selfishness and crime as we have
shown in India can only be paralleled by the present
state of affairs in France, where wickedness reigns
supreme.

CAMP DELHI,
Saturday, 20th, 1857.

We were quiet yesterday till 5 p.m., when the enemy attacked our right rear and we had a most serious engagement with them, in which we lost many men and officers killed and wounded. We seem to get under a hotter fire each time. Poor Yule was grievously wounded in the thigh and afterwards brutally mangled. Major Daly was badly wounded through the left shoulder. Frightfully exposed as we were, it pleased a merciful God to preserve my life again. I cannot describe to you the confusion that ensued in the dark, and how grand it was to see the battle raging in the dark, when one could see the flash of every matchlock. Money's guns were very useful. I do not know what we should have done without them at the latter end of the battle, though one of his tumbrils blew up, at least, I believe it was his, for it blew up within a hundred yards of where we were, and could hardly have been the enemy's. We got into a fearful scrape. Horse Artillery guns and Cavalry having to cope with the enemy's all arms, most strongly posted behind garden walls and villages and copses. It was a mercy the camp was not sacked. It was all we could do to repulse the enemy after dark, when we could not see what we were about. Goldie is missing and has, I fear, either been killed or taken prisoner. I had not forty winks last night, so strange and eventful had been the scenes I had gone through ; besides, I was captain of the day and had to spend two hours of the night in visiting my picquets. At

3 a.m. this morning we were again in the saddle, and Hope had a very pretty little battle of his own, as he had a good force of Infantry and Turner's guns, and two squadrons of ours and one of Carabineers ; and his object was to bring in all the dead and wounded from last night's scene of action. As we approached the place the enemy were seen in great numbers, and scampered off before the well-directed fire of Turner's guns. The Infantry fired a village in which there were a number of the enemy's wounded, and we returned to camp about 8 o'clock, but had not been in more than ten minutes before we were turned out again, the enemy attacking our rear with guns and absolutely shelling our camp. A strong force of Artillery went out against them and they were repulsed. As yet I have heard no particulars. The enemy seem determined to worry us and do for us if they can before the arrival of our reinforcements.

CAMP DELHI,
Sunday, June 21st.

Up to this, 2 p.m., we have had a very quiet day, disturbed only by the sound of our advanced batteries pounding away at Delhi, which they will eventually make too hot for the rebels, who are, I think, beginning to show signs of losing heart, but who will yet doubtless give us some very sharp work in the way of destroying them. Owing to poor Yule's death, I have now a the responsibilities and anxieties of temporary command again, and shall probably retain them for a fortnight and more, since

Hope does not expect Ouvry before then.   Under so much pressure was he at one time regarding his wife, that he was on the point of leaving her at Jumnoo under Golab Sing's charge, but he did not like the idea of trusting him, and has, I believe, brought her down to Sealkote.   This is a particularly hot day, and I have been streaming all day long.   I am much better than I was at first starting, and do not now feel the same utter exhaustion of strength just before dinner that I did for the first week in June.   I saw Mr. Rotton bury ten (Yule and five of ours, and Alexander, 3rd N.I., and three 60th Riflemen) last evening.   Mr. R. knows the burial service by heart, and had no book with him.   The corpses were all tied up in their Guthries, and looked so snug and comfortable in their little graves, which were, how-ever, hardly deep enough.

The general's horse is much the worse for his hard work on the 19th.   He cannot stand hard work. A spent ball struck him on his left hind-quarter ; and did I tell you how nearly I lost my left leg below the knee?—a piece of shell tearing a great hole in my trousers.

Monday, 22nd.— I have not much to add this morning.   We passed a quiet night, and have been quiet up to this.   Hope had a very narrow escape on the 19th.   He had to catch hold of his orderly's horse's tail, and was thus brought out of immi-nent danger.   Most fortunately for him his horse carried him fifty yards before he fell dead.   Upton has gone on picquet.   We have mounted a heavy battery in rear of our camp, and have now two

officers' picquets. All the clouds have dispersed, and
there are at present no signs of the rains. We are
pitched in a perfect hollow (the officers' tents, I
mean), and must be particular about draining the
ground. Baird Smith is coming to be our chief
engineer.

CAMP DELHI,
June 22nd, 1857.

Up to this, 3 p.m., we have had a very quiet day,
but a terribly hot one. A reinforcement of artillerymen is coming in to-morrow, together with a handful
of troops from Meerut to fill up the casualties in the
Carabineers and 60th.

23rd June.—The report at mess last night was
exceedingly warlike. It was said that the enemy,
nearly driven to desperation by the misery of the
place inside, by the blowing up of some bridges, and
by constant desertions, had resolved on coming out
in force to attack us this morning. We were ordered
to be ready to turn out at twelve o'clock midnight.
It happened that we were not disturbed, and up to
six o'clock, now, all has been quiet, but we literally
know not what an hour may bring forth. Poor
General Johnstone got an upset from the mail-cart,
and was obliged to lay himself up at Paniput for
some days. His force is close at hand, under the
command of Major Olpherts, H.A. It consists of
about 350 Europeans, six guns, and 500 Sikhs. It
brings us some supplies. We drank our last drop
of beer last night. Upton has just come in quite
tired from picquet, and the stench out there close to

the scene of the action of the 19th is something
very dreadful. The batteries are firing away most
vigorously.

CAMP DELHI,
Tuesday, June 23rd, 1857.

This has been rather a busy day for us. Soon
after despatching my letter, I was ordered to go
with two squadrons and protect four of Money's
guns, and prevent the enemy from interfering with
the long string of supplies, ammunition, and baggage
that arrived this morning under Olpherts. General
Johnstone has, I hear, hurt his spine, and has been
obliged to return altogether. We were out from
about 9 till 11.30, and saw the baggage well in,
though not without an alarm, for we heard firing
in rear of it just as we were returning to camp, and
had to go right about and trot about a mile to learn
the cause of it, and found out that Olpherts had fired
two shots at a party of the enemy who were disagreeably close. We had another incident. Blair
saw three unarmed men skulking along a wall: he
captured them, and, after examination, Money
ordered them to be shot as spies. When the
pistols were presented at their heads, they made
a clean bolt of it for their lives. It was their only
chance, and a poor one, too, for they were pursued
and shot down and lanced. There has been much
musketry firing to-day on the right, and our batteries
have been unusually active. Sarel went out with us.
He did not expect to be called on so soon. He
turned out quite spruce, though he is far ahead of al

his traps. He came and told us that he had seen
you all. I have recommended French for poor
Yule's vacancy ; rather hard upon Head, who has
been so much under fire, but one must stick to the
roster. We have all raised choppers for our horses
and servants, and these have quite spoilt the beauty
of the camp, being most irregular in their fashion.

Wednesday, 24th.—There was a good deal of fighting yesterday afternoon. The enemy brought four
guns outside the walls of Delhi, and fired shell into
our batteries, which suffered more than usual. Moreover, they swarmed up on our right, and occupied in
force a village about 600 yards from it, whence they
were, however, dislodged. Jackson and Ward, 1st
B.E.F., were killed, and two officers missing, Colonel
Welchman wounded in the arm, Shebbeare wounded,
and there were a good many men killed and wounded—
some seventy, I believe. The enemy suffered a loss
of 450 killed; but what is that to them ? They fought
from behind the cover of the village (a strong one,
with pucka (brick) buildings in it), and took aim at
their leisure, our men not knowing where to return
the fire, seeing no enemy. I felt quite knocked up
after my three hours' sunning, but a greater portion
of the Infantry, Artillery, and the Cavalry picquets
were out all day. I was glad to hear from House
that Drysdale had reached Kussowlee on his way
back to us. We expect to see him to-morrow or
next day.

CAMP DELHI,
Wednesday, June 24th, 1857.

Drysdale came in safe this morning, with Chamberlain. They were, however, both surprised at coming in safe, so utterly insecure and unprotected is the road into camp. Cuppage, of the 6th Cavalry, has been attached to us ; he is a nice-looking young fellow, who can ride well. House has just come in to say that there is no brandy to be had at Umballa and that there has been such an immense demand for soda-water, that in eight or ten days the machinery for making it will be worn out, and no more can be made. Very pleasant news, considering that I have just been made Mess President, and have sent an order to McDonald to supply the mess with 150 dozen monthly, and to Crump & Co. to send us every month fifty dozen of beer, twelve dozen of claret, and nine dozen of brandy. A southerly wind is blowing to-day, and the rain looks close at hand. What miserable work it will be, then, for us, on picquet especially. Yes, Friday is a very favourite fighting day with the Mussulmen. I have observed that they always fight after having received reinforcements. We have done all we can to destroy the bridge, but it seems to be too difficult an operation for us. We shall take Delhi eventually, but not just yet. Young Anson * is in the Headquarters camp, on his way to join his regiment, the 84th, which appears to have had plenty of fighting at Cawnpore. Yes, Becher rode in amongst a number of the enemy, in the dark, mistaking them for our own people. They turned upon him, and he escaped with a slight wound in the arm. Showers does not

* Colonel Hon. A. H. Anson, V.C.

seem to get on well as Brigadier. He is, I think, the worst abused man in camp.

Thursday, 25th.—I took a ride through Cantonments. A most melancholy sight do they present. Nice large houses, where different people have known so many of the joys and sorrows of life, roofless, charred, and in ruins. Compounds, that formerly revelled in every shade of green, have now their trees and shrubs nearly all cut down, or eaten by the elephants and camels. A strong south-westerly wind is evidently blowing up the rain, which cannot hold off much longer. Do you remember the fat merchant, Elihu Bux, in the Suddur bazaar? Well, he was impudent to some officer, who reported him, and Maitland immediately had him flogged; not a bad joke that for everybody else but E. B. himself. Maitland seems to have acted, and to be acting, with uncommon nerve, vigour, and coolness at Umballa; but yet I cannot think it a safe place for ladies. Young Anson called yesterday. He is for the present attached to Headquarters, and will wait for the arrival of his regiment here. He is highly spoken of as possessing the most determined courage, together with a great amount of intellect. All that we shall be able to do for some time is to hold our own. We are not strong enough yet for an attack. Hope's favourite Irregulars are beginning to waver. Some of the 4th have joined the enemy, and a few of the 9th have skulked off. Young Ward, of the 2nd B.E.F., is not killed; he had only a sunstroke. I am so glad to hear you are well. So long as you keep well, I do not care what happens to me. May God bless and preserve your much more valuable life.

CAMP DELHI,
5 p.m., Thursday, 25th June, 1857.

This has been, up to the present, a remarkably quiet day, the batteries even have had some repose. After morning parade I went to the flagstaff picquet, where I met Herbert, who said he was as well as such an old fellow could expect to be. Young Sheriff and Bishop and Dirom of the H.A. I also saw in good health and spirits. We cannot expect such a very quiet day to-morrow. Yesterday evening I went to see Showers, and found poor old Welchman stretched on his bed suffering pain from his badly wounded arm, the ball having entered above and gone out below the elbow. I also saw Seaton and Money and Turner. Money is looking uncommonly well and T. seems to have quite recovered from the effects of his fall. Yes; the Lord may sacrifice us as a wicked and adulterous generation, but there is nothing more certain than that He is on our side, and that after justly punishing us for our sins, He will grind the heathen to powder. There is no doubt that there have been great disturbances at Cawnpore. We heard that fighting had been going on there for eleven days. I have never been able to hear whether my draft for 700 rupees ever reached Agra in safety, I strongly suspect that it did not. Communication with down country seems to be just now quite shut up.

Friday 26th.—Another quiet night, and up to this, 6 a.m., quiet morning, but I have just heard the Infantry bugles sounding the alarm, so suppose that the Pandies are bent on mischief of some sort. I went to see Becher this morning, but he was asleep.

Young Anson is attached to us, and Hope has made him his A.D.C. He was dining with me last night, when Betts came to say that all the claret was out. We shall soon, I see, be reduced to Commissariat rum. I very much fear that we shall see nothing more of our 600 rupees worth of claret and beer that left Umballa on the 8th. The reports last night were that Agra was invested by the Gwalior force, and Meerut attacked by the Bareilly one ; that Colonel Handscombe and other officers at Lucknow had been killed.

CAMP DELHI,
Friday, 26th June, 1857.

All has been quiet up to this, 3 p.m. I am so glad to see the moon getting up again, for there is nothing so unpleasant as poking about a large camp in the dark. French has been gazetted as a captain. House gets 180 rupees a month for being Acting-Paymaster. Hamilton is drawing more than 1,000 rupees a month just now. An impostor went about camp yesterday collecting money and clothes for (he said) a poor conductor's wife and three children, who had been twenty days in the jungles, having escaped from Delhi. He succeeded in getting 28 rupees from the Carabineers, with clothes, &c., and some rupees and clothes from the 9th, and he turns out to be some rascally scoundrel of the Fusiliers. It makes my heart long so when I see the bheesty playing with his children. In spite of his hard work, he seems to be the merriest and most paternal of the servants. Showers is coming to dine with me this evening.

Saturday, 27th, 6 a.m.—There was some slight disturbance in the night from small arms, and this morning we are all on the *qui vive*, and the picquets have been strengthened, the enemy showing an inclination to fight along our front. Upton is on rear picquet. We shall probably have a busy day of it.

CAMP DELHI,
Saturday, June 27th, 1857

Up to this, 10.30 a.m., from 6 a.m. there has been a good deal of skirmishing, for the Infantry and the batteries have been firing away very vigorously. Our supporting troops returned about 10, and now there is only a dropping fire of small arms, with, however, a heavy fire from our batteries. We are in camp, but only just out of range of their shells, which sometimes come an enormous way and pitch close to camp, indeed, on the right beyond camp. We have just had our first shower of rain. Thirty-six dozen of soda-water reached us to-day from McDonald. We are afraid to send back our empty bottles, for fear of their being looted. We are in great want of saltpetre and potatoes, neither of which can we procure. It is no joke being Mess President in these times, when nothing is to be had. Young Anson has been appointed to my troop. How oddly things do turn out. Who would have thought that he would ever have been serving with me in the same regiment? It is now about 5 p.m., and it has been pouring since 1 o'clock. The camp is already flooded, and there is no appearance of its leaving off; on the

D

contrary, it looks as though it would rain all night. Imagine how miserable everything looks outside. I dread these rains more than the enemy. Have you heard of the shameful behaviour of some of the Europeans, 2nd B.E.F. and our 8th, at Umballa, where they broke into the E troop barrack, and looted all Goldie's things, as well as other officers' property, stole claret and beer out of the canteen, and regaled themselves so that about 100 were drunk at the same time? To-morrow we expect another large reinforcement in, with heavy guns, &c. Perhaps the heavy rain may detain it. Our regiment will probably have to escort it in. When it comes we shall advance our batteries and prepare for the assault of the place. About 1,000 of the 8th and 61st, besides Artillerymen, are expected.

6 *a.m., Sunday, 28th.*—It rained till 6 p.m. yesterday. No more cool nice nights in the open air. Except just in the hollow where the staff line of officers' tents is, the ground we are encamped on is well drained and was walkable over an hour after the rain, of which there seems to be plenty more coming. The 8th, about 350 of them, under Greathed, marched in this morning, with an immense amount of small and large ammunition. The 61st and Coke's corps, and the 4th Punjab Infantry are expected in in three or four days. I was sorry to hear from Hope yesterday that Ricketts is missing and cannot be found. I was introduced to Sir T. Metcalfe yesterday evening; he was dining with Anson. He told me that J. Hutchinson was killed in the palace with Douglas and Fraser. The enemy

got severely punished yesterday. We lost seven killed and wounded.

CAMP DELHI,
Monday, June 29th, 1857.

There was no post in yesterday, owing, I suppose, to the rain ; and, moreover, they say that the dâk horses are quite knocked up, so that from this date we must not expect to have our letters as regularly as they have hitherto been coming. Last night was very quiet, and nothing has occurred to disturb our equanimity this morning. Baird Smith has arrived, and, doubtless, by the end of this week things will be far more advanced than they are, at present. A young civilian from Bijnore of the name of Palmer dined with F. Grant yesterday. Greathed, who seems to be the great civilian here, has ordered him to Mozuffurnugger, but he doesn't appear to relish going there at all. I wish I could hear something of our friends in the 28th N.I. None of them seem to be at Naini Tal. It is far better for officers to be killed on service here than to be murdered in Cantonments ; and how I have felt all along for the unfortunate ladies. Singularly enough, as soon as ever the damp weather sets in, I begin to feel out of sorts, heavy about the head, sleepy, and lethargic. We have had nothing to complain of in the way of heat during the last two days. Smith is the only officer sick. My messing is horribly expensive, but this I cannot well help. The Mess Consammah came to me yesterday, in a very doleful state of mind, saying that the wind and rain had

nearly prevented his cooking the dinner, and that
two ducks and five fowls had been drowned in the
rain.   Walker, who married Miss Scott, has joined
the camp.   I shall be glad to see him, for I took a
great fancy to him.   Captain Roberts has been
appointed D.A.Q.M.G. to the Cavalry Brigade, which
is swelling out in its proportions.   I do not think
Hope will ever command the regiment again.   Should
he be all right at the end of a successful campaign,
he will most probably become Major-General Sir
Hope Grant, K.C.B., and richly will he have earned
his honours.

CAMP BEFORE DELHI,
Tuesday, June 30th, 1857.

I have written to General Johnstone, offering to
buy his horse, since there seems no chance of his
being able to use him.   They tell me that he is now,
poor man ! mentally diseased.   I am very sorry for
it, for few have glorified their Saviour more than he
has.   Throughout tremendous affliction he exhibited
a truly Christian character, such as could not fail to
command the regard and esteem of his fellow-
Christians.   I am very sorry to learn that I had
grieved and vexed you by what I said about myself.
All I meant to do was to prepare you for all contin-
gencies, and to counsel you not to be downhearted,
whatever might happen to me.   You may depend
upon my taking all proper care of myself; but I cannot tell you how comforting and consoling it is for
me to think that you have faith and mind and heart
enough to support you under great difficulties, and

that you will daily call upon the Lord to be your helper. I want all the strength and courage He, and He only, can give me; and it is such a blessing to be able to say, " Our Father, which art in heaven, and to pray to Him through Christ for all our wants. We had a quiet day and night yesterday, but there is hard fighting going on this morning on our right, and we are in readiness to turn out at a moment's notice. I dined with Showers at the 1st Fusiliers' mess yesterday, and met Seaton, Hodson, Wreford, Simpson, Wemyss (whose wife has got two Christian Ayahs from Mrs. Newton ; they give her great satisfaction), and others. Showers had just received a very clever sketch, from Atkinson, of an incident that occurred on 23rd, viz. : two European soldiers and a Goorkha were resting themselves against a village wall, when a hostile Sepoy (a Pandy, in fact) put his head out of the window to see what was going on. The Goorkha seized him by the hair of his head—his top-knot—and cut his head off with his kookree. All the faces are inimitably pourtrayed. I saw Welchman. He is doing well, but suffers considerable pain and annoyance from his wound. We were on the point of changing our ground yesterday, but the spot fixed upon for the new Cantonment was so extraordinarily filthy and abominable, that we have been allowed to remain where we are. Some supplies came in yesterday—champagne, brandy, soda-water, and tea and sugar. Hamilton treated the mess last night to champagne on account of his promotion. I was away, and thus, fortunately, escaped a headache.

CAMP DELHI,
Tuesday, 30th June, 1857.

Shortly after closing my letter we were turned out
for half an hour in support of the troops engaged on
the right. We were home by 9, and it has been
pretty quiet up to this, 3 p.m., when from Upton's
troop (the inlying picquet) having been ordered out,
the enemy, I suppose, are on the move again. This
has been a hot, steamy day, not so bad, however, as it
might have been, for the sun, though powerful at
times, has been much obscured by a thick haze.
Best thanks for yours of 28th. Our worst fears will,
I fear, be realised in reference to Shahjehanpore.
What a diabolical atrocity. We never could have
conceived such a horrible fate as has befallen so
many people that we were intimate with. How
thankful we ought to feel that you are all comparatively safe at Kussowlee. I had a very long visit
from Lieutenant C. W. Packe, of the 4th N.I. He
seems a nice, gentlemanly, clever young fellow.
He has been employed in the Grand Trunk Road
between Attock and Peshawar, and is on his way
down to an appointment in Ajmere, but, finding himself unable to get further than this, has got himself
posted to the 4th Sikhs The 61st are just marching
in, band playing most cheerily. It is quite a treat to
hear it. There were some hearty cheers given them.
About thirty men were killed and wounded yesterday. Poor Yorke, of the 4th Sikhs, is, I fear, mortally wounded through the chest, and my little friend
Packe was shot through the ankle, I must go and see
him this afternoon. I was captain of the day yester-

day, and had a beautiful moonlight night for visiting my picquets. I met Young, of the Artillery, busily engaged in sending shot and shell to the batteries which they have strengthened, and from which a vigorous fire will be opened to-day. The strangers at mess last night were Campbell, the civilian,* Campbell, of the Irregulars, Norman,† Light, and Maisey. I went over to Hope's and he kindly allowed me to read Mrs. Alexander's letter. There is, I fear, no doubt of the fate of our friends, and it is truly dreadful to think of. Only fancy the wretches murdering twenty-five children at Hansi and Hissar. Poor Mrs. Wedderburn was quite a young creature, with an infant only a few months old. Mrs. Barwell was also a newly-married lady. If it had not been for the telegraph we should have been all murdered at Umballa. God bless and strengthen you to bear up against all the ills of life.

CAMP DELHI,
July 1st, 1857.

Barring a more vigorous fire from our batteries, and consequently theirs also, the day up to this, 4 p.m., has passed off quietly enough. The sun has had fierce play, and it has therefore been hotter ; but a cool, pleasant wind has been blowing all day.

Thursday, July 2nd, 6 a.m.—A remarkably quiet night and morning. Now our mortars have just commenced playing, and there is a good deal of noise. We silenced one of their batteries, the Moree

---

* Sir George Campbell, M.P.   † General Sir Henry Norman.

Gate one, yesterday, but they have doubtless repaired
it during the night. Poor Yorke, of the 4th Sikhs,
died yesterday. Upton is better this morning and
has gone on picquet. He is very thin and scarcely
takes sustenance enough, I think. The expense of
mess staggers him, as it did me when a subaltern.
Coke's Corps is to march in this morning, and then
all the reinforcements will be in for the present. I
made a mistake the other day, saying Baird Smith
had arrived; he is only on his way. Some of the
men of the 2nd Fusiliers committed a very barbarous
act two days ago, in killing an unfortunate native
who, at the risk of his life, had brought in a letter
from Agra to Young, of the Artillery. The letter
contained good news from Agra and Cawnpore
(where there had been a good deal of fighting, but
Wheeler had been able to hold his own well), and
Benares. I am so glad to think that your dear
parents are out of the country. The worry and
anxiety of all this would have been highly
injurious to your father's health. By the middle of
November we shall have about 15,000 Europeans in
these parts. The civilians cannot collect the revenue
about here, and seem to be ludicrously nonplussed.

CAMP DELHI,
Thursday, July 2nd, 1857.

We do not expect any down-country reinforcements just yet, though Europeans have been reaching
Benares at the rate of 150 a day. At present it is
as much as they can do to keep all serene down

country. So far as we can look ahead, we shall have force enough in the country by November to act with the utmost vigour, and punish the villages and towns that have shown such a bad disposition, and reclaim all our revenue. By the end of next cold weather we shall have done enough, I think, to promise our spending next hot season somewhere in Cantonments. The whole of the cold weather must be employed in reconquering the country. Matters are fast approaching a crisis here.

Friday, July 3rd, 6 a.m.—A pretty quiet night. About twelve we had an order to be ready to turn out at a moment's notice, there was some anticipation of an attack from the enemy. This morning we are carrying some design (either advancing the batteries or obtaining cover for them), for the 8th and 61st marched down early to the right. Yesterday, treason reared its head in the camp itself, and ended in three executions and the disbandment of about seventy Mahommedans of the 2nd Punjab Cavalry. The head man of Nicholson's Sikhs was found openly tampering with Coke's men. He and two other native officers were hung. William Ford has come into camp, and dined with me yesterday. For the last six weeks he has been in danger of having his throat cut every day, and has had some narrow escapes. He lost between four and five thousand rupees worth of property, and the Government treasure, 15,000 rupees, fell into the enemy's hands. All this treasure which they have seized will make their resistance more obstinate. Campbell lost 25,000 rupees on his own account. Blair, who has

numerous correspondents at Mussoree, tells me that
he cannot count upon receiving a letter safe, and
that his letters often miscarry. I saw Martin this
morning, and he observed how much more comfortable you both were at Kussowlee. Murray
McKenzie and Fagan were slightly wounded in
the batteries yesterday, and Evans and Blair had
narrow escapes from round shot. I hope Mrs. Grant
is better. Colonel Jones, of the 60th, dined at mess
last night, and was called to a consultation at
Showers' tent about 9 p.m. He is an old-looking,
worn-out man, to whom this sort of service must
be exceedingly irksome. We all of us get up
terribly languid of a morning.

CAMP DELHI,
Friday, July 3rd, 1857.

Up to this, 1 p.m., we have been very quiet
indeed, the batteries even having scarcely fired; a
regular lull there is. Packe and Allen have just
written to say that they cannot get a rupee at
Umballa, and would I be so kind as to give them
an order on the Divisional Paymaster for 400 rupees
to enable them to push along with. These waterproof things are so horribly expensive that I must
try and do without them, particularly as I cannot
help my mess bills being so extravagantly high,
obliged as I am occasionally to ask people to dinner.
Were I not so high up in the regiment, I would not
think it my duty to dine at mess, but holding now
rather a conspicuous position it would not do for me
to eat alone in my tent and abstain altogether from the

society of my brother officers. I am, however, disgusted at the great but unavoidable expense which the mess entails. All I eat, too, is soup, meat, and onions (the potatoes being very bad), and bread and butter washed down with sherry and water. I have a strong idea that if Delhi is taken in a strong off-hand manner, and a terrible example made of these detestable Pandies, it will go far to restore peace to the country, frightfully disorganised as it is ; witness the presence of so many civilians in camp treasureless and powerless. Campbell, of Moradabad, says that the officers there would not believe that they were in so much danger, that while the civilians used to go to church with swords and revolvers, the officers never took their swords even. Alas ! for the poor Lysaghts and Sneyds. The old lady will never survive such a blow. I wish I could hear of her safety.

Saturday, July 4th.—Anything but a quiet night last night. About 5 p.m. yesterday it was reported that between 3,000 and 4,000 of the enemy (Cavalry and Infantry), with six or seven guns, had found their way into our rear, and intended attacking us during the night, while another party would engage us in front. Well, this put us all on the *qui vive*, and a strong force under Coke, consisting of two squadrons of Dragoons, 1,000 European Infantry, twelve guns, and Coke's own corps, besides Irregulars, was detailed to march to Alipore, encounter the enemy at all hazards, and rout them out of our rear, where it is preposterous to allow them to remain one moment longer than we can possibly help. Well, during the night, between twelve and one o'clock, guns were heard, firing in our left rear, about five miles off, and the whole camp was immediately on the *qui vive.* What the enemy were firing at we don't know at present; but we made sure they meditated a descent upon our camp. I had no comfortable sleep after this, and feel jaded and used up this morning, which in camp has been quiet enough. Hope sent for me yesterday, and treated me (a great treat, indeed, in these times, when beer is so scarce) to a glass of good beer, which I thoroughly enjoyed. He has a small supply of his own, about 2½ dozen, and said he would always share his bottle with me if I came about three o'clock, when he has a glass, and some good mutton broth. I shall be very glad to hear that you have received my yesterday's letter, containing drafts. Till those fellows are out of our rear we can depend upon nothing being right there.

Sunday, July 5th.—I had the hardest day's work yesterday since I have been in camp, and feel uncommonly tired to-day in consequence. We heard Major Coke's engagement with the enemy in our rear begin about 9 a.m., and a very fierce artillery fire it was. Well, in about two hours he sent in for reinforcements, and all the Cavalry mounted and trotted away, six miles, to his troops, who had beaten back the enemy. We remained about an hour, and then walked steadily back into camp. We had not returned more than one and a half hours, when a fresh requisition for aid was made by Jones, who, with some of the 61st, had been left there by Coke, who had withdrawn his corps and the Artillery, thinking that

the enemy would not bother us again. But he was
mistaken. They surprised Jones' party at tiffin, on
the banks of the canal, and the 61st flew to their
arms, the Cavalry mounted, and a serious skirmish
took place. We trotted out again at 1.30 with some
H.A. to their assistance, and arrived just in time to
disperse, by the fire of the H.A., a large body of their
Cavalry, who were meditating mischief; and there
we remained, guarding the canal bridge till the
Engineers were ready to blow up another bridge over
the canal, about a mile from us. We did not get
home till past 8 p.m., men and horses completely
done up. This bids fair to be a quiet day. They
say that it is the Bareilly force that has been bother-
ing us so. They got to Alipore, drove away the
Irregular guard, looted the place, killed a few sick in
the serai, and were caught by Coke on their way
back, and made to drop all their loot. No dâk came
in yesterday, in consequence of this disturbance in
our rear.

CAMP DELHI,

Sunday, July 5th, 1857.

Up to this, 3 p.m., we have had, I am thankful
to say, a singularly quiet day. Another hard day's
work would have knocked me up. I made a light
breakfast this morning, and feel myself now all right
again. The general's horse, being so large and
powerful and difficult to make to walk, is a very
fatiguing animal to ride fifteen miles on. I rode
the Cape horse seven miles, but had some difficulty
in keeping him on his legs over such heavy ground

as we passed over. The enemy have repaired their
bridge, and don't much care for the loss of the canal.
The Meerut people were much to blame for allowing
the Bareilly force to pass the Ganges in boats at
Ghurmucktesur so successfully as they did. A very
small force with guns would have effectually prevented them. We have heard of the death of Sir
Henry Barnard. Poor man, a happy release for him
from his painful command so full of responsibility.
It is fortunate that we have Chamberlain and Baird
Smith in camp just at this juncture. It is just going
to pour, and a proper wet night I shall have to go
round my picquet as captain of the day. Fawcett
has kindly promised to lend me his waterproof cloak.
I do not think the general's horse is worth more
than 1,000 or 1,100 rupees at the outside ; I am
afraid I shall have to give one or the other sum for
him. I am sorry to hear that —— is making such
a goose of himself. The fact is, though, that the
mistrust of natives, Mahommedans especially, is
pretty general throughout the service. How singu-
lar that, just after concluding a bloody war in favour
of the Turks and Constantinople, the chief seat of
the " Crescent," we should be now fighting for our
lives and India against the vile Moslem.

Monday, July 6th.—Chamberlain, I hear, had ma-
tured a plan of attack three or four nights ago, but
Barnard* could not be persuaded to carry it out, so
deeply sensible was he of the awful responsibility
of his position. Reed is now the nominal com-

---

* General Sir Henry Barnard, Commander-in-Chief.

mander, while Chamberlain* will be the real one. I had such a miserable ride round my picquets last night, which was a very rainy and stormy one. I dozed in my chair at mess till past eleven, when, the heaviest rain being over, I mounted my horse and had a wearisome trudge of six miles all round the camp. It was nearly two o'clock before I got back. I tumbled into bed, and was in my first sound sleep (and a sound one it was, because, being wet, I took off my clothes and regularly turned in, which I have not done more than twice during the campaign) when Upton was turned out to go to Alipore and escort three lacs of treasure into camp. That is the worst of chumming. One subjects oneself to just double the disturbance one would otherwise have. I would give a good deal to be alone. I was truly delighted to hear of old Mrs. Sneyd and Louie's safety. It is quite a load off my mind, though, poor old lady, I daresay she wishes that she had been killed too with her son and the Lysaghts. A Sepoy of the 5th N.I., fully armed and accoutred (he had fifty rounds of ammunition in his pouch), came and gave himself up to our picquet yesterday, saying that he was tired of his life. He was hung. I doubt the good policy of hanging those who voluntarily surrender themselves. Young, of the Artillery, asked me to join him and Heatley and Baker at Divine Service in Y.'s tent, but it was far away and I was too tired to go ; besides, the rain would have prevented me. We have been quiet up to this, 7 a.m.

* General Sir Neville Chamberlain, K.C.B.

A regiment of mutineers (the 72nd) from Neemuck, aided by one from the Gwalior contingent, are meditating a descent upon Agra. The Europeans there under Riddell, with some guns, intend marching out to meet them if they come near enough. The Muirs* have been all ready for a start downwards for the last six weeks, but they are still living in trepidation at Agra, which seems to be the general rendezvous for the broken-up civilians. A large force of Europeans will soon be collected at Allahabad.

CAMP DELHI,
6 a.m., Tuesday, July 7th, 1857.

No dâk in yesterday, so I suppose I shall have two letters to-day. My sugar ran out yesterday, and I am now paying the mess man R1. 4. for one seer of lump sugar. A cup of tea in camp is an extravagant treat; it is far preferable, however, to beer in the middle of the day. Hope takes more exercise than I do, and finds that it agrees with him well. He has been generous enough to give Daly, of the Guide Corps, six bottles out of his small stock. Young Anson and I tiffed with him yesterday, but I would much sooner have had my tea and mangoe-fool than beer and mutton broth, and mean to avoid the snare for the future, except on special occasions of fatigue, &c. The mess has bought all General Anson's wine and beer, to the amount of £400 and more. The Ewarts, father and son, dined with Hope yesterday. They were both looking well. The father

* Sir William and Lady Muir.

is not going to Umballa after all. The son is really a very nice lad, and reminds me much of his amiable mother. Please mention young Packe in your next letter home; he cannot write himself. I saw him this morning; he was not so well, he was a little feverish and suffering a good deal of pain from his nasty wound, which will, I fear, lame him somewhat for life. He is such a nice, gentlemanly fellow, I quite grieve to see him laid up. Upton has just received the small parcel, and is now reading the Bible it contained. I like him for the attention he pays to it. He is certainly about the best chum I could have. If he did not suit me, I should be miserable indeed, for I am not fond of chumming. I went to see Showers and Welchman yesterday evening. The latter is progressing very slowly. The doctors are afraid that he will have to lose his arm, and that he will hardly have strength to bear the operation. He was more cheery than I expected to find him. Robertson, of the 8th, called upon me yesterday.

CAMP DELHI,
3 p.m., Tuesday, 7th July, 1857.

It was a great relief to me getting yours of the 5th, and hearing a better account of yourself. What beautiful verses those are culled out of the Psalms for the day, and how specially adapted to our present position. " O let not them that are mine enemies triumph over me ungodly, neither let them wink with their eyes that hate me without a cause. Awake and stand up to judge my quarrel, avenge Thou my

E

cause, my God and my Lord. With Thee is the
well of life, and in Thy light shall we see light. O
continue forth Thy lovingkindness to them that know
Thee and Thy righteousness to them that are true of
heart. Commit thy way unto the Lord and put thy
trust in Him and He shall bring it to pass. The
arms of the ungodly shall be broken, and the Lord
upholdeth the righteous. And the Lord shall stand
by them and save them. He shall deliver them from
the ungodly, and shall save them because they put
their trust in Him. The angel of the Lord tarrieth
round about them that fear Him and delivereth
them." I wish I could take all the heavenly comfort
of those verses to myself. I feel I am not spiritually
minded enough to have the privilege of richly enjoying the sublime sentiments. We had a heavy
thunderstorm about ´2 o'clock, and the air now is
delightfully cool and refreshing. Robertson paid us
another visit to-day, and was much pleased with
your milk-punch. He looks upon this as a very strong
place (and he is well acquainted with it, for during a
month that he was here doing nothing he amused
himself with surveying it all round), and always
thought that a large force would be required to take
it. He asked me whether it was true that —— had
grossly insulted General Anson, who fully intended,
had he lived, to call him to a reckoning for it. What
a thousand pities that Anson had not Tucker by his
side. Though I had no great personal liking for
Anson, I feel sure he would have come well out of
this scrape in the end. Young Barnard left camp at
3 p.m. yesterday for London ; an only son, his pres-

ence at home is imperatively required. The Sepoy
of the 5th was hung yesterday. The rope broke
twice ; the second time the bystanders laughed, and
he laughed too. Three volleys put an end to his
existence. Did I tell you that yesterday evening
one of the enemy's shells burst right over part of the
camp? They are following our example in burying
their mortars in the· ground, and thus obtaining a
greater elevation for the shell. Three faithful hardworking bheesties were wounded at Hindoo Rao's
battery two or three days ago, by shot bounding
back from the walls of the house. James Brind *
accosted me in the Headquarters camp yesterday
evening. He has grown so old and grey that I
hardly knew him, though he is one of my oldest
friends in the country. I saw him first in '38. He
jumps about the batteries as unconcernedly as a
monkey, believing that every bullet has its billet.
We are going to add a filter to our luxuries at mess,
and buy all the General's jams, &c., for F. Grant,
Blair, and Jones are great devourers of sweets of that
sort. Your account of poor Mrs. Knox and Mrs.
Mowatt affected me much. Mowatt was a very
worthy man. I have been out since 2 a.m. to-day
(8th), and only returned at 2 p.m. frightfully worn
out by the blazing sun. We blew up the bridge.
No enemy was to be seen ; they were coming to
attack us, but, seeing this heavy column *en route*,
scampered into Delhi again.

* General Sir James Brind, K.C.B.

CAMP DELHI,
Thursday, July 9th.

I was so tired when we returned yesterday, from
blowing up the bridge, that I was obliged to close
my letter abruptly.   I was so glad to get home
yesterday, for, from F. Grant's not warning me for
the duty, I started in a hurry, and without my usual
comforts.   The heat was very intense.   We went
about fourteen miles altogether.   This morning is
quiet   enough,   though   there   is   a   report   that   the
Pandies are going to attack us to-day in consequence
of the arrival of a distinguished leader from Oude.
The King of Delhi has been chaffing us.   We can
enter upon no conditions till we have avenged the
blood of our murdered countrymen and women.

CAMP DELHI,
Thursday, July, 9th, 1857.

We had a sunning yesterday, and have a ducking
to-day.   Nice young plants shall we be.   The batteries, observing a stir about the gates of the city,
were pounding away most vigorously, when suddenly
the   enemy,   consisting   of   a   hundred   sowars   of the
8th Irregulars, from Bareilly, and some footmen,
positively had the pluck to make an irruption into
the very camp itself, and to surprise, as it were, the
Carabineer picquet.   You may imagine how soon the
alarm   sounded,   and   how quickly   we   all   repaired   to
our posts.   I saw three unfortunate camp-followers—
two men and a woman—lying dead in camp, and a
European drummer in hot pursuit of a Pandy, who

was bobbing in the middle of the canal like a duck, but who was finally shot. Hope's party saw two of the sowars trying to take their horses across ; finding themselves pressed, they abandoned the nags, and saved themselves by flight. Tombs and Hills, of the H.A., pursued a sowar, who turned round and wounded the latter in the hand, while the former ran the mutineer through the body. A number charged our picquet ; some of our men behaved very badly, absolutely running away and leaving their officer Stillman, to cut his way through the enemy, who were audacious enough, too, to let the artillery horses loose to add to the confusion in camp. Some five or six Carabineers were wounded, and some artillery having been quickly brought to play upon the mutineers, about thirty of them were killed, and the remainder escaped to Delhi, where doubtless they will receive an ovation. We were out for about two and a half hours in the rain (it has been raining all day), ready to act when and where called upon, and of course were drenched. It is said that these men of the 8th expected to draw off all our remaining native troops by this bold proceeding. I certainly don't like the look or bearing of the Irregulars in our camp. A court-martial was trying two prisoners the other day, when the alarm sounded, and the members betook themselves to their respective posts. On reassembling, they asked where the prisoners were. "Oh !" says the provost-marshal, "not knowing when you might return, I, to save all further trouble, shot the prisoners directly you left."

Friday 10*th*, 6 *a.m.*—A very rainy night, but a quiet

one, and it is peaceful enough this morning. A court
of inquiry has been ordered to investigate the ugly
Carabineer affair. I hear that Tombs saved Hills'
life in the following way : Hills was lying wounded
on the ground, and was on the point of being speared
by a sowar, when Tombs presented his revolver, and,
at twenty yards, shot the man right through the
heart, so that he dropped down dead instantly.
The enemy, after doing all the mischief they could,
had the impudence to walk close by Martin's picquet,
who, mistaking them for friends, let them pass unmolested, and did not find out their error before they
were nearly out of cannon-shot. Light, of the H.A
let fly at them, and did trifling execution.

CAMP DELHI,
Friday, July 10th, 1857, 10 a.m.

This is one of those drizzling, misty, rainy days
so inimical to compound walls. Upton went on
picquet (the picquet, too, that was surprised yesterday) this morning, and will not, I fear, have a
comfortable time of it. Hope sent for both of us
yesterday for beer, broth, bacon, and cherry-brandy.
I did not feel inclined to go, but Upton went and ate
a hearty dinner, and came back quite thirsty from
his unwonted imbibitions. As it was wet, I did not
feel disposed for mess. I ate my bread and butter
and beef and drank my glass of brandy and water
at home, and we spent the evening together. Fancy
some of the 8th Irregulars, on their way back from
our camp, coming across Hodson, and entering into

familiar talk with him about the campaign, and taking him in so completely that he thought they were some of our own Irregulars, till one of his own men discovered whom they were, then off they scampered like roes, only one of them being killed. Were I in power, I would disarm at once all our Irregulars in camp, for, in spite of Hope's fondness for them, I have, from their insolent air and demeanour, a very strong impression that they would not be true to us in action ; that they would turn against us at a critical moment and prove very thorns in our sides. I never dreamt of being six weeks before the walls of this place, or I would have brought more kit, especially warm regimental clothing, with me. I have got my little supply of books out, and am never at a loss for mental occupation, though I am sadly so for physical. Whenever the tent is devoid of Upton's bed (which he takes on picquet) I take the opportunity of working my arms and legs about a bit. From want of doing this as regularly as I used to do at Umballa, I am not so strong as I was there.

CAMP BEFORE DELHI,
Saturday, July 11th, 1857, 6 *a.m.*

Rain, rain, nothing but rain, sometimes soft, sometimes hard, making everything, particularly boots, horribly damp, and every person dull and miserable. I am captain of the day, and am already thinking of my wretched ride round the picquets to-night. I have a note from Johnstone, selling me his horse for 1,200 rupees. Were he killed in action to-

morrow, Government would give me only 800 rupees
compensation for him.   On the 9th there was some
hard fighting in the Subzi Mundi quarter.   Our
casualties amounted to 212 killed and wounded.
The enemy's to seven or eight hundred.   Mount
Stevens, of the 8th, was killed, and Captain Daniell
wounded.   Tombs, in his fight with the sowars, had
a very narrow escape ; one of their blows took effect
on his head, cutting through his basket cap, and
shaving off a large lock of his hair.   The shot by
which he saved Hills' life was quite a chance one,
and Hills should view it in the light of a merciful
stroke of Providence in his favour.   The Carabineer
business is not such a bad one after all.   A panic
seems to have seized the whole picquet, and one
of the guns was the first to make off, conscious, I
suppose, of being very ill-manned, there being only
two gunners present with it.   There seems no doubt,
however, of the complicity of the 9th Irregulars with
the enemy.   One of their vedettes having been seen
parleying with the enemy, the 9th Regulars have
been disbanded.   Drysdale was ailing a bit yesterday, and stayed away from mess.   Boils of the most
laying-up sort are prevalent in camp, especially
amongst the Carabineers, who have three officers
laid up with them.   Custance amuses us very much.
He has been so thoroughly let in for the disagree-
ables of life, in spite of his independent means, and
has a decided penchant for a quiet, easy, luxurious
mode of life.   Delhi is a very large place, some eight
miles in circumference, fortified all round.   Two
thousand five hundred Europeans are not equal to

taking it and defending their own camp at the same
time. We may do something shortly, but I should
not be surprised if we waited for Wheeler's four regiments before assaulting.

CAMP DELHI,
Sunday, 12*th.*

I can only give you a hurried line this morning,
since we are momentarily expecting a visit from the
Pandies, who have turned out in force. I had a fine
moonlight night for my picquet duty, and went to
church this morning, and heard an excellent sermon
from Mr. Rotton, a man evidently of strong intellect.
I saw there nearly everybody in camp. The Jhelum
business seems to have been a tough one for the 24th,
who at one time got the worst of it. The 14th N.I.
having a river in their rear, fought desperately, took
one of our guns, and threw it into the river. Colonel
Ellis was badly wounded. There has also been a
disturbance at Rawul Pindee, where a Mr. Miller has
been wounded. Since the Pandies do not seem disposed to disturb us, I may as well resume the chain
of my communication with you, so abruptly broken
about an hour ago. There was certainly a deep and
earnest feeling of devotion very manifest among the
congregation this morning. The sermon must have
emphatically convinced us of our want of genuine
faith in, and love for, Christ. While the mart, the
theatre, the exchange, and the senate occupied men's
minds most passionately and intensely, in nine cases
out of ten the effect of religion on society was
the chilling, damping, and quenching of all cordial

social intercourse ; and he traced this to our unbelief and want of daily communion with Christ by prayer and meditation. Captain ——, of the Irregulars, has made himself the laughing-stock of camp by some very curious behaviour. He was on duty at Alipore, and, dreaming that he would be attacked, wrote, in anticipation, a despatch (imaginative, of course) of how he had seen the enemy's cavalry in large numbers, of how they had advanced upon him, and compelled him to a precipitate retreat, and how much he was in want of support. This despatch he entrusted to a faithful servant, bidding him wait for his orders to take it to the Headquarters camp. The servant, however, through some misapprehension or other, started off for camp with this precious document, and delivered it over safe into the hands of B——, the greatest alarmist in camp. It created quite a sensation, and people were, finally, but too delighted to find it all a romance. Can you conceive such a thing happening? We have had two warnings to-day to be ready to turn out at a moment's notice, proving much restlessness on the enemy's part. It seems they have come out twice on mischief bent, but, seeing us wide awake, bobbed in again. I saw young Grant to-day ; he is a little better, but very seedy. Hope was reading the Bible to him. He has a great affection for the young man.

Monday, 1 *a.m.*—I am just going off to escort a large convoy in.

CAMP BEFORE DELHI,
July 13*th*, 1857.

It was fortunate I had my letter written yesterday,

or you would have received none to-morrow. About twelve o'clock, midnight, Drysdale was at the bottom of my bed, pulling at my toes, and calling out my name. He warned me to be ready to start at 2 a.m. on escort duty. Being senior officer, I commanded the party, which consisted of two guns under Lieutenant Elliot, 100 Irregulars under Probyn and Davidson, one squadron of ours under Jones, 100 of Coke's men under Pollock, and eighty men of the 4th Sikhs under Rothney and Wauchope, and formed the largest party I ever commanded in my life. Luckily the enemy did not attack the convoy, which consisted chiefly of magazine stores, &c., and thus saved me the indescribable hubbub, hurry, and disorder, as well as the frightful responsibility, of a fight. Soon after starting I had to wait nearly three hours for some bullocks that were to have accompanied me, but which never made their appearance. There I was, sitting on a doubled up cloth, in the very middle of the Pukha road, with my head on my knees, and the heavy dew falling fast around me, listening to the devil Hindoo cry of the jackals and the unmusical voices of the pea-fowl on some neighbouring trees. Peacocks and hens are just as common here as barn-door fowls at home. I made the acquaintance of some agreeable fellows. Probyn * is about the nicest and most gentlemanly man I have met in India.

* General Sir Dighton Probyn, V.C. Elsewhere my father describes him as the handsomest man in India. It may not be without interest to members of the family to know that my father was 6 ft. 2½ in. in his socks, and that four different people told me he was the finest man they had seen.—H. S. A.

Rothney is a very taking sort of fellow. Wauchope, who is a first cousin of the Spottiswoode who was in our regiment, is an agreeable youngster. We had a most tedious ride back to camp, at about one and a half miles an hour. It was twelve o'clock, and I immediately dressed, and ate my breakfast, and went to a regimental court-martial at the mess till nearly four. At six there was a parade, after which I went down to see young Lambert, and found him very much changed indeed. He is, however, nearly well again, and told me that he frequently heard from Mrs. Montgomery, whose mind had been somewhat uneasy by tidings of the Jhelum and Sealkote mutineers. I am very sorry for Brind and Dr. Graham, both of whom I knew very well. There has been some fighting at Agra. The enemy attacked the Cantonments, and have burnt some bungalows. The Muirs must have taken refuge in the fort. The Kotal contingent behaved very treacherously, and took one of our guns. Our volunteers, however, sallied out of the fort, beat the villains back, and took two of their guns. I hear heavy firing now (7 a.m.) going on in the direction of Meerut, and fancy it must be General Hewitt punishing some refractory villagers. Wheeler is supposed to be at Allyghur with three regiments, and 4,000 Europeans are at Allahabad by this. This news came last evening by electric telegraph from Sir John Lawrence. On the 9th the European Infantry killed seven camp-followers by mistake. It was a crying shame, and excusable only under the very peculiar circumstances of the sudden attack on our camp.

Yes, there is the greatest comfort to be found in the Old Testament, in reading the account of the many battles that God fought for Israel ; and the one you mention has often made an impression upon me.

CAMP BEFORE DELHI,
Tuesday, 4 p.m., 14th July.

Memorable, indeed, in the annals of India will the year 1857 be. There has been hard fighting all day from 10½, and it is by no means over yet. We mounted at 11, and my squadron only has come back ; the other two are still out as supports. Mine came home because it was on picquet all day yesterday. The musketry fire is just now fiercer than it has ever been, and I fear I shall have to give you a long and painful list of casualties before I close this. On our return home we met the 1st B.E.F. going to the scene of action, and I saw young Brown at the head of his company, and Captain Green, a volunteer. Turner, too, with his 9-pounders, was going to render his powerful assistance. We thought at first that our rear was going to be attacked, because a large party came out last night and got round there ; but it seems that they doubled back again, and lent their aid to keep up the attack (a most determined and long-continued one for Pandy) on our right, under cover of the gardens and walls of the Subzi Mundi. We must, I fear, have suffered very much. The enemy had the impudence to fire a salute last night, in honour of their victory at Agra over the volunteers. The firing is so fierce in front that I have just

sent off Fawcett to let me know what is going on, as
I am the senior officer in camp, and may have to turn
out again. I have got yours of the 12th. I am
sorry to see that it is written in rather bad spirits,
but I am not surprised. We shall eventually have
the Lord on our side. Let us cast our burden upon
Him. He will not suffer the righteous to fall for
ever. God shall send forth His mercy and truth,
though our souls may be among lions. Hodson is
not to blame. Anyone might have been taken in
under the circumstances. Saunders, of the C.S., is
going to make himself useful between Kurnal and
this. He is an active, energetic man, and will do his
best to keep the district in order.

Wednesday, 15th, 6 a.m.—We passed a quiet night
after the turmoil of the day. I was so tired that I
could not go to mess, but dined at home, and turned
in immediately afterwards, waking this morning very
much refreshed. I have been out trying to glean
particulars of yesterday's most noisy fight. All their
guns and all ours were banging away. It seems that
from 11 to 3 not much was done on either side. The
enemy occupied their usual posts behind walls, &c.,
and resisted all attempts to dislodge them. About 3
we sent out a fresh column, composed of Turner's
guns, Coke's corps, 1st Fusiliers, and some of the 8th,
all under Showers, to take the enemy in rear. This
they effected ; and then commenced a stir amongst
them. They fell back, and were pursued up to the
very walls of the town, from which the enemy fired
grape upon our troops, who suffered much in consequence of their close proximity. Turner had two

men killed, two severely wounded, and had his own horse hit in the belly by a shot which went through his sabretache. Lieutenant Thompson was wounded. Chamberlain, the Adjutant-General, badly wounded in the arm. Our Walker shot through the thigh. A great number of men appear to have been wounded, but few killed. The enemy kept up the spirit of their troops by pouring out numerous reinforcements. It is certainly the hardest day's work our troops have had, and since Wheeler is near, the chances are that the enemy will try and give us plenty to do before he can join. I saw Packe this morning; his doctor seems to be most attentive, and sleeps in his tent.

CAMP DELHI,
Wednesday, July 15*th*, 1 *p.m.*

All quiet up to this. I received the following in answer to my note to Showers: "We were under a very heavy fire of grape from the fort and our loss is severe. The 1st Fusiliers have lost one killed, two missing, and sixty-one wounded. The Goorkhas are said to have lost thirty-five killed and wounded throughout the day. Coke's corps must have lost some, but I have not heard the number. Artillery, two killed and four wounded. The enemy must have lost heavily, as our nine- and six-pounders were playing upon thick masses of them, and the heavy batteries from Hindu Rao's house were seen to play upon a thick crowd who were running towards one of the gates, when it was shut upon them. Being in the open plain, we had no opportunity of ascertaining the amount of their loss. We took the assailants of Hindoo Rao's mound in flank and by surprise, and observed several wounded or dead carried across the road. There was a place where about twenty mutineers were caught, and there were killed." I have sent the three last *Lahore Chronicles* to our hospital. Those men in hospital who can read entertain those who cannot with all the reports that find their way into the *L.C.*, and thus while away an hour or so of their tedious time. What a sad and frightful finale for two such old Indians as Brind and Graham. Brind, it seems, was very obstinate, and would not disarm his lot, but chose to confide in them to the last. Ouvry has arrived, looking very well. We hear from him that when the 4th were being disarmed at Umballa, —— made a donkey of himself by stepping forth and saying that he protested against the measure, and chose rather to resign his commission than see it carried into effect. Can you conceive anything more preposterous than this behaviour, now, too, after so many bloody, treacherous scenes, and after his having himself been made an animated target of?

Thursday, 16th.—A remarkably quiet night and morning. I went to see Showers and Welchman. The latter leaves to-morrow for Umballa and Dugshai, with a number of sick and wounded. I accompanied the former on his ride round half the camp, and had a good look at the enemy's bridge through his splendid telescope, and saw only foraging parties, escorted by numerous sowars,* crossing over to the

* Native Cavalrymen.

other side. We were nearly incommoded by some bullets from our own 61st, who were discharging their muskets towards the open country instead of into a bank. The Gwalior force has arrived, and will, I suppose, soon give us something to do. Captain Daniel, of the 1st Fusiliers, is badly wounded in the arm. The casualties altogether on the 14th amounted to 209.

Friday, July 17th, 6 a.m.

A remarkably quiet night and morning. Were it not for an occasional shell bursting just outside our camp and the fœtid atmosphere one breathes, we might fancy ourselves a camp of exercise only. Young Anson told us that Lord Canning had sent for Wheeler and his troops to keep the peace in Bengal, but I should think this highly improbable. There has been a great clearance of the Headquarters camp this morning. General Reed, too old and feeble to stand such hard work, has resigned, and Brigadier Wilson* is now commanding the field force, with Norman acting for Chamberlain, who, poor fellow, is exceedingly restless under his painful wound, which has split, not shattered, the bone of his left arm about four inches from the shoulder-joint. They expect to save his arm, but he is a very bad patient. When the coolies helped him out of the dhoolie, they let him fall on his wounded arm, and caused him so much pain that McKinnon, the surgeon, could hardly help crying out for sympathy. As soon as he was pretty easy he burst out laughing, and said " Did you see that sowar's horse topple

---

* General Sir Archdale Wilson, Bart.

F

over?" alluding to one of the Pandy Cavalry, whose horse and himself got hit by something in such an extraordinary manner that the next moment he was underneath the back of the animal, whose four legs were straggling up in the air. The sudden transition from a state of comparative repose to the performance of such a wonderfully active somersault seemed to tickle his fancy very much. There were a good many strangers at mess last night. Norman and Hocken were dining with Hope. Dr. Innes, of the Rifles, was dining with young Anson. Tombs with Sarel. Ford with Ouvry. Dr. Davenport, of the Carabineers, with Smith. We had a mild sort of alarm about midday yesterday. Hope received a note from Headquarters saying that the enemy were coming out, and that they looked to him for the defence of the rear. Whereupon he ordered all to saddle and bridle, and we remained so for an hour. It was very fortunate that we did not turn out, for it was a very hot steamy day—just the day for *coup de soliel.* Twenty-one lacs are expected in a day or two.

CAMP BEFORE DELHI,
July 17*th,* 5 *p.m.*

This has been a frightfully hot day, and it is a great mercy that we have not been turned out. The flies are something awful. Upton was good for nothing till the post came in and brought him his usual letter, which roused him to something like exertion. From 10.30 to 12 o'clock I felt dreadfully lethargic myself. Drysdale is just going to Alipore to escort the sick. He will be out all night, and will bring in a convoy of eighteen lacs, besides munitions of war and supplies. The thermometer ninety-nine degrees at 5.30 p.m.

Saturday, July 18*th,* 1857, 7 *a.m.*—We passed a very quiet night. In consequence of Drysdale's absence, I went round the picquets between 10 and 11. There was a good deal of thunder and lightning. I expected every moment it would rain, but it has not done so up to this, though the wind is easterly, and it is very cloudy. I am glad of the change, for we lost one man from apoplexy (Taylor of A Troop) yesterday, and the heat gave old Sergeant-Major Spence an attack of fever. Upton went out sketching in the evening, and brought back the outlines of a very picturesque old ruin of a temple and tree. Ouvry went to Bagh-ke-Serai to exhume Delamain, who was buried with only one more man. He had no difficulty in recognising the body from it having only one arm and the dress. He had it brought in, and paid it the last honours with Mr. Rotton at 11 p.m. It is reported (one of the shaves about camp) that Pandy is coming out to-day in two large columns, one of Mussulmen and one of Hindoos, and that when the Neemuck force joins him, he intends treating us to a pitched battle. The Artillery officers, now that Wilson is commanding, are likely to hear authentic intelligence. Martin, of the 75th, and Perkins, ex-engineer, have both gone away sick. Hope had Colonel Jones, of the 60th Rifles, and Colonel Custance, of the Carabineers, dining with him yesterday. I was obliged to finish abruptly for the " turn out " sounded. We are standing to our horses.

F 2

CAMP BEFORE DELHI,
Monday, July 20th, 1857, *6.30 a.m.*

We are getting turned out and kept on the alert every day regularly. The alarm has just sounded, and the Infantry have sallied out to meet the Pandies, who must be infuriated to attack us before they have "cooked." Mr. Rotton read and preached to the Cavalry Brigade yesterday evening. The service, which lasted about one and a quarter hours, was too long, and many of the men fell out, my legs ached again from standing so long. His text was from Isaiah lvii. verses 4 and 5, and he preached a sermon thereon applicable to these times, telling us (to Drysdale's and others' great displeasure) that God was punishing us for our sins ; but that He would no doubt eventually exalt us. Three thousand French troops originally destined for China have arrived at Calcutta, and it admits of a question whether Government will employ them in India. I don't think they will. We must fight our own battles. They might seriously complicate matters too. In six weeks' time we may hope to see some reinforcements, meanwhile Pandy seems bent on worrying us. The goats are the greatest comfort to Upton and me, giving us delicious milk, morning, noon, and eve. While the Infantry were out yesterday, I was sent with my troop to patrol and prevent any disturbance in their camp. Fortunately we were not out more than three-quarters of an hour, or would have suffered from the sun, which was blazing hot. Hope paid me a visit. He cannot help feeling somewhat anxious about our getting too weak in the end to hold our own here if

not speedily reinforced. Every day now some thirty
or forty Europeans are expended by the enemy, the
sun, disease, and fatigue ; and as the season advances
we may expect more sickness. Indeed, there is just
now a good deal of sickness amongst the officers. The
poor watchmaker, Ellis, was seized with cholera at
1 a.m. this morning ; the symptoms were subdued, and
it was thought he was going on favourably, when
apoplexy set in and carried him off at 6 a.m. I was
very sorry to hear of his death. Rivers, of the 75th,
has also just died of cholera. One Walker is dead—
not ours. We have heard nothing in camp about
Meerut, but I think your news regarding it very
probable.

Monday, 2 p.m.—It proved to be a kind of false
alarm in the morning ; the picquets, however, have
been popping away, and Pandy evinces every inclination to pop out of the gates ; but he is narrowly
watched and knows and feels it. To-morrow, however, he is determined to have a slap at us, and a
good one too. The news from the up country is
cheering. Golab Sing has caught 200 of the 14th,
and is going to blow them away from guns. A small
force came up in rear of the Jullundur mutineers, and
with Nicholson in their front they were, the Infantry
at least, nearly all destroyed. So long as we continue
rooting them up like this, branch and stem, the Punjab will be quite safe, and the country is ours from
Allahabad downwards, so that the mutineers already
find themselves cabined, cribbed, and confined. In
Rohilcund there is no strong place for them to hold
out in, and the mere presence of the European force

will suffice to crush rebellion in that quarter. Hocken's
Irregulars were distrusted, and he has been obliged
to take them off to Loodiana. I received yours of
the 18th. I am suffering more from want of sleep
than anything else, and get up of a morning much
more tired and worn than when I went to bed. This
feeling, however, wears off as the day waxes, but
comes on again as it wanes. From 2 to 6 I always
find it trying. The Gwalior contingent, it appears
now, is not near Delhi ; it has not, in fact, passed the
boundaries of its own district. We shall be delighted
to welcome the Kumaon battalion, and if a wing of
the 52nd could be spared, so much the better. I am
glad to hear that our things in the canteen have
escaped the wet.

Tuesday, July 21st, 7 a.m.—Yesterday evening just
as we (Drysdale, Jones, and myself) were going to
poor Ellis's funeral, the alarm sounded, and we heard
that a large body of sowars were about turning our
right and getting into our rear, and that the enemy
were attacking the picquets all along the front. We
mounted in hot haste, trotted down a mile to the
menaced flank, and the alarm turned out to be in a
great measure a false one ; so, after waiting three-
quarters of an hour, and seeing the Guide Corps
march back into camp from the Subzi Mundi, to the
shrill, but tuneful and inspiriting, sounds of their bag-
pipes and tom-toms (and a most picturesque scene it
was in the dark of the evening, their head-dress being
very Oriental and peculiar), we returned to camp in
time for dinner. Captain Spring, of the 24th, who
was killed at Jhelum, has a wife. He and Robert-

son left Roorkee in the same conveyance, and Mrs. Spring was congratulating herself upon her husband's going to a safe part of the country. Mr. Parker says, "We hope soon to hear that Delhi has fallen, and that a part of the troops are busy superintending the prisoners in the work of demolishing the city. If one stone is left upon another it will be a great mistake; but I think it has been good policy to wait till now. If you were inside your force is insufficient to secure the supplies, and as it is, Delhi is a sort of rat-trap for mutineers." I do not think there is much chance of Delhi falling before the middle of November. Sandford and Willuck have been appointed to the Guide Corps.

CAMP DELHI,
July 21*st.*, 2 *p.m.*

Ouvry is determined to pay all suitable honour to poor Delamain's remains. It is, I think, a good trait in his character. He is now bent on a marauding expedition down to Metcalfe's house to secure one of the marble slabs that are lying about there to place as a tombstone on D.'s grave. He is going down in one of the hospital bullock-carts, and since where he is going is perfectly within range of cannon-shot from the walls of the fort, the enemy, thinking that he is bent on some mining operation with his cart full of powder, will be sure to have a crack at him. He says he feels sure that he will be transferred to one of the new regiments coming out here. In that case Drysdale will command, and I should be second in command, a post which has its privileges. Poor

young Greensill, of the 24th (a captain) met, about
10 p.m. last night, with a most melancholy fate. He
is attached to the Engineer Camp here, and was examining the ground in front of the battery picquets,
having previously concocted a signal with them by
which they would know him, when, on his return,
he was challenged by an officer of the 75th, and,
not answering, was fired on and shot through the
stomach. He lingered on till this morning in great
agony, and then expired. It was a most unfortunate
circumstance. Greensill was a nice little man, and is
much regretted. A Calcutta dâk of the 1st June
arrived in camp this morning. Did you hear of the
fate of General Hewitt's old scoundrel of a kitmutgar
at Meerut? He had been twenty-five years with his
master, and on the evening of the Delhi massacre
Captain W—— suddenly discovered him dancing
round the dinner-table and throwing the tumblers
up against the wall, loudly exclaiming against the
Feringhees and their rule, whereupon Captain W——
out with his revolver and shot him on the spot. If
the 52nd and Kumaon Battalion come down here,
we shall be able to hold the Subzi Mundi, and hem
the enemy in completely.

Wednesday, 22nd.—I had to patrol for two hours,
from 9 to 11, last night, up and down in front of the
camp. This morning I thought we were going to
be attacked; there was such a smart fire of musketry
in the direction of Metcalfe's; the batteries, too,
opened, and so "Boot and Saddle" was sounded,
but nothing came of it. The Neemuck force has
joined; there is, I believe, no doubt of that, and

Murray McKenzie will have the satisfaction of being fired at by his own guns. The enemy make no end of powder daily, and have manufactured 15,000 percussion caps, which are useless, however, at present, because they don't know how to make the detonating composition. They are very much down in their luck since they have heard that a village near Agra has received orders to prepare supplies for 4,000 Europeans, and that twenty ships have arrived at Calcutta full of soldiers. Good-bye. Grace, mercy, and peace be with you.

CAMP BEFORE DELHI,
July 22nd, 1857, 2 *p.m.*

Though I am on inlying picquet, and consequently first for duty with my troop, and I fully expected passing more than half the day in the sun, all has been very quiet up to this. The post brought me in a good many letters, and C——'s was a great treat to me, breathing, as it did, of green fields and country life at home. I am very glad to hear that Havelock has got the command of the troops coming up country. He will lose no time in joining us, and I fully expect to see him here by the 8th or 9th prox. If 3,000 Europeans join us we may make a dash at the place about the middle of next month. Poor Bessie (Lady Muir), why did she not start off at once to Calcutta, like Mrs. Sneyd and Louie? The young family was the hindrance, I suppose. She now seems to be in the thick of it all, and I pity her from my heart. You will see how handsomely I catch it over the face and eyes from Mrs. C. for venturing to express an opinion on her brother's case. She is evidently Bonteau's "Woman of Mind." It is natural enough for her to take her brother's part, but it would require much cleverer advocacy than hers to exculpate him from all blame of dilatoriness in the pursuit of the "treacherous miscreants," nor do I see much wisdom in consenting to bear the blame which he can so readily fix, if he chooses, on others. Notwithstanding she has a good theme, she makes a very bad case out for him. No question but that he ought to have attended to Sir J. Lawrence's repeated suggestions, and disarmed the "base traitors."

CAMP BEFORE DELHI,
July 23rd, 1857.

I was obliged to close my letter very abruptly this morning in consequence of the alarm sounding, but nothing came of it beyond the hurrying out of our supports, and a heavy fire of artillery from both sides. This may yet prove a busy day. Norman has just galloped past, and there seems to be a stir in camp. Showers paid me a long visit this morning, but gave me no news. He is coming to dine with me on Saturday. House is the tidiest and most luxurious man in camp. Many wings of roast geese have I helped him to. It is a troublesome dish to carve, I assure you, and so are the ducks, a highly favoured dish. Jones and Upton and Martin and Goldie are very much afraid that their respective applications for transfer to the 2nd and 3rd Dragoon Guards may be attended to. They had much sooner

remain where they are, and quite dread the idea of
seeing their names in the *Gazette*. I am not at all
sorry that I cancelled my request. Should it please
God to spare me through this, I shall have had quite
enough of India. There is a very hot musketry fire
going on just now, 10 a.m., at Metcalfe's. This is, I
think, the twenty-third small battle that has taken
place.

CAMP BEFORE DELHI,
Friday, July, 24th, 1857.

The engagement yesterday was soon over. It did
not last more than two hours. We had twenty-three
killed and wounded, and an unusual proportion of
officers amongst them. Law, of the Sikhs, killed.
Colonel Drought hit in the small of the back, near
the spine, wound supposed to be mortal. Colonel
Seaton badly wounded, hit on the left side, rib
broken, but the rib turned the ball, which instead
of passing *through* him, went *round* him under the
skin. Money, H.A., hit in the knee. The ball went
in just below the knee-cap and came out sideways,
thus sparing the joint, and consequently the leg,
which would have had to be amputated if the joint
had been touched. Bunny was slightly wounded in
the face. Turner had a graze on the shoulder.
Showers had a horse shot under him. Colonel Seaton need not have been there. He was on no duty,
but meeting Showers on the road when the scrim-
mage began, Showers said to him, " Come along,
Seaton, and see what's going on. You have nothing
better to do." The skirmish seems to have been in

favour of the enemy, who had only three killed.
Young Anson is going up to Simla for a week, to
settle his uncle's affairs. He means to call upon you
either on his way up or down, and I told him that
most probably you would give him a small parcel for
me. He starts this evening by the mail cart from
Alipore. There was a good deal of rain yesterday,
and this is a remarkably cool, cloudy, pleasant day,
but, oh! the flies. I fully expect to be a mass of
sores. There was no dâk yesterday, but House has
just brought me yours of the 21st, and the *Lahore
Chronicle.* God grant that we may meet again.
That was a hasty speech of mine, but when a man
approaches forty he is sometimes apt to entertain
extraordinary views of life. I suppose the easy
kind of death must have been uppermost in my
thoughts, and faith and submission to the will of
God in temporary abeyance. I cannot tell you how
much I miss my children. They are as necessary to
the sunny health of my whole soul and body as sun-
shine is to the world. The one-year-olds are my
special delights. I often fancy I see you walking
into the dining-room just before prayers with your
arms full of the day's work, &c.

CAMP BEFORE DELHI,
Saturday, July 25th.

Yesterday was a remarkably quiet day. There
was a good deal of rain at different times, heavy
clouds, and a high wind, which made it very nice and

cool. To-day is a regularly rainy day. The heavy clouds have amalgamated, and there is one continuous downpour. I went to see Money at 5.30. p.m., and found him free from pain, and in very good heart and spirits. I met Turner and Greathed in his tent, which, by the way, is so nicely paved. Turner was not looking well. I congratulated him on his narrow escape, and he said, " Didn't they whizz the bullets into us, that's all?" It is not fair fighting for us. There the enemy lie, snugly ensconced behind walls, nullah banks, and large stones, and plying you well at from 150 to 300 yards with their deadly small arms. We must advance to drive them away, and thus present them with very fair shots. Poor young Jones, of the Artillery, died yesterday. French arrived by the mail-cart yesterday evening, and Wilkinson is expected in to-day. French came *via* Murree, and met many troops on the road between Lahore and this. I thought I had mentioned something about the Pandy Queen. I don't know what became of her. She was not, however, sent back to Delhi. There is a talk of the enemy getting into our rear again. They are no doubt very anxious to do so, but it is rather a risky operation, since they must proceed in force, and with guns, which Europeans have a knack of taking if placed in their way. Hope is naturally very sensitive about our rear, for on him has been devolved the whole responsibility of protecting it. Chamberlain is doing well. Drought is not mortally wounded after all, and is mending fast. I saw Blunt yesterday evening looking very well.

CAMP BEFORE DELHI,
Saturday 25th, 3 p.m.

It has been raining almost continuously up to this, but we happen to be so well placed on the parade-ground, which slopes downward to the canal, that the water incommodes us but for a short time. Hope came to see me this morning. He is looking remarkably well, and, from the exercise he takes, indulges in all manner of food. So quiet has been the day, that one is almost tempted to forget that there are within two miles of us twenty thousand " base traitors " and " treacherous miscreants" thirsting for one's blood.

Sunday, July 26th, 9 a.m.—Very quiet night; somewhat rainy morning. Went to Church at 6 a.m. Mr. Rotton preached an excellent sermon from " Being justified by faith, we have peace with God through our Lord Jesus Christ." About 9 p.m. yesterday evening I received, per Kossid, through Greathed, another wee (so wee, that I have unfortunately lost it) note from Bessie (Lady Muir), dated Agra, July 20th. She gave no particular news in it ; merely said that they were well, though much crowded in the fort. That they were anxiously looking forward to the arrival of European troops as well as good news from this, and begging me to write, through Greathed, asking what news I had of Mary (Mrs. Havelock) from Kussowlee. I answered the note this morning, and sent my reply through Greathed. Saunders and Ford left camp this morning for their respective duties at Paniput and Hissar. The carriage of General Anson's wines down to Kalka cost 166 rupees.

CAMP BEFORE DELHI,
27th, 1 *p.m.*

Just a few lines to say I have returned safe from Alipore, but a miserable trip, indeed, we had of it. Major Scott, H.A., commanded. We started at 11.30 p.m., got there about 2.30 a.m., when it began to rain. For two mortal hours I was sitting on my morah, in the middle of the road, well cloaked, and with a chattah over my head. Can't you fancy me? We started on our return at 5 a.m., and so bad were the roads, and so large and slow the convoy of provisions and ammunition that we did not get home till twelve. There is no doubt, I believe, that Wheeler and his small force at Cawnpore were obliged to capitulate, after holding out for twenty-two days, and killing numbers of the enemy. His powder magazine and hospital were fired, and he and party allowed to go on board boats, where they were murdered. I very much fear that Goldie has lost all his relations— killed at Futtyghur. At Futtehpore Havelock encountered the mutineers, killed 1,500, and took twelve guns and seven lacs from them. This is the best piece of news we have heard for some time.

CAMP BEFORE DELHI,
Tuesday, 28th July, 1857.

Thanks for parcel, which Sergeant Woodward safely delivered to me yesterday. A report came in yesterday evening from Younghusband, commanding the Irregulars at Alipore, to the effect that he expected an attack on his post in force, and would have to retire to Bagh-ke-Serai, where the battle was fought on the 8th. It was thought advisable to send off two guns and a detail of troops for his support if necessary. Havelock, directly after relieving Lucknow and looking after affairs a little at Agra, is to bend his steps towards us. We can hardly expect him before the 20th prox. There is a strong rumour flying about that the enemy are bent on disturbing our communications with our rear. The late heavy rains have evidently shown them the difficulty of operating in such a swampy country, and we being forewarned, are, I trust, forearmed. Mr. Rotton has kindly consented to give us a Wednesday evening service. It is to take place in my tent, because it is larger than the generality of other tents, and is to begin at 8 p.m., in order that Hope may have plenty of time to visit all his picquets beforehand. Mr. Rotton seems to have an extremely good memory, and is in the habit of preaching extempore with only the Bible before him. While Ouvry was bathing at the Flagstaff, the day before yesterday (he was F.O. on duty) a shell came and fell so close to him that he was obliged to throw himself flat on the ground under a bank to escape from it, a large piece flew innocuously over his head while in that position.

Five hundred and fifty rupees is an enormous saving out of what I have sent you. You had better keep it for a time of need. You will see what arrangements I have been making for paying Johnstone. I hope they may succeed. I am rejoiced to think that you have 550 rupees by you, and am charmed with the spirit of self-denial that prompted

you to offer it to me in part payment of the horse.
I wish you to consider it your own, to spend on
yourself and the children, or, if any be over, put it
aside for passage money home. Flannel vests and
cholera belts would to acceptable; for though the men
are obliged in quarters to have two of each, the things
get lost and wear out very fast campaigning, and
there are but scanty means of replacing them. What
they want most just now are padded curtains to their
cap covers. Their heads, owing to the small size
and shape of the forage caps they wear, are very
inadequately protected from the burning sun. This
is a very cool, cloudy pleasant day, inclined to be
showery.

CAMP BEFORE DELHI,
July 28th, 1857, 4 *p.m.*

The heavy rain has certainly been another kind
stroke of Providence in our favour, keeping the
" miscreants " at home, and swamping the country so
as to render any movement to our rear impracticable
What an atrocious, traitorous scoundrel that " Nana '
has turned out. I am so sorry that Havelock did not
catch him and make an immediate example of him.
He it was who headed the troops opposed to Havelock. What a providential thing your parents being
at home. They would otherwise have been murdered
to a certainty. Smooth-faced villain Nana—how well
I recollect him. His doom is sealed. Your father
(General Manson), too, always looked upon him with
an eye of suspicion. Poor Sam Fisher—he little
anticipated such a fate. I dined at mess, and sat

G

opposite Hodson, who knows better than most what is going on in camp.   Brigadier-General Wilson is very uneasy about our rear, and it is by no means improbable that the enemy may trouble us there. Fancy young —— writing up to Rawul Pindee that some part of our regiment had run away the day the camp was attacked.   French, on his way through, saw the latter, and has made him apologise for the false statement.   He said that he (——) had only just arrived in camp, and hearing the news, had confounded between the 9th Irregulars and our regiment. He has got off wonderfully cheap considering the atrocious calumny.

29th July.—This morning I went down to Metcalfe's house, and was surprised to see it such a wreck and ruin as it is.   Being completely commanded by the enemy's river battery, it is riddled through and through with shot, and there is hardly one whole pillar of the noble verandah left.   The enemy fired three shots at us—one hit the wall at our feet, the others came crashing in over our heads. The shot often go inside the once happy home, which now looks desolation itself.   The view of the river and the bridge of Selimghur, the palace, and a good bit of the well-wooded right bank, is exceedingly beautiful.   The compound looked green, and therefore not so bad.   It is quite a small, undulating park in its way.   I went there with Drysdale and Blair.   This is Wednesday, so we are going to have a beefsteak at 4.30, to be ready for service at 8.   The mess man has consented not to make an extra charge, though he has a right to do so, for, properly speaking, you can only have your dinner from the mess at dinner-time. As he charges one rupee eight annas for dinner, and will furnish us only with a beefsteak, and bread and butter, he will not be a great loser. Captain Ward, of the 8th Cavalry, arrived with the last convoy—a stout, happy-looking party.

CAMP BEFORE DELHI,
Thursday, July 30th, 1857, 4 p.m.

The post is resuming its good habits. Yours of the 28th, together with three *Examiners* arrived before noon to-day. Yes, I can never forget, for it is indelibly impressed on my innermost heart, the affectionate and assiduous care and diligence with which you nursed me through that dangerous illness of last November. I am sure that if I had not had the frequent sustenance and unremitting attention you bestowed upon me, I should not have made such a rapid recovery. I recollect once or twice waking up in the very early morning wretchedly faint, and feeling quite revived from what you gave me. I pity a poor bachelor in illness severe, left to the tender mercies of his bâtman and native servants. I went to see Showers, who sent me over two of the last *Punches*, and asked me to come and talk over J.'s defence with him. He does not think it a strong one, but, like myself, deems it a great shame that General H., who had not Punjab officials to deal with, should have been so leniently dealt with. J. would have done very well as a brigadier in this army, if he had not so grossly disappointed and disgusted Sir J.

G 2

Lawrence. I look upon Sir John as sure of a peerage after this business, for he has rendered incalculable services at this crisis. Showers gave me a glass of port-wine, which I mixed with water, and some delicious English biscuits. He had had good accounts of Mrs. Showers and children, and enquired kindly after you. There has been another fight at Cawnpore, when the mutineers were most signally defeated, and all they had taken from them. Such is Hope's news to-day. The enemy here are fortifying the head of the bridge on the left bank, which looks as if they were afraid of Europeans coming up that side.

Friday 31*st*, 6.30 *a.m.*—The alarm has just sounded. We shall probably have some work to do to-day.

9.30 *a.m.*—We have been formed up in front of our lines for the last three hours, and have just been turned in for breakfast for men and horses, the saddles remaining on. The enemy have come out in two strong columns, but they do not seem inclined to advance, and as yet there has not been much fighting. I accompanied Upton out sketching yesterday afternoon. The ride was a nasty one, all through the back slums of camp; but there was much to see and examine in all the old ruins about, and small country houses of Delhi baboos and jewellers. He took a sketch of a pretty old mosque.

Rothney and Craigie dined with Hope last night. All is quiet just now, 10 a.m.

CAMP BEFORE DELHI,
Friday, 31*st*, 5.30 *p.m.*

This has been a very rainy and a very noisy day—

our artillery vying with Heaven's own in thundering form. The very heavy thunderstorm seems to have kept Pandy quiet, though he showed a great disposition to fight to-day, and in addition to giving us two false alarms, he kept our batteries in full play, or fire, for some six hours. The rain began about twelve, and it is raining hard now. The enemy are trying to work round our rear, for a large body of Cavalry and some Infantry and Artillery were seen to leave Delhi this morning, and proceed Rohtuk-wards, with a view, it is said, of making a dour (raid) on Paniput. We have detailed a movable column under Coke to start at seven this evening, for the purpose of frustrating their attempt   A squadron of ours, the 4th, under French, Blair, and Sarel, forms part of the force. Did I tell you of young Sandford's good behaviour some time ago? While roving about the Subzi Mundi, he entered a house and found a book as large as a family Bible. On opening it he found it full of the most obscene pictures imaginable, beautifully, nay, artistically, executed. It was a most elegantly bound volume. What does he do but tear it up there and then in presence of his Irregulars (some of the 9th Irregulars), who fully understood the import of the devilish work. Many less scrupulous youngsters would have boned it as a *rich prize*. To-morrow will be sure to be fine after all this rain, and August, you may depend upon it, will be a month of excitement for us.

Saturday, August 1st. — Tremendous heavy rain. It began about five, and it has been thundering down up to this, 9.30. French's squadron went out only

to help bring in a convoy.   It came in half an hour
ago, all drenched and dripping.   Our guns are firing,
in spite of the rain.   I have not heard whether the
enemy's force that went out yesterday returned
again.   Should they not have done so, orders will
probably have been sent to stop the Kumaon battalion and hurry on Nicholson to fight the enemy's
detachment.   It is all we can do to keep our tent
from being flooded, we shall not succeed if it goes on
pouring much longer.   I dined quietly in my own
tent last night.   You have set me such a noble
example of economy, that the oftener I save the two
rupees for mess wine the better.   Atkinson says that
we shall be the laughing-stock of all Europe for
having sat down before the walls of Delhi for three
months.   It has no pretension to the name of a
fortress.   Mooltan had, and took twenty-two days
of open trenches before it fell.   Delhi, once we begin
in *earnest*, cannot possibly take so many.   The native
country places and gardens about here put me much
in mind of the vineyard described in 5th of Isaiah.
Read also from verse 16 to the end of the 3rd
chapter.   Our poor murdered women went through
it *all*.   You seem to have been spending only 150
rupees a month, wonderful to say.

CAMP BEFORE DELHI,
August 1st, 1857, 1 *p.m.*
It is just now beginning to clear up a little.   The
camp is one mass of water.   An order has just come
for the horses to be saddled ; so Pandy is, I suppose,

peeping out. You hear more news than I do of the
down-country force. Oh, that villain Nana. I should
really like to see him blown away from a gun. What
a narrow escape you all have had. What could have
saved you at Bithoor, isolated as it is? About
6 p.m. the alarm sounded, and the enemy have been
attacking us up to this hour.

    7.15 a.m., Sunday, August 2nd.—About 11 p.m.
they seem to have come on in force; before that they
contented themselves with long shots at the picquets;
but from eleven to six there has been quite a battle.
I never passed a more noisy night, for the enemy
kept firing into the camp from some guns they had
brought out, and all our guns on the ridge were
blazing away. The Infantry have been fighting for
thirteen or fourteen hours, and sometimes very hard;
I hope to tell you with what result before I close
this. Poor Willock, of the 6th Cavalry, got a very
bad fall yesterday. The horse seems to have rolled
over him, and hurt his kidneys very much. Tombs
fainted away while on escort duty yesterday; he had
been ill with diarrhœa, and started very weak. Blair
was so ill from diarrhœa and spasms that he was
obliged to return to camp. He was looking very ill
yesterday evening. Upton has just come home from
patrolling the camp, while the Infantry are out fighting, a duty which devolves on the Cavalry; and he
tells me that he saw a ten-inch shell (a huge monster)
close to the Headquarters camp. I have just seen
Ouvry, who was field officer yesterday. The old
story, he said, the enemy occupying the Subzi Mundi
and annoying us. At one time they came close

enough to suffer from a discharge of grape. I saw Light this morning—a perfect wreck from dysentery.

CAMP BEFORE DELHI
Monday, August 3rd, 1857.

Well, the great Buckra Eed fight proved a miserable failure. The Infantry waited for the enemy behind their breastworks instead of exposing themselves in the jungle and open, the consequence of which was that the enemy, after trying every dodge they could think of by false bugling, that is sounding the advance while they were retreatiug, the charge, &c., &c., to draw our Infantry out approached close enough to throw hand-grenades amongst them. This gave our men the opportunity they longed for, namely, of pouring some volleys into them. In front of one picquet some thirty dead Pandies were found. The enemy, however, were altogether so prudent and kept firing such a way off that it is supposed that they did not suffer a loss of more than two hundred men. Ours appears to have been something short of twenty, with one officer, Eaton Travers, killed. He was shot through the right side of the head and lingered a few hours. Last night was perfectly quiet and I slept like a top. I awoke once and heard Upton talking in his sleep about picquets, for which the puffs and beef he ate at dinner would fully account. I had a very pleasant rest yesterday underneath the curtains, which the horrible flies are beginning to make beastly dirty. Best thanks for yours of the 31st containing the treasure of a vei' and thus rendering me somewhat independent of them. I got it late last evening. I could not go to church in the morning because the Buckra Eed battle was raging. At 6 p.m. Mr. Rotton read prayers and preached a very good sermon extempore from 9th of Isaiah, verses 16 to 19. It all turned, you may say, on the words, "The effectual fervent prayer of a righteous man availeth much," adducing Abraham's intercession in favour of Sodom and Gomorrah. He deduced high encouragement from this to the cause we have in hand, and spoke much in praise of the immense importance and wondrous efficacy of the prayers of really pious men. The Kumaon battalion and Knatchbull's battery arrived yesterday. They have made handsome marches, but convoys even make this in three days from Kurnal. We have strengthened our defences in front with breastworks, &c., very much. A 60th Rifleman complained the other day that whereas before there was a chance of his being hit in the body, he now could only be hit in the head. The men will thank you for good flannel waistcoats and belts, but certainly not for those hairy inferior hill stuffs. You have contributed handsomely out of your private store. Wise and young Plowden have arrived and have been made honorary members of our mess, so their comfort is secured. Wise, in addition, is one of Hope's orderly officers. Nicholson with the Ferozepore siege-train cannot be here till the 18th, and we expect Pat Grant two days after. Delhi will, I fancy be taken by the first week in September.

CAMP BEFORE DELHI,
Tuesday, August 4th, 1857.

Here I am on picquet commanding a squadron in
the rear of the camp. I have been fortunate in not
having much picquet duty this campaign. In wet
weather, when the roads are bad, it is very disagreeable having to potter along patrolling in the dark,
tumbling into mud-holes as Blair did the other night,
and with the water in some places up to one's saddle-
girths. Hutchinson, Goldie, and Evans are on with
me ; our four charpoys are under the permanent picquet chopper. Hutchinson and Evans have regular
mosquito curtains, and look very comfortable. The
flies, of course, are worse here than in camp. Your
veil will come into great use. The night was quiet
enough, except for the frightful noise made by
numerous pariahs snapping, barking, and fighting
close to the tent. I have just (7 a.m.) received yours
of the 1st, and am sorry to hear that you felt so
uneasy during the Buckra Eed, and M.A.'s reports
were not calculated to make you feel more comfortable. The enemy suffered more than was thought,
for on Saturday night and Sunday morning some
500, they say now, were killed and wounded. Bad
news came in yesterday evening from Havelock.
Sir Henry Lawrence died on the 4th from wounds
received on the 2nd. What a loss to India and to
the Lawrence Asylum in particular, to which he used
to subscribe £1,000 a year. Havelock with 1,500
Europeans and nine guns had signally defeated the
enemy on three different occasions, and Pat Grant
was hurrying up with great reinforcements and going

to take the field at once in person. Mr. Allen's introduction to camp was not a propitious one. It rained very heavily all the day of his arrival, and at night there was this noisy attack. He is about the best-dressed man in camp. Drysdale induced me to have coffee for breakfast yesterday morning, and it made me quite ill. It was such nasty, blue-looking adulterated stuff, tasting like a decoction of liquorice. Upton was taken in too, and we both determined on having no more.

Wednesday, August 5th.

On picquet yesterday Evans caught a venomous snake which had bitten Hutchinson's small dog. He made the reptile bite his cap, and then seized it by the back of the neck, and holding it tight exposed its awfully sharp and venomous fangs most richly to view. The cool way in which he held it, and poked its mouth about amused me much. He is fond of stalking musk-rats round the walls of the house, pouncing on their necks with his finger and thumb with great dexterity. He and Goldie have been amusing themselves with blowing up with powder thousands of flies ; they are a horrible plague indeed. In the afternoon Metcalfe, Forster, 6th Carabineers, and Lowe the A.D.C. came down to the picquet and had an hour's chat. Forster was at Eton with my brother Anchitel. He is a remarkably good-looking man of about thirty, senior captain, and very fond of the stage. The horrible fœtid smell at the picquet, proceeding

from a number of dead carcases about half a
mile off, very nearly made me sick. The three
had a goose, rice pudding and stewed guavas for
dinner. I had a beefsteak and bread and butter.
They drank claret-cup—I had a bottle of beer.
Yours of the 2nd came in about 9 a.m. this
morning. We have had such very heavy rain
that I am not surprised at your dâk being late.
A horrible business, that of the 26th. Why did
Spencer go unarmed amongst them? We could
not go to the sacrament last Sunday in consequence of the great disturbance in camp. I am
on camp patrolling duty again to-night, but will try
only two hours at a time this turn. Mrs. Grant's
resolution is a very wise one. It would take 22,000
rupees to give each of our men two first-rate flannel-
shirts. I went to see Frank Grant the day before
yesterday. He seemed quite grateful for my visit.
Young Anson came back yesterday, and everybody has been chaffing him about House's keys,
which he failed to deliver going up. He had a
miserable trip, he says. Rain all the way there
and back. He was so wet on passing through
Kussowlee, on his way back, that he could not
go anywhere. I have written to Pila Doss for fifty
cap curtains for my troop. I am about the only
one who has done so, but it was Ouvry's order
that captains of troops were to take measures
themselves to supply their men with them. This
is a hot day—few clouds. The batteries are blazing
away at each other, but Pandy keeps at home. I
do not wonder at your feeling nervous. There is

not, I believe, a native in the country who would not be glad to see us all hashed up. Martin went out peacock shooting yesterday with Fawcett, who was kind enough to send me down a bottle of the most delicious eau-de-cologne to drive away the stench at the picquet. Ewart has a good deal to do. Both he and his son are well. Good-bye. May God be your rock and refuge now and ever. Blessings on the children.

CAMP BEFORE DELHI,

12.30, *August 6th,* 1857.

We have not been called upon to act as yet, though the batteries have not ceased firing and the picquets are engaged with the distant enemy, who will keep firing at our Infantry behind breastworks at from three to four hundred yards. From the number of shots fired by them, one would suppose that there was another Sobraon going on. Some 300 sowars about three hours ago came charging up the Metcalfe Road, shouting and yelling as if determined to charge through camp, but one well-directed volley from the picquet sent them to the " right about " like a flock of sheep. Wise, who saw the affair, said that it bore a most ridiculous appearance. The Engineers sent an infernal machine against the bridge, but it unfortunately stuck upon a sand-bank and blew up innocuously. To prevent such a catastrophe for the future they have put up beams across the river. The "Extra" came in this morning, and Ouvry is now a Lieutenant-Colonel in the 3rd Dragoon Guards. In ten days or so Drysdale will have the command, and I shall be again second in command and thus avoid picquets, which I abhor, because they are such filthy spots, and you are so teased by vermin of all sorts. My wine bill for June is Rs.73 14a. 11p., and mess for July Rs.70 15a. 4p., making a total of Rs.144 14a. 3p.—enormous sum, I think. I can, by screwing to avoid mess oftener, bring it down to Rs.100; one must live generously. Upton, I am sure, does himself harm by his abstemious habits. I am in such a state of prickly heat : when quite a griff in Calcutta I do not think I was worse. The enemy made a very feeble attempt at a night attack about 1 a.m. this morning, August 7th. Two or three volleys from the Metcalfe picquet sufficed to stop them, but the "alarm" sounded, and the whole camp was roused. I was not home from visiting the picquets until 11.30, and when I laid down I could not sleep, it was so horribly hot and muggy. To-day it is piping hot, and the sun ready for any amount of *coup de soleil.* Poor Brown, of the 33rd N.I., but doing duty with the Goorkhas, was mortally wounded yesterday. He died during the night. Temple, also doing duty with the Goorkhas, was wounded. There is some mention made of Kenyon too. It is said that the enemy are asking leave for the next two months, promising to return and fight us in the next cold weather. Another report is that within three days from this they mean to loot the city and then decamp. They have been bored by a number of wounded fugitives from Cawnpore coming amongst them. They have had the impudence to erect another battery, which we have been hoping to silence all the morning. There is a "shave" in camp, emanating from Douglas, the baggage-master, that the 52nd have had a fight on the Guggur, close to Umballa. Yes, Bithoor now is a scene of utter waste and desolation. Your father will hardly believe it; and there is a report into the bargain that Nana Sahib and all his wives were drowned in the river while crossing in a boat. You seem to do wonders with your money, buying yourselves gowns and bonnets, and sending me stamps and eau-de-cologne, and a veil, &c., &c. All the merchants have increased their prices. Greathed was dining with Hope; Robertson with Ouvry last night. I dined with Showers this evening.

REAR BATTERY PICQUET, CAMP BEFORE DELHI,
August 8th, 1857.

Here I am again, and a piping hot day it is; few or no clouds. Such a roar of artillery all night to keep the enemy from repairing their new battery, which suffered greatly from our fire yesterday, and which there is a talk of storming to-day. I was up at the flagstaff about 6 p.m. yesterday, and saw the enemy firing rockets into our camp. Three came into camp, and others fell into the ruined lines in front. I had a very nice little dinner at Showers' yesterday. There were only four of us—Showers, O'Callaghan, Wriford, and myself, and the conversation was very interesting; Pandy, of course, having his share. The enemy lost a great deal of their powder, or rather the powder they were making, yesterday. There was no explosion; but an immense column of black, sulphurous smoke apprized us of the happy circumstance. The

Infantry, consisting of thirty of the 2nd B.E.F., under
Lieutenant Hunter, have just been taken away from
my picquet. They want every available man I
suppose. My goodness, what a plague the flies are.
You are obliged to battle for every mouthful. Young
Pemberton is the Artillery officer on duty; only ten
months in the country, and working like a galley
slave in the batteries. I shall never forget the trouble
you took with your children; it seemed to me quite
killing, so I am not surprised at your feeling somewhat astonished at Mrs. ——'s *laissez aller, laissez
faire* system. Nicholson himself is in camp. His
force will be here about the 12th. I called upon Mr.
Rotton, Robertson, and young Anson yesterday.
Frank Grant has bought General Anson's stud-bred
chestnut for 670 rupees, and Hope bought a young
Arab for 700 rupees, with which he is much pleased.
Willis, Rich, Mills, and Upton have been transferred
to the 2nd Dragoon Guards. Upton would sooner
have remained where he is. I saw Turner yesterday, and Light, looking much better; also Grindall,
Wemyss, Green, and others sitting outside Showers'
tent. I must stop for the flies.

CAMP BEFORE DELHI,
Sunday, August 9th, 1857, 8.30 a.m.

I do not know when I passed a more miserable day
than I did yesterday on picquet. The flies, added to
the damp heat without a breeze, were something too
abominable, and almost unendurable. Hutchinson
and Evans both went away sick, leaving Goldie and

me to carry on the duties. Evans came sick. I shall take my own shuldaree another time. There is so much eating and drinking going on under the chopper, that the flies congregate there by myriads. It was hard lines, however, in the evening not to be able to eat one's dinner in comfort because of the flying bugs, which make a most nauseous smell indeed. They dropped into one's plate by half-dozens at a time. I went to church this morning directly I came off picquet, and found about fifty people collected together in the Fusilier mess-tent. About forty stayed for the sacrament, which I was quite rejoiced to have an opportunity of taking. I sat between Showers and Turner. Hurford has arrived looking very well. Mr. Rotton preached an excellent sermon on the text " Awake, thou that sleepest, arise from the dead and Christ shall give thee light." Mr. R. is certainly one of the most painstaking pastors I have met in the country. There has been a good deal of firing from the batteries this morning, and not a little musketry popping, betokening that Pandy is out and mischievously disposed. Pat Grant is, I believe, somewhere this side of Allahabad. I fully expect to see him by the end of the month. Fancy your having had such an undeniable earthquake. Some of these days Kussowlee will be rolling down upon the top of Kalka.

CAMP BEFORE DELHI,
Monday, August 10*th*, 1857.

Another season of discomfort is in store for me

H

You must know that at first we had three or four, or more, spare Government tents, and it was one of these that House lent me ; well, what between permanent tents for picquets and the others having been called for by the exigencies of the Service, there are now no spare ones, and in consequence of Clifford's demanding the three hospital tents that he is entitled to, I have been called upon to give up mine, and am therefore once more reduced to the shuldaree. I am more sorry for Upton's sake than my own, because he is too poorly to bear much hardship. In consequence of our moving about half a mile further from the hospital, thus making it now about a mile from camp, he is going to establish a temporary hospital in camp to admit serious cases at once into, and remove them to the bungalow in the ruined lines at his leisure ; not a bad measure, but he does not absolutely require three tents to carry it out. I am under orders to proceed to Alipore at 1 a.m. to-morrow morning, to escort 400 hackeries into camp. One troop of ours and one of Hodson's are going. Sandilands and Hutton of the 8th were wounded to-day in the Subzi Mundi by shrapnel.

CAMP BEFORE DELHI,
Monday, August 10th, 1857.

We have shifted our camp in order to make room for the Infantry, 52nd and 61st, expected in on Wednesday next, and have gone about half a mile to the rear, on the other side of the canal, to some high ground formerly occupied by all the camels in camp.

It required laborious cleaning, and the spot on which my tent is pitched is so uneven that it will require a day to level it in and make it at all comfortable. I am writing, therefore, under difficulties, the table sloping away from me like an inclined plane. There has been no great stir on the enemy's side. There has been a good deal of heavy firing on both sides, and the enemy are knocking Metcalfe's stables to pieces. They have now hit upon the range so nicely that they killed with a round shot yesterday a sergeant of the Fusiliers, who was standing on the top of them looking through a spy-glass. The same shot wounded two other men. There was no dâk in yesterday. Goldie and Evans are on my left, young Anson about ten yards in my rear, and Hope about the same. Jones has been appointed D.A.Q.M.G. Hope has got his buggy with him. Grain is cheap, about fifty seers the rupee ; so is attah, about twenty-seven seers the rupee. Yes, poor Platt! I cannot tell you how sorry I was to hear of his melancholy end. He was a very brave man, and you may depend upon it died most heroically, but how terrible the infatuation that led him into the danger. What worse than fiends he had to deal with. He was a particular friend of mine, and I lament much his untimely and horrible fate.

CAMP BEFORE DELHI,
Tuesday, 11th August, 1857.

I had a heavy dâk in this morning, and having just despatched a four-anna packet to you, sit down to answer yours of the 8th, for which, and for *The*

Home News, accept my best thanks. We were caught in the rain returning this morning from Alipore, but thanks to the waterproof coat and my cloak and jack-boots I did not get wet in the least. The wind was very high. It was quite a storm, in fact. An ugly incident happened at the mosque just now on the ridge, while Hope and young Anson were there. The enemy fired a round shot, which took off young Anson's syce's two legs above the knee, carried them off slick. The mosque (which is an old tomb) seems to be the most exposed place on the ridge, there being no battery there to protect you from the enemy's shot. A live shell fell right into the building itself, and, lighting on the staircase, smashed an unfortunate man who happened to be on it. Another shot brought down a ton or two of bricks and mortar on the head of another unfortunate European, who happened to be just below where it struck. Hope, good fellow that he is, is doing all he can to keep the tent for us. So long as it continues cloudy and there is the least breeze the weather is very cool and pleasant, but two days' unclouded sun renders the heat almost intolerable. We shall find it very hot and unhealthy here from 1st September to the 15th October. All who know Delhi dread those six weeks, even when living in the most comfortable way. Rothney has just written and asked me to find out something for him regarding his sister-in-law, Mrs. Dempster, whose husband was killed at Cawnpore. He has some hopes that she left Cawnpore before the attack on Wheeler, and proceeded to Agra, and he wants to write to Farquhar, at Agra, to

get news of her. What a disjointed sort of society
we are just now in India. These vile Mahomedans
must be laid low. *All* will not run away from Delhi ;
a lot of Ghazees, fanatics, will remain and fight unto
death. I am pretty sure that by the time we have
everything ready for the assault numbers will have
run away, but I am also convinced that we shall
finally have to contend with seven or eight thousand
fanatical desperadoes. Should I be spared through
this business I will make a point of going to you at
Kussowlee. There is a comfort I want, and which I
must screw out a gold mohur for if I can, viz., a set
of net, the best net mosquito curtains. The only
real repose I have had in the day since I have been
in camp has been under Upton's. Let me know
what you can get them me for. They do not yet
appear at home to have their eyes half open to the
gravity of the crisis. There may have been a sup-
plement to the *L.C.* of the 1st. This the mess-
sergeant did not send me. I have no doubt that
intrigues are going on all over the North-West. The
52nd, &c., &c., come in to-morrow. We shall no
doubt extend the line of our operations, and commence forthwith a regular siege. Poor Dr. Graham
was shot in his buggy, and his daughter drove him
into the fort in a dying state.

Wednesday, August 12*th.*—Well, it has pleased
Almighty God to preserve me untouched through
another brilliant little affair, while men and horses
were killed and wounded by my side. We (my
squadron, the 2nd) left camp at a quarter to three
this morning, and went to the place of rendezvous,

where we met 200 more Cavalry (Guides), 1,200 Infantry (8th, and 75th, and Fusiliers), and eight guns
(details of troops under Bishop, Remington, and
Elliot). After waiting there about an hour, Showers,
who commanded, arrived, and arranging us in order,
marched us towards the enemy, our object being to
drive them from a position which they had taken up
rather too close to us, and capture four field-guns
they had with them. Well, about ten minutes before
dawn of day the fight began, and for about half an
hour there was a murderous fire. Our Infantry made
a bold dash at the guns, which were obstinately
defended, took, and brought them away in triumph,
and succeeded in driving Pandy away altogether
from the spot. We were not actively engaged, but,
what is much worse, I think, we had to sit mounted
under fire the whole time. Strange to say, what
between Pandy's fright and his having been caught
napping, he fired so high and badly, that we had only
two men wounded and five or six horses. One man
was wounded close to me, young Whelan, by a spent
ball. The ball did not go through him, but lodged
in his side, inflicting a dangerous wound. What a
spank it made when it hit him ! and what a groan he
gave, for it took the breath out of his body. Showers,
noble fellow ! is, I regret to say, wounded in two
places, one long, slanting wound through the surface
of his chest—a flesh wound, but an ugly one, and
one of the fingers of the right hand smashed, for
so it looked when, in passing to the rear, he showed
it to me. Coke was wounded. They say that his
life is valuable, because he manages his men so well.

They would not mind anyone else, being properly independent and averse to discipline. Poor young Shireff was killed, and Captain Greville wounded in the hip. Being on duty after the fight in Turner's camp, I asked him to give me a cup of tea, as I had none before I started, and felt somewhat done. He gave me a most refreshing cup, and I saw Bunny, Light, Remington, and Dr. Brown. I am afraid that our shifting camp will put a stop to our Wednesday evening service. Some of Nicholson's lot are to come in to-morrow. There are some more guns to be taken on the Subzi Mundi quarter, and Nicholson will probably have the command of that expedition. We heard that Havelock had beaten 40,000, and taken thirty-three more guns at Lucknow. Young Anson has just been here, lamenting that he was not present this morning. It is just as well that he was not, for, being a volunteer, he would probably have come to an untimely though honourable end.

CAMP BEFORE DELHI,
Thursday, August 13*th*, 1857.

I have had a very heavy cold. It was very bad yesterday ; it was all I could do to sleep, tired as I was. I am much better to-day. I find the veil uncommonly useful. One hundred and thirteen were killed and wounded yesterday morning, the 12th. My man is not dead yet ; indeed, I went to hospital yesterday evening to see him, and found him sitting up, being bled, and wonderfully well, entertaining good hopes of himself ; but Smith, whom I met there, told me he had no hopes of him. Mr. Rotton came yesterday evening in spite of the distance, and Hope and Frank, Hamilton, Rothney, Upton, and myself formed the party. Mr. Rotton read the 37th Isaiah, expounded it at length, and gave us a long, appropriate prayer. Mr. Ellis paid us half-an-hour's visit yesterday. He says he has lost 1,500 rupees' worth of things at Umballa. It was kind and generous of Ouvry giving the women one hundred rupees. How it must have pleased Mrs. Grant distributing it. Hope has succeeded in keeping the tent for us; but I have sent two camels with the bearer, who left this morning, to bring up a similar one from House's store at Umballa, so that I shall be independent for the future.

CAMP BEFORE DELHI,
Friday, August 14th, 1857.

Best thanks for yours of the 11th, and for writing a few lines to M. A. Fancy young Anson telling me the other day that the General did not know that I was Sir George Anson's son, that, in fact, he knew nothing about his own family, and hardly ever saw one of them but his own immediate brother, Lichfield, with whom he was very intimate; but he knew little or nothing even of *his* family; didn't know how many brothers and sisters young A. had, nor how many of the latter were married. He was, in fact, notorious for ignoring his own kith and kin. Nicholson's force marched in this morning. It was quite refreshing hearing the 52nd band. Five big guns, viz., two 24-pounders and three 18-pounders, arrived with them.

You should have heard the Europeans in camp cheering the advent of their fellow-soldiers. The space that we vacated is now swarming. The Cavalry Brigade, being on high ground, looks down on the whole Infantry and Artillery camp. We are very prettily and commandingly situated, having a fine view of the flagstaff, mosque, observatory, and Hindoo Rao picquets and batteries. I had a long, wearisome ride last night round the picquets, and was obliged to report one that I found fast asleep, sentry and all. The excuse that they gave was that they had been up nearly all night (it was nearly four when I visited them) listening to the enemy's fire on the Metcalfe picquet. Their mode of attack is this: They steal up in great numbers to within eighty or ninety yards of the picquet, and, firing off their muskets, run away as hard as they can, one of our batteries helping them to do so with a good grace. Our men being safe behind breastworks, their noisy volleys are perfectly innocuous. The veil is useful, but though a capital, fine, thin one, it is somewhat stuffy from the proximity to one's face. However, I am very grateful to it for saving me from fever twice on picquet, where, if it had not been for it, I could not have had a moment's rest. The immense cobra that was found in Jones's small tent under his box has made me very anxious to have curtains by way of protection against reptiles of all sorts. Our youngsters' great amusement is going down to the river to shoot alligators. Fawcett shot a large one last evening. Many people have been complaining lately of sickness at stomach. Young Anson was obliged to hurry out of mess last night in a fainting state, and Wilkinson had only eaten three spoonfuls of keer for breakfast when he was sick. I felt queer yesterday at dinner, and could not make it out, except it was from emptiness, for I had only soorgee for breakfast, and nothing more till 8 p.m. I am always going to have some bread and butter for the future at 2 p.m. I went to see Hope yesterday evening, and found Frank sprawling upon his bed. We had a lively conversation about Pandy, &c., and I read Tucker's letter to him out of *The Home News*. How busy you seem to be about the men's affairs.

CAMP BEFORE DELHI,
Saturday, August 15th, 1857.

Thanks for yours of the 12th. We have put up our chicks, and are now so free from flies that we seem to have entered upon quite a new state of existence. How I dread going on picquet to-morrow after the last two days' happy exemption. We go on picquet now by squadrons, and so, of course, I am on every fourth day, and the flies and heat and stench make it the most disagreeable duty it is possible to imagine. I shall be quite glad to be like Drysdale, second in command, and thus off the roster. The next mail will, I hope, bring out official intimation of the changes, and place Drysdale at once in command. We had a very heavy fall of rain yesterday evening, the first we have had since our camp has been pitched here, and we were very glad to find that almost any amount of rain might fall without much inconveniencing us. Clifford was glad to hear what you said about the pillows. You are a perfect wonder to me. Your resources seem to be inexhaustible. Our camp now, with the 2,500 reinforcements, looks a very respectable size. One hundred and fifty of the 52nd went down to the Subzi Mundi this morning for the first time. All is quiet. The enemy's bounce has passed away. It was mere bounce that induced them to make such a noise night and day for forty-eight hours after the loss of their four guns.

REAR BATTERY PICQUET,
CAMP BEFORE DELHI,
Sunday, August 16th, 1857.

Here I am again on this tormenting picquet with Hutchinson, Evans, and Thonger. Hutchinson is very comfortable under a punkah (just big enough for him) that he has rigged up. Evans is under mosquito curtains, and Thonger on his bed fanning the flies off with his handkerchief. The two former are reading novels. I am sitting on my favourite morah at the bottom of my bed scribbling away. I should have liked to have gone to church this morning and heard the special service ordered by the Bishop. There has been, as I expected, a regular row among the Brigadiers. This system of super-seding Queen's officers by parvenus will never answer. The Horse Guards must put it down, or be content to be served with a very small modicum of zeal. I cannot tell you what a fume they are in about it, and very justly too, for it is not only an insult to them, but to the service at large. I feel myself exceedingly annoyed about it. —— was cracking jokes with the doctor (S——), saying what an objection he had applying to doctors in general, and particularly to him, inasmuch as he nearly killed him between Kurnal and this. "The busiest six hours I have had since I have been in camp were owing to you," said he. I saw the largest black scorpion yesterday that ever came under my notice. Imagine a young lobster, and you will have a good idea of the loathsome reptile.

CAMP BEFORE DELHI,
Monday, August 17th, 1857.

That horrid picquet has, as I fully expected, given me the mulligrubs. The night was dark, rainy, and damp, and I had to get up before three and patrol over swamps, into ditches and holes, and over embankments for about four miles; horrid work, I assure you, and most uncongenial to me. If I had had only light it would not have mattered so much, but I lost my way into the bargain and got sadly bewildered. Upton has received official intimation of his transfer. Ouvry no longer commands, and, thank goodness, there is an end of picquets for me for some time. I can do now without the net curtains. The chicks keep the flies out well, and I really can do without them. I am going to buy a new mess-tent. It is rather a reflection upon us, its having lasted so short a time. The inner fly is only now pitched, and that leaks like a sieve. They had at breakfast this morning to take refuge under the table. The cap flies have come from Pila Doss, and he has been ordered to supply all the regiment.

CAMP BEFORE DELHI,
Tuesday, August 18*th,* 1857.

I was lying down feeling poorly at six o'clock yesterday evening when I received intimation that my squadron was to leave this at one o'clock this morning for Alipore to escort 250 carts of ammunition. I have had a good deal of this Alipore escort duty, and am quite sick of the dirty-smelling road, at every 200 yards of which you meet with an enormous mass of putrefaction in the form of a dead camel or bullock. The camels are very unhealthy just now, and many die daily. Jones is kept very busy removing them by means of elephants. We met the convoy half-way and had the good fortune to be in camp again by six o'clock. The ride, if anything, did me good. We stopped about two hours by the roadside to let the convoy pass us and have a good start, and Evans took the opportunity to go to sleep in a puddle. He is the strongest man I know. Yesterday he was for two hours up to his breast in water under a burning sun surrounded by alligators, which he was attempting to catch by their noses. He has only got a slight cold to-day.

CAMP BEFORE DELHI,
Wednesday, August 19*th,* 1857.

My heavy cold makes me feel so stupid that I

cannot write *con amore.* Thanks for yours of the
15th. I am sorry to hear that dear sweet little B.
has had a touch of croup, spurious though it may be.
I saw Martin this morning; he has still a very
heavy cold on him. He was in a state of mind at
having his troop changed again. Upton is now sitting on his bed smoking and wrapt in the contem-
plation of one of his fondly-beloved productions. He
certainly draws very well, and may probably, some of
these days, become an artist. He has just finished a
spirited sketch of a Horse Artillery gun and its escort
of Lancers, and is sending it off to-day. The thermometer was 96° yesterday at 2 p.m., but even that will
give you little idea of the very trying, sapping sort
of day we had, and of which this bids fair to be a *facsimile.* I felt sure that such a day could not pass
without proving fatal to someone, and so it happened,
for on going to hospital this morning to see my
wounded men, the first thing I saw was poor Sergeant
Wynn stretched on a table with a sheet over his face.
He died at 11.30 last night of congestion of the brain.
Wonderful to say, Matthews is still holding out.
They have no hopes of him, poor lad; he bears up
right well under it all. Lloyd, who was shot right
through the right shoulder, was not so well this
morning, having passed a bad night from the pain he
was suffering. I am very sorry to lose his services.
He is one of my bravest and strongest dragoons. It
is very kind of young Perkins sending us his *Home
News.* He would be pleased to hear that it finds its
way finally into our hospital here. I am better to-
day, though I had such sharp pains yesterday that

I quite dreaded the return of the serious illness of last November without you to nurse me through it. I should not mind being ill again if I had you to nurse me, and, left to myself, I hardly think I could pull through a serious illness. The mutineers in Delhi are sending off their wives and children to some secure place. The bridge was crammed with their covered carts, &c. The report is that Havelock is at a standstill somewhere near Lucknow for want of powder.

CAMP BEFORE DELHI,
Thursday, August 20th.

We had quite a *levée* in our tent yesterday, and the visitors complained much of the heat, for though the chicks keep out the flies, they do us a bad turn in keeping out the air. Hope, Drysdale, young Anson, Blair, and Hunter, of the H.A., were all in the tent at the same time. Hope wrote and invited Upton and myself to dinner, but as Upton would not go, I got leave to take Hunter instead. We had an exquisite little dinner: grouse, soup from P., A. and Co., to remind Hope of the grouse shooting season at home, and a green young goose, with some very good fresh-looking peas from a Parsee merchant just come here, hash and fricassee, and a nice pudding. We drank a bottle of beer each, and enjoyed our dinner very much, Hope slyly observing he did not know what his wife would say to his extravagance. When we had finished dinner a note came in from the advanced picquet on the right to say that a regiment of Infantry were in the jungle about half a mile in their front.

Hope went immediately to look for himself, and
found that in consequence of our boning forty-five of
the enemy's camels, some of them came out to see
what was the matter, and finding all quiet, went home
again. Hodson has had a skirmish at Rohtuck, where
he found no enemy but the Goojurs, who, directly
that he had made himself and party comfortable
in a serai, surrounded the place and attacked him.
He got his men out, formed them, and charged, cutting up a few, and then sent in word to camp for
guns and troops to make an example of the rascals.
Nicholson's brigade started off last night, and will
doubtless give a good account of them. This morning the enemy attempted, after doubling the strength
of their picquet, to encroach on our ground at Metcalfe's, and we were obliged to keep up a smart fire
from our guns on the left to drive them away.
Hunter knows the Thomases very well. He lived
a month with them at Murree, and gives a splendid
account of him, his earnest, genuine piety; how he
visited all his parishioners and tried to make himself, like St. Paul, all things to all men; how at
Jhelum he found them all indifferent about religion,
only two or three attending church, and how in two
months his church was crowded; how he worked like
a slave at Murree, out all day and coming home quite
tired out in the evening. He has knocked himself up
and is going home directly he can. We expect the
siege-train here about the 1st, and five days after it
arrives our batteries will open a fire under which the
walls of Delhi will soon crumble to pieces. You will
be sorry to hear that poor Hope had what might have

proved a very bad fall while visiting his picquet yesterday evening.   He was riding at speed when his horse
put his foot into a rubbish hole and fell head over heels.
Hope came on his head and neck and cut his lip a
little.   His neck is a little stiff, but altogether he escaped wonderfully well, and is quite fit for duty.   A
woman, by name Mrs. Leeson, has made her escape
from Delhi.   She came into camp about two days
ago, but could give us little information about the
place and people, having been kept in close confine-
ment.   An Afghan befriended her.   She escaped as
an ayah.

CAMP BEFORE DELHI,
Friday, August 21st, 1857.

As I passed Money's tent yesterday evening on
my way to Showers', I saw him sitting comfortably
in an armchair outside, and stopped to have a few
minutes' conversation with him.   Showers was not
quite so well, he looked worn and depressed.   Wilson
had just been to see him, and Hope spoke a kind
word to him as he passed.   He is, however, doing
altogether very well.   Turner is, I regret to say, laid
up with fever.   Young Salway, H.A., has got inflammation from a cold caught on picquet ; and Light is
improving so slowly, if at all, that he must go away on
medical certificate.   Poor Mrs. Leeson's tale is a most
heartrending one.   Her husband was murdered, how
and where she knows not.   A brutal Sepoy came to
her quarters in Delhi, and finding her in bed with her
two children, a boy and a girl of four and three re-
spectively, he took the boy up by his head, cut his

I

throat from ear to ear, and otherwise gashing him, threw him on the top of the poor mother. He next seized the little girl of three, and cut her about the mouth from almost ear to ear. She lived six hours, poor little dear, asking or signing for water from time to time. The mother herself was wounded. Some good-natured Mussulman's family took care of her, and when the King went out the other day to slaughter the camels himself, two Afghans persuaded her to escape in ayah's clothes. She had one or two very narrow escapes, but at last presented herself before our picquet dreadfully exhausted. Nicholson's force returned about eight next morning. They went to Alipore, but from that they could get no further, the country was such a swamp. There was a good deal of firing yesterday on our left. Scott's two nine-pounders were trying to destroy a house, from the top of which the enemy kept annoying our Metcalfe picquet. They fired forty rounds with little or no good, and it was resolved to try and blow the place up at night. To-day the enemy have been firing rockets from an island in the river on the Metcalfe picquet, but they proved a failure. We are all most anxious to hear something of Havelock. We have heard something of an engagement, in which we lost one officer and seven or eight men killed, and gained a complete victory under Havelock. We hear to-day that 3,000 Ghoorkhas have taken Lucknow before Havelock could get there—that's good news, if true. Wilson here has been made a major-general, so that he cannot be superseded by Havelock, and he pockets 1,000 rupees a month more. The Umballa Artillery lost all their rich grain-fed mutton the other day. Their scoundrel of a shepherd drove them all into Delhi. They mess much cheaper than we do. Colonel Waugh has got the Royal Geographical Society's Patron's gold medal, a much-coveted acquisition in a scientific way.

CAMP BEFORE DELHI,
Saturday, 22nd, 8.30 a.m.

Pandy gave out yesterday evening that he meant to favour us with a night attack, so all proper dispositions were made to receive him, but, barring a little more noise than usual from the guns, the night passed off quietly enough. Hope has just casually made the acquaintance of a queer fish in Captain ——, who is by way of being merrily religious, and thinks that all religious meetings should partake of the nature of soirées, musicales, and literary converzationes. I used to know him at Cawnpore and he has, I hear, been enquiring after me, but he has evidently become a little too strong-minded for me. There have been two Kossids murdered between Meerut and Agra, and the last man from Cawnpore was sixteen days *en route*. In a letter received yesterday from C. he speaks very ill of the transport-train, and so long as —— is at the head of it, it will not, I fear, be up to much. C. says this is a bad establishment, everybody is disgusted with its arrangements, nothing could be worse. The manager, instead of being on the spot, lives at the hotel, and the deputy is difficult to find out. Poor Willock, who got such a bad fall a month ago, is dying from the effects of it. French

I 2

has had an attack of fever, something quite new for the little Hercules. General Anson's binocular sold for 133 rupees; his telescope for fifty-two. Two Parsee merchants have arrived with an entensive assortment of goods. I have no patrolling to do now—another privilege.

CAMP BEFORE DELHI,
Sunday, August 23rd, 1857.

The last three days have been tolerably cloudy and cool, and the rains are evidently thinking of another good flood or so before taking their final departure. They have greatly befriended us. Poor Willock, after much suffering, died at 2 p.m. yesterday, and was buried this morning. His death is not wholly to be ascribed to the bad fall he had, but to an access of fever and bad erysipelas when he was recovering from the effects of the fall. He has left a young widow and child. Upton is a little better, but he gains strength very slowly.

I went with Hope to the hospital stables this morning. He has two horses under treatment there, and it was all he could do to keep from interfering with ——, who was doctoring them in a very cool, phlegmatic manner. His three-year-old grey Arab that he gave 800 rupees for the other day is at present a bag of bones, and a year or two must elapse before he can make anything of him. Howard writes from Umballa, 21st, that the siege-train was expected in next day.

CAMP BEFORE DELHI,
Tuesday, August 25th, 1857, 10 *a.m.*

This is a regular rainy day, and it is pouring heavily just now. Everything is, and smells, so damp. I have such trouble in putting my boots on and off. Pandy issued forth yesterday with twenty-four guns and a strong force of Infantry and Cavalry, with the evident design of cutting somewhere into our rear and opposing the dignified elephantine progress of our siege-train. This movement on his part has necessitated a counter one on ours, so at 4 a.m. this morning Nicholson's Brigade, with eighteen guns, one hundred Lancers (the 3rd Squadron), and some Guides, marched out of camp with their tents and provisions for five days, and they are now about seven miles off, watching the villains, who have as yet made but very little progress. I am sorry to think of our poor fellows exposed to all this drenching rain. I went to see Showers last evening, and found him well enough to take a long stroll up and down the street in front of his tent. We were joined by Colonel Seaton, Light and Bunny. I met Blunt on his way to pay Upton a visit. Blunt was looking so well and stout and war-like with his beard that I scarcely knew him. Jones has been transferred to the 2nd Dragoon Guards, or " Queen's Bays," and in consequence of being fortunate enough to hold a Staff appointment, he loses nothing by the exchange. Young Nicholson and Sandford were dining with Hope last night. Sarel, French, Evans, and Goldie have volunteered for the Artillery, but their services are wanted at home. Perhaps one or two, Sarel and Evans for instance, may be allowed

to serve in the Artillery. When I got up this morning I saw Clifford, Drysdale, and Wilkinson (who live
together), sitting outside without a tent over their
heads. They looked like three disconsolate mer-
maids dripping with dew. On enquiring I found
out that the little doctor had run rusty with his
colleague, Smith, for striking one of his hospital tents,
(Smith, you must know, had orders to take a tent with
him, and he must have either taken a hospital tent or
the one in which Clifford & Co. lived). Smith did
not know that Clifford, sooner than part with one of
his hospital tents, was prepared to strike the Government hospital tent he and his friends were using.
When he heard that Smith had taken one of his
hospital tents, he, Clifford, immediately struck his
own and sent it off to replace the one Smith had
taken. Hence the mermaid *exposé* of this morning. Hope is all right again. There are rumours of
the 32nd having come to grief at Lucknow. How
heartrending and sickening is the list of the names
of the people murdered at Cawnpore—so many old
friends of ours.

CAMP BEFORE DELHI,
Wednesday, August 26th, 1857.

This was a very beautiful morning after the rain.
About 3.30 a.m. I heard Nicholson's tomasha going
on. He has, I am glad to say, been very successful,
in spite of bad weather and bad roads, and has
taken twelve guns and killed about 200 of the
enemy, with the loss of forty-one killed on our side,

and one officer, name unknown at present. The
enemy, in order to save their remaining six guns,
were forced to blow up two bridges. The twelve
guns that were taken were on our side of the canal,
the six on their side. The force has not yet returned,
and we have only heard thus much for the present.
When I was at the flagstaff this morning I saw the
two explosions caused by the blowing up of the
bridges. Buktowar Sing, the Bareilly villain, commanded the enemy's force, and he was either to
destroy the siege-train or reckon on being hanged on
his return if unsuccessful. The King, they say, let him
off the sentence of a court-martial on those express
conditions. I fell in with such a pleasing passage
in a review of Dickens' " Little Dorrit," that I must
fain transcribe it for you. " Then again, we have in
Little Dorrit's character the nature of duty, the for
getfulness of self, the thoughtfulness for others, the
constant patience, the noiseless endeavour to be
straightforward and right in little as in great things,
and the habit of doing everything in the most kindly
manner. Selfish relations do not weaken in her heart
the filial tie. She is laughed at, patronised, nomin-
ally held in low esteem ; but she wins more or less of
love and reverence from all, and in an hour of need
even those who affect to laugh at her rely upon the
wisdom of her counsels." You have heard, I suppose, of Delafosse's letter from Cawnpore, from
which he and a Mr. Thomson, a gunner, and a private
of the 53rd alone escaped. His letter is too long to
transcribe. It will doubtless find its way to Kussowlee, and its harrowing contents will rend your heart.

Reality, as I have always said, beats fiction into fiddle-strings, and nothing more truly horrible have I ever read of than that fearful Cawnpore tragedy. We have given over expecting any more reinforcements, and Wilson is hardening himself by degrees for the assault, the whole responsibility of which our present force must take. We are sadly in want of the heavy guns coming up with the siege-train. All we have at present serve only to defend the camp; we have none to spare for breaching. The enemy are thinking of attacking, for a troop of ours has just been ordered to patrol, a sign that the Infantry have all gone out to fight.

CAMP BEFORE DELHI,

Thursday, August 27th, 1857.

The roads are improving, for yours of the 24th reached me last evening instead of this morning. I saw the *thirteen* guns this morning taken by Nicholson. He certainly had a glorious success, and deserved it, too, for pushing ahead in the gallant, determined way that he did, coming up with the enemy at 4 p.m., and attacking them at once without hesitation. The only place where they made anything of a stand was in the village of Nudjuff-ghur, which was carried by the 61st at the point of the bayonet, and here it was that we sustained our chief loss. Dr. Ireland, of the H.A., was shot through the left eye, the ball taking a diagonal direction and coming out under his right ear. The wound, though dangerous, is not necessarily mortal. Lieutenant Elkington, 61st, mortally wounded in the head,

Lieutenant Lumsden killed, and Lieutenant Gabbet wounded, and dying of his wound and cholera combined. The victory will have a wonderfully good moral effect on all the petty rajahs and villages round about, and make all smooth for the advent of the siege-train, which we expect next Tuesday, the 1st. "If the Lord Himself had not been on our side when men rose up against us they would have swallowed us up quick." Our great sin in this country has been paying too much attention to their religion and too little to our own. In building up India we have thought too much of Mammon and too little of God, and you know that "Except the Lord build the house their labour is but lost that build it. Except the Lord keep the city, the watchman waketh but in vain." It is our "leanness, our leanness" that has brought this woe upon us and caused the people to deal treacherously — so very treacherously—with us. Henceforth let us all pray that we may trust more in His Word and that our help may stand in the name of the Lord, Who hath made heaven and earth. I think we may now say that the snare is broken and we are delivered, though we shall not be, humanly speaking, much indebted to the good people at home for the happy result of our exertions and endurance before Delhi. Their apathy, culpable in the extreme, seems to reign supreme, and they will require to hear the news of the fearful Cawnpore massacre before shaking it off. Mr. Rotton came as usual last evening. Hope and Frank and Hamilton were present. He read the 116th Psalm, expounded it, and prayed at length afterwards. The service was most comforting and strengthening, and we feel, I am sure, very much obliged to him for his ministry. It is a pity we are so much out of the way, for it makes people think twice before they come, especially when there is no moonlight. Hope was boasting at dinner the day before yesterday that he had never felt the sickness at stomach we all, more or less, have been bothered with. Well, to show what a bad thing boasting is, he had hardly swallowed his breakfast next morning before he brought it all up again. He has received intelligence from the Horse Guards to the effect that the 9th Lancers are to be kept up to their full strength, so I daresay some of the transfers may be retransferred ; at all events, Powys will become a major, *vice* Ouvry. I am going to lend Showers the buggy this evening to take a drive in. He asked me to drive him, but I begged to be excused, having no fancy for driving in this crowded camp. The camels are always in the way, hundreds of them going about in troops, blocking up the road and frightening the horses. They are a dreadful bother, all so scabby, diseased, and stinking, too. I keep steadily away from the Headquarters camp. Perhaps there is no one in camp of my standing and position that has seen less of the big wigs than I have. The truth is that unless they are wholly unaffected, like old Parsons, for instance, and Hope, their presence is much more of a pain to me than a pleasure. Wilson, to my surprise, bowed to me this morning. He knows, I fancy, who I am, and has been intimate with some of my people.

CAMP BEFORE DELHI,
Friday, August 28th, 1857.

Blair, Evans, and Cuppage have volunteered for the Artillery, and their services have been accepted. They will have to work in the heavy batteries and be exposed to much heavy fire. Ouvry has been appointed extra A.D.C. to Wilson and attached to us. Nicholson lost twenty-four killed and sixty-six wounded, and there were twenty-nine killed and wounded on the ridge the same day. We have had three such beautifully cool mornings, one would imagine that the cold weather had really begun. We shall, however, for the next six weeks have to suffer a good deal of heat in a dry place, without the shadow of a cloud. We have fifty-three in hospital, *i.e.*, about one-eighth of our effective force. There was a good deal of loot taken at Nudjuffghur, and, amongst other things, a lot of baby linen, a parasol, some silk dresses, and 6,000 rupees. Our native allies are dead hands at looting. The hope of plunder seems to be with them a main excitement to the fight. If we have 3,000 of Golab Singh's army we shall be perfectly set up for the sack of the wicked and adulterous city, which must be smitten and left desolate. I am much afraid that after the fall we shall be broken up into small detachments and sent scouring the country under a parcel of mad civilians. Four captains of Carabineers are ready to be off home for good at the first convenient opportunity. Young Anson is very anxious to have a game at chess with me. He is very fond of the game; it seems to run in the family. My sister

M. A., will beat five out of six old generals.
Anson has got a chess-board from the Headquarters
camp and is intent on having a game, so good-bye
for the present.

CAMP BEFORE DELHI,
Saturday, August 29th.

It takes some time to stir up strife in England's
mighty heart, but by the next mail I fully expect
to see her roused to a proper pitch of anxiety and
earnestness. There was so much firing last night
that I could not sleep soundly, and consequently feel
tired this morning. The firing was in consequence
of a new battery that our Engineers are constructing
on the right, by way of raking the ground outside
the city walls and thereby facilitating our approaches
to the city on the left, where we intend opening a
battery at about 300 yards, which will soon smite
the wall to the ground, bring it low, and lay it even
with the dust. Meanwhile the siege-train has been
delayed a day or two crossing the Markinda, and
will hardly be in before the 2nd or 3rd. Five
hundred hackeries, indeed, laden with ammunition,
came in this morning under a strong escort, for the
enemy, feeling this to be their last chance, have again
assembled in force in our rear with a view to molest
its progress. This force there is a talk of our sally-
ing forth to-morrow morning to encounter, and I
shouldn't wonder if Hope had the command this
time, for probably the whole of the Cavalry will have
to go. May he have as good success as Nicholson,
though of course he will have to deal with an enemy

grown very wary by defeat, and therefore more difficult to get near to. One hundred and nineteen
officers have been killed and wounded since the 1st
of June, and between 1,800 and 1,900 men. Bloodthirsty Pandy would give his right arm not to be engaged in such a mortal struggle ; he simply counted
on killing us all and having it all his own way, having
an idea that our country was very small compared
with his, and could not send out many soldiers.
They say that Sir Colin Campbell is positively in
Calcutta, having left England the day that the mail
did, *i.e.*, the 10th July. We cannot do without a
small native army, especially on the frontier beyond
Peshawar ; but the new native army will be as small
as we can make it, and there will be no monsters of
Poorbeas in it. It will also be much more strongly
officered and disciplined, and under the strictest sur-
veillance of an army of Europeans double its present
strength. Strong fortifications will be built at the
principal stations, and powerful brigades kept as
moveable columns, ready to march at an hour's
notice. This you will see will be the new *régime*
when the present troubles are over, which I fully
expect they will be by the end of the cold weather.
Havelock, finding the enemy too numerous and too
strongly posted between him and Lucknow, has
thought it prudent to place the river between them
and him and wait quietly at Cawnpore for reinforcements. The Dinapore mutineers have been caught
and punished by the 10th and other troops. The
Benares ones also have come to grief, but the whole
of Oude being up in arms, we must make a com-

bined and concentrated move on Lucknow, whither we shall probably bend our steps when this affair is over. Golab Singh's contingent is within a week's march of this. What devils all these natives will be at sacking the dung-hill city. I am anxiously looking out for the *Home News*, to have a quiet spell over the speeches in Parliament about India. The mess papers have come in, but I seldom go to mess except to dinner. I bought Willock's printed flannel warm dressing-gown at his auction yesterday for four rupees eight annas. It will last me ten years if I live so long. All his things except the uniform sold very well. Anson and I had a long tussle at chess yesterday, in which I came off victorious.

CAMP BEFORE DELHI,
Sunday, August 30th, 1857.

This bids fair to be a sneezing hot day. The thermometer is ninety degrees now at 10.30 a.m. Yesterday Upton had a severe attack of ague and fever. Drysdale happening to come in, and seeing the state of affairs, hurried off for Clifford, who immediately came, and decided on giving him medical certificate at once. The Board will sit upon him either this evening or to-morrow morning, and the probability is that he will make a start of it to-morrow evening, and that he will reach Kussowlee on Thursday or Friday. He was very ill all yesterday afternoon, and moaned so that I thought he was going to sink into his last sleep. He is, however, much better this morning. Showers may be said to be quite well again. Nice doings at Umballa. The 5th N.I. have caught it at last. How pleased young Ward will be. Sir John Lawrence will take vengeance on those who have dared to fire the native lines at Umritsur. There was a good deal of firing last night, and, being on inlying picquet, it kept me awake for many hours. I heard this morning that our troops had attacked and demolished a hostile breastwork from which the enemy had been annoying our wood-cutters. We lost one rifleman (60th) killed and one wounded. Poor Matthews, who was wounded on the 12th, died two or three days ago. Thanks for yours of the 27th. I am glad you hear all the camp news so quickly. It is supposed that 600 men, women, and children perished at Cawnpore. Havelock is reported to have relieved the troops at Lucknow. Twenty-five pairs of warm socks were given over to each troop yesterday as a present from the ladies at Kussowlee. Dr. Brown is laid up with fever. I am sorry to think that you should feel nervous at Kussowlee, but stay your mind on the Rock of Ages, and He will keep you in perfect peace. His loving spirit will not suffer you to be tempted beyond endurance, but will assuredly make a way of escape for you. We may soon hope now to drive these bloodthirsty, dastardly villains into the Tartarus from which they spring, or they shall send us to the Heaven we pray for. Hodson reports our rear clear. I beat Anson another hard game yesterday. Mr. Ellis is laid up with fever, and unfit for duty.

CAMP BEFORE DELHI,
Monday, August 31st, 1857.

The siege-train is at Paniput to-day, and will
positively be in here on the 3rd. Active operations
will then immediately commence. We are to serve
in the trenches fifty men by day and fifty men by
night. Sixty guns are to open fire on the place
eventually, and one gun will be fired every three
minutes. One thousand guns played at once on
Sebastopol. Sir Colin Campbell has arrived in Calcutta. A thousand Marines are to defend Calcutta.
A number of sailors are coming up to join us.
Clifford had a letter from Mrs. Nuthall. She said
all was quiet at Calcutta, but that they could not
help feeling some little apprehension from the very
large native population, that might be infatuated
enough to rise at any moment, and that her husband
had received orders to make vast preparations for
forwarding heavy numbers of Europeans up country.
Wilson, I hear, after conquering the city, intends
pursuing with all the troops he can muster. We
were told to expect a night attack last night, and
when I went my rounds as captain of the day, I
met an European Infantry support marching out,
and found that the Carabineer picquet had been
warned to be ready. The night, however, passed
over without the least disturbance. Poor Hope's
fall must have given him a good shake. His neck
is even now stiff from it, and he has some little pain
in swallowing. Best thanks for yours of the 28th.
Dear sweet little B. with her rag doll. How it would
delight my heart to see her. Existence without wife

and children is much of a blank to me, but duty must be a diadem of beauty to me for some time to come.

CAMP BEFORE DELHI,
Tuesday, September 1st, 1857.

Our men have too much to do to work (tailoring) ; I will just wait till Pila Doss comes, and then give him the stuff to make up my jackets with. I fully expect to have to go to Alipore, if not to Rhaiee, to-morrow or next day to help escort the siege-train in. Yesterday the King had the impudence to send us terms to the following effect : that he would make the mutineers lay down their arms and would give up the murderers of our women and children and allow us to enter Delhi, provided that we did him no harm and kept him on the Musnud. Of course, they were scouted, and an order given for all the batteries to open and sound their roar of defiance. When I was at the flagstaff this morning, they made a good shot with a shell from their battery across the river. The shell burst right between the two picquets down at Metcalfe's, and must, I fear, have done some mischief. The tent looks so large now the other charpoy is gone. I shall have lots of room henceforth to fling my arms and legs about without a witness. Having so long been used to see Upton sitting on your chair opposite me, it seems rather strange to me being alone, but I feel quite grateful and contented with being <i>a solitaire.</i> Nicholson mentioned Sarel in flattering terms in his despatch as commanding the cavalry and rear-guard. With

K

regard to Tombs, he said, " This officer's merits are so well-known that it is needless my touching upon them." The coolie, Lechman, has served me very well as a bearer during the Sirdar's absence. I expect the latter will be in to-day or to-morrow, and he is bringing all sorts of things for other people. What will C. say to the Cawnpore massacre? Unparalleled, indeed, has been the treading-down of our lives, and the laying of our honour in the dust. But the Lord abhorreth the bloodthirsty and deceitful man, and is preparing for him the instruments of death, and he will fall into the destruction and be buried in the pit which he dug for others.

CAMP DELHI,
Wednesday, 2nd September, 1857.

There was such a nasty smell pervading the camp all last night that I could not sleep, but kept kicking and tossing about and feeling sick every now and then. I wish I had not such superb olfactory nerves. Drysdale is similarly circumstanced. We have neither of us an ear for music, but we can smell corruption miles off. We rather envy Hope, who cannot smell a stench under his very nose, but whose ear for music is, as you know, something wonderfully excellent. I was calling upon Colonel Greathed last evening and he introduced me to his brother, the civilian, who had just heard from below, to the following effect: that our European troops were concentrating at Benares, prior to a move on Oude *viâ* Fyzabad ; that Havelock was as busy as a bee, fighting the enemy wherever he could find him ; that

affairs were much in *statu quo* at Lucknow, and that
his wife, Mrs. G., had heard from Mrs. Sneyd in
Calcutta, enquiring about her son and daughter. I
have just received my orders to proceed to Alipore,
and perhaps to Rhaiee, at 11.30 to-night, with my
troop and fifty Carabineers and 100 Native Cavalry
and Bourchier's * troop H.A., to help escort the
siege-train in on the 4th. I shall not, therefore, be
able to write to you to-morrow, and perhaps not
on the 4th, but that will depend upon the time I
get back to camp, which will, I fear, be late, so
do not be nervous if you do not hear from me
for two days. I was on duty this morning for two
and a half hours valuing horses of the 4th Irregular
Cavalry, for Hodson's Horse and the Guides, and have
to attend again this evening, at six, for the same
purpose. Major Richardson, of the 3rd Cavalry, who
got his brevet-majority for being at Kertch, in the
Crimea, is President, and Forster, of the Carabineers,
the other member of the committee. There is a
report that the assault will be made on the 8th
September, the day that Sebastopol fell. Certain it
is that once the siege-train arrives it will not take
long to prepare everything.

CAMP DELHI,
Friday, 4th September, 1857.

I must send you only a few lines to-day. I got
back this morning, about 7 o'clock or 7.30, earlier than
I anticipated, but very much done with my two nights'
work, and sleeping on the hard road, in the midst of

---

* Lieutenant-General Sir George Bourchier.

dirt and stench. Fortunately, at Rhaiee, I met the
bearer with my tent, so that I was able to put Smith,
the doctor, up, and we both were independent, and
much more comfortable than we deserved to be for
going so shiftless. We left camp a few minutes before
11, and arrived at Rhaiee at 5.30 a.m, after sundry
halts *en route*. The siege-train, under the command of
Colonel Farquhar, soon came in, and we all encamped
there for the day only, for at 5.30 p.m. the train,
which was certainly six miles long, started for camp. I
commanded the rear guard and did not leave till 8.30,
and that was much too soon, for we caught up the
tail in an hour, and halted a quarter of an hour; then
on again and halted one hour; then on again and
halted two and a half hours at that dirty place Alipore,
where we found the Artillery dhoolie and refreshed
ourselves with some nice hot tea. In Bourchier, commanding the Battery, I found an old Cawnpore
acquaintance, who was very friendly, nay, cordial.
Most thankful was I to pitch into his saddle of mutton
about 6 p.m., and how I did enjoy the bottle of beer I
brought out. The two combined, with the tea *en route*,
made me quite equal to the long, tedious grind of
eighteen miles. On our way back, about two miles
from camp, we met Hope, as fresh as a lark, and he
kindly told us that, having escorted the train in safety
thus far, we might march straight into camp without
any delay. Two elephants were harnessed to each
big gun and drew it along like a toy. I made the
acquaintance of Dr. Waghorn and Lieutenant Sconce
(a nice young lad) *en route*.

CAMP BEFORE DELHI,
Saturday, September 5th, 1857.

Having quite recovered from the fatigue of my two nights' deprivation of rest, I must have a good long chat with you. I was indeed very glad that the siege-train reached camp unmolested. A thousand plucky Cavalry would have made confusion worse confounded. Six 24-pounders, eight 18-pounders, four 8-inch howitzers, and four 10-inch mortars, in all twenty-two, with about 400 rounds of ammunition per gun, have come to us all right. Large working parties are now very busy preparing the batteries and approaches, and in three days from this, if not sooner, there will be a flame of devouring fire and a tempest of shot all about the place. Two or three days after the fire has once opened we shall, like a flood of mighty waters overflowing, storm the walls, and I fervently hope and pray destroy these murderers and burn up their city. Prize agents are being appointed, and everything is beginning to look like work in earnest. What a fright that clap of thunder seems to have put you in. Your poor hearts just now are in such a state of flutter from the fiendish atrocities that have been committed that I am not surprised to hear of the least incident throwing you into an agony of terror. The last horror I have heard of is the murder, by the 12th Irregulars, at Segowlee, of Holmes and Gardner and their wives. They were set upon while at dinner and cut to pieces. When Pandy became aware of our new right battery a consultation was held, as he thought that it looked like the beginning of the end. One brave Pandy stepped out and swore that he would destroy it, even if it cost him his life, but no such attempt has as yet been made. Pandy is under the impression that we intend attacking him on our right ; that is the reason, I suppose, he allows our working parties on our left to get on unmolested. Three days ago a deputation of Pandy soldiery went up and asked the King for pay, &c. He flew into a rage, and, raising himself a bit, flicked the velvet cushion he was sitting on right into their faces, saying, "There, take all I have, you'll rob me of my clothes soon."

CAMP BEFORE DELHI,
Sunday, September 6th, 1857.

This bids fair to be as hot a day as yesterday, when the thermometer rose to ninety-four degrees. For the last twenty-four hours we have been pretty free from horrible smells. Colonel Custance, driven nearly wild by them, set out on exploring the purlieus of the camp, and discovered no less than sixty-five huge putrefying carcases, all huddled together at no great direct distance from the camp. The removal of these will slightly benefit us. The enemy has been surprisingly quiet, considering that they must know that we are bestirring ourselves a bit now that the siege-train has arrived. They do not fire on our working parties ; indeed, there is less noise now than there was before. I met a crowd of Europeans and natives on my way to church this morning, and Nicholson was in the middle of it haranguing the Europeans, and bidding them for their own interest and comfort conciliate the affections of the Punja-

bees lately arrived in camp, saying that even the vile
refuse who have so deeply revolted from us could and
did, as in the instances of the 35th and 26th, appre-
ciate brotherly regard from Europeans ; that it was
just now of more importance than they imagined to
keep on the best of terms with the brave northern
levies, and that they were sure to reap the reward of
doing so in ensuring their hearty friendship and co-
operation in the field.   I stopped and listened to him
for some time ; he has a bad voice but spoke with
good and earnest feeling.   He has said that no permanent brigadiership in this part of India would
compensate him for the loss of his Frontier Commis-
sionership in the Punjab.   Strange that nearly all our
best civilians should be military men.   Baker, of the
60th N.I., accompanied me to Rhaiee in command of
100 of Hodson's Horse.   He had only joined this
new levy three days before, and found himself suddenly metamorphosed into a cavalry officer commanding a squadron of raw recruits !   See what
shifts we are put to.   There was no sermon this
morning, in consequence of the celebration of Holy
Communion.   About twenty-five remained.   I saw
Showers, Money, and Blunt yesterday morning.   The
two wounded men are getting on famously, though
Money has thrown himself back a trifle by attending
to the doctor's orders and beginning too soon to walk
about on crutches, two handsome pairs of which I saw
standing up against the Kurnauts (sides of the tent).
He has also been amusing himself with inventing a
most satisfactory and comfortable rest, or splint, for
his leg ; one or two more slight additions and altera-

tions will make it quite perfect, and it will add much
to the comfort of men in hospital with broken legs.

CAMP BEFORE DELHI,
Monday, September 7th, 1857.

I am sorry I cannot write you a long note this
morning, because I am on a court-martial at 11
o'clock. So all the transfers have been cancelled and
Ouvry reverts to the command and Upton is still in
the regiment, and Martin does not gain his five
steps, but is still in the "break," and I am quite a
"chota" again, and shall have to go to that horrible
rear battery picquet, which has been reduced to one
troop, and since I am the only officer in my troop I
should have had to go under any circumstances.
Four officers were buried on the 5th, I know the
names of two only, viz., Tyler, 61st, and Elkington.
Walker has made a wonderful recovery from his bad
attack of cholera. Wyld's Rifles marched in this
morning. Our batteries are to be armed to-morrow
I believe. Meanwhile the enemy's Bareilly force
has marched out of Delhi and taken some heavy
guns with it, whether with the intention of protecting
the Pandy retreat or taking up some new position in
Rohilcund or anywhere else we do not know. I am
sorry they have moved out, for it will, I fear, have the
effect of prolonging the business, inasmuch as we
must move against them, wherever they may choose
to ensconce themselves. Doctor McAndrew arrived
two days ago and is living with Clifford. I have
voted for Robertson as Prize Agent. Sir E. Camp-

bell seems to be the popular candidate. The days now are cloudless and very hot. Thermometer yesterday ninety-four degrees at 2 p.m. We found Mr. Rotton's evening service very trying.

CAMP BEFORE DELHI,
September 8th, 1857.

The siege of Delhi has commenced in earnest. This is a regular fighting day, and the popping puts one in mind of the old Subzi Mundi days. During the night we made a battery for ten heavy guns, which opened fire early this morning, and which the Infantry are now defending. It is between 600 and 700 yards from the wall. To-night there is to be one made for twenty guns, so that in four or five days we may expect to be ordered to the assault. I cannot do better than transcribe for you Wilson's admirable order of yesterday's date :—

" The force assembled at Delhi has had much hardship and fatigue to undergo since its arrival in this camp, all of which has been most cheerfully borne by both officers and men. The time is now drawing near when the Major-General commanding the force trusts that their labours will be over, and they will be rewarded by the capture of the city for all their past exertions and for a still greater endurance of fatigue and exposure. The troops will be required to aid and assist the Engineers in the erection of the batteries and trenches, and in daily exposure to the sun as covering parties. The Artillery will have even harder work than they have yet had, and which

they have so well and cheerfully performed hitherto ;
this, however, will be for a short period only, and when
ordered to the assault, the Major-General feels assured
that British pluck and determination will carry everything before them, and that the bloodthirsty mutineers against whom they are fighting will be driven
headlong out of their stronghold and be exterminated.
But to enable them to do this he warns the troops
of the absolute necessity of their keeping together
and not straggling from their columns ; by this only
can success be secured.   Major-General Wilson need
hardly remind the troops of the cruel murders committed on their officers and comrades, as well as their
wives and children, to move them in the deadly
struggle.   No quarter should be given to the mutineers ; at the same time, for the sake of humanity and
the honour of the country they belong to, he calls
upon them to spare all women and children that may
come in their way.   It is so imperative not only for
their safety, but for the success of the assault, that
men should not straggle from their columns that the
Major-General feels it his duty to direct all Commanding Officers to impress this strictly upon their men,
and he is confident that after this warning the men's
good sense and discipline will induce them to obey
their officers and keep steady to their duty.   It is to
be explained to every regiment that indiscriminate
plunder will not be allowed.   The Prize Agents have
been appointed, by whom all captured property will
be collected and sold to be divided according to the
rules and regulations on this head, fairly among all
men engaged, and any man found guilty of having

concealed captured property will be made to restore
it and will forfeit all claim to the general prize and also
render himself liable to be made over to the Provost-
Marshal to be summarily dealt with. The Major-
General calls upon the officers of the force to lend
their zealous and efficient co-operation in the execution of works of the siege now about to be commenced.
He looks especially to the regimental officers of all
grades to impress upon their men that to work in the
trenches during a siege is as necessary and honourable
as to fight in the ranks during a battle. He will hold
all officers responsible for their utmost being done to
carry out the directions of the Engineers, and he
confidently trusts that all will exhibit a healthy and
hearty spirit of emulation and zeal, from which he
has no doubt that the happiest results will follow in
the brilliant termination of all their labours." There,
it has cost me some trouble writing this out, but it is
so good an order, and so much to the purpose, that I
thought I would give you the benefit of it. We seized
a place this morning, the Koosea Bagh, within three
hundred yards of the wall, and where doubtless we
shall erect a battery to command the bridge.

CAMP BEFORE DELHI,
Wednesday, September 9th, 1857.

I thought that duty would have prevented my
writing to you to-day, for I received orders yesterday
evening to proceed to the trenches at 4 a.m. this morning with twenty-four of my men. We had all our white
pugrees dyed and were ready to go, when they found

they could do without us, and we were told to hold ourselves in readiness if wanted. I am not sorry we had not to go, for the battery is within 500 yards of the wall, so that we should have been under fire the whole day, and the sun would have been terribly oppressive. Hildebrand, of the Artillery, was killed in the battery by a three-pounder shot, which hit him on the head, and a Lieutenant Bannerman was wounded. The casualties of the day amounted to about twenty altogether. Last night the mortar battery was finished and armed, and is, I believe, now dosing the town with its pills. To-night and to-morrow will be erected a large breaching battery for knocking the wall down; as yet we have only been trying to subdue the fire of the Moree Bastion and Cashmere Gate. I should not wonder if the assault were ordered for the morning of the 11th, the very day that Lord Lake took the place in 1803. This must be an anxious time for Wilson, who is not altogether pleased with the way in which the Engineers have been conducting the siege, trusting too much to dash, and neglecting the rules of art. It is strange that they should do so after the warning we had at Mooltan, when such proceedings utterly failed. There is now nought but a dark perplexing future before me, and "Sufficient for the day is the evil thereof." The Bareilly force has not marched out after all. We had a most refreshing storm yesterday afternoon, which brought the thermometer down to eighty-four degrees from ninety-six degrees.

CAMP BEFORE DELHI,
Thursday, September 10th, 1857.

I have got young Ward sitting opposite me. He arrived in the middle of the night, slept in his shig-ram till the morning, when he found me out. He has applied to serve in the batteries, and his wish is sure to be granted. There has been some little delay in erecting the breaching battery, which was to have been ready to open at daybreak this morning with the mortar battery. The Engineers discovered last night that they could advance the breaching battery some eighty yards closer, and determined to do so. In consequence of this alteration in their plan the breaching battery will not be ready till to-morrow, if then, for just at this moment there is a very heavy fire of musketry from the enemy, who are beginning to feel the pressure they are under. Turner has been feeling the worse for his exposure to the sun. The loss in two days in his troop amounted to six killed and ten wounded. Wilson issued a complimentary order yesterday regarding the excellent conduct of the working parties, and mentioning Lieutenant Pelly's name as having shown his men a very good example. I got the following last night from Great-hed, with a request to send it and the letter from Colonel Neile to Colonel Cotton on to Mussorie :

"Cawnpore, 25th August, 1857.

" MY DEAR MUIR,—For reasons which I cannot at present divulge, the relief of Lucknow became as a military operation impracticable. I was obliged as a general to come to this painful conclusion ; however, as a man my feelings might prompt me to a different course. May that Providence which in its inscrutable decrees has imposed on me this stern necessity continue to watch over those most dear to us! Young Charles Havelock is safe at Benares. I gave the troops in Oude a parting thrashing on the 12th, and at Bithoor on the 16th defeated the mutineers from Saugor and took their two guns."

Colonel Neile writes from Cawnpore the 27th August " that the health of the men was improving; that H.M.'s 33rd is escorting up munitions of war arrived at Bombay. Sir Colin most energetic. Martial law proclaimed in Calcutta; a battery added to the Calcutta volunteers. European yeomanry cavalry being rapidly organised. Recruits pouring in. The Battalion of Marine Light Infantry brought on the Bengal establishment, under Captain Peel, R.N., and ere now on their way up the river to be stationed at Allahabad. They have ten 68-pounders with them. Four hundred men have left Allahabad for Cawnpore; the 5th and 90th are following hard on them. The road is open to Allahabad, but off the trunk road civil power not entirely re-established. I wish we could make a move toward you and smash the Futty-ghur fellows. There is a vagabond at Calpee on the Jumna doing much mischief; a brother of the Nana is now with him and is casting guns, and has in his possession some uncovenanted Civil Service men and their families. He is playing a fast and loose game; has several times promised to send them in, but has failed as yet. I have told him if a hair of their heads is hurt neither himself, his family, nor estate will be spared. On the Nana's brother joining him the other day, after his defeat at Bithoor, he fired a royal salute for the victory at Bithoor and the reoccupation of this by the Nana, who had driven us out. The news from Lucknow is most cheering. The enemy had assaulted and been repulsed with vast slaughter. They and the troops there now declare if Lucknow holds out for two years more, they won't attempt to storm it again. We are there scarce of provisions for Europeans, but on half-rations have them for long. They have no end of wheat and grain. They are now, I consider, all right, and will be saved when the reinforcements come up. The fellows on the opposite bank are throwing up earthworks, but we can turn them. A Nawaub fellow here, who is with the Nana at Lucknow, whose son there commands four regiments before the place, left their womenkind in their house here. I have had the ladies made prisoners and had it intimated to them that if one woman or child of ours is hurt or injured in Oude they will be publicly exposed and subjected to every indignity. We are justified in *threatening* reprisals."

CAMP BEFORE DELHI,
Friday, September 11*th,* 1857.

There has been a good deal doing and done during the last twenty-four hours, which, as you may imagine, have been noisy enough. There have been some thirty or forty casualties ; not to be wondered at when our left breaching battery at the Custom House is within 180 yards of the wall. Hope and his staff and young Ward went down there last night about two o'clock, to see what was going on.

While in the battery they were saluted with two dis-
charges of grape, which fortunately did them no
harm. They returned in about two hours, having
satisfied their too eager curiosity. Ward is in orders,
and will have to serve in some battery to-day.
Sanctuary, whose wife, by the way, is in England, is
now fighting away under the walls with the Belooch
corps. One of our men was killed and two wounded
yesterday. Somerville, of the Artillery, was also
wounded. The large breaching battery and mortar
battery are to open to-day at twelve o'clock. Their
fire will be, they say, most destructive ; and if found
adequately so, the place may be assaulted to-morrow.
The mutineers have been doing their best to-day to
annoy the working and covering parties, keeping up
a heavy and constant fire on them from the walls. A
large body of their Cavalry rode out of the Lahore
and into the Cashmere Gate yesterday afternoon,
by way of bravado, I suppose ; but they got well
punished for the useless display of gallantry, for one
of the batteries fired grape into them, and killed
between twenty and thirty. We had a heavy shower
yesterday afternoon, and I was much vexed to find
that my new tent leaked like a sieve. Had the rain
continued, I should not have had a dry thing in it ;
so I have sold myself rather, for the other was as
tight as a cup.

CAMP BEFORE DELHI,
Saturday, September 12th, 1857.

I had a touch of fever and ague last night, and feel
so stupid and heavy-headed this morning, that I fear
I must curtail my letter a bit. There was a decided

change in the weather yesterday, and the night was quite cool enough for a blanket. I suppose we are reaping the benefit of the immense fall of rain you have had. A sudden change like this generally upsets me a little by hindering perspiration, that healthy safety-valve. I went to bed about seven, without my dinner, but passed a very restless night, for my brain bothered me dreadfully. It would keep working, and there seemed no end to its eddies and whirlpools. I am much better this morning, and shall be all right to-morrow if I eat no dinner to-day. This is an awkward time to get ill, for the assault is sure to take place in two or three days. The fire of our batteries has silenced the enemy's Moree and Cashmere bastions, and I fancy by to-morrow morning the Engineers will report all ready. Young Ward has been away ever since twelve o'clock yesterday. Poor lad! he is entirely dependent for food and drink on the good nature of his friends there, for he has no servant, and none of mine are disposed to risk their lives for him. Yesterday afternoon there was a brilliant little Cavalry skirmish at our rear picquet. Two hundred gaily-dressed Delhi sowars came out and attacked it, killing one man. Some of the Guides and Hodson's Horse, under Probyn, Watson, &c., were immediately sent out. On nearing the spot, they found these fellows ready marshalled across the road, and apparently determined to fight. The Guides, &c., charged them, and they lost heart and fled. Twenty-two were killed in the pursuit, and amongst them two swells of Ressildars. There is a council of war to be held at eleven to-day. I have

L

no doubt but that within the next twenty-four hours
we shall have effected a lodgment inside the walls,
and be banging away at the interior defences.

CAMP BEFORE DELHI,
Sunday, September 13th, 1857.

Hope led the Brigade a dance from 5 to 7.30 yesterday evening. We went about two miles to the bank
of the river, by way of leading the enemy to suppose
that we intended crossing, and capturing two or
three guns of theirs that are a great plague to us,
enfilading our batteries, and, in a measure, commanding the Pucka road that leads down to the Cashmere
Gate, and down which all our munitions of war and
provisions for the men in the advanced batteries have
to go. Yesterday evening Smith, the doctor, was
walking quietly along this road, on horseback, when
a round shot killed the horse under him, and three or
four dead bullocks and camels testify to the enemy's
having got the bearing of the road. Our left, and
most important, breaching battery, the one near the
Custom House, was found to be so faultily con-
structed with regard to the direction of the embra-
sures, which were made so as not to allow a gun to
point where it was wanted to point, that the embra-
sures had all to be altered, and great delay and in-
convenience were experienced. It is now banging
away at the Water Gate, and by to-morrow, or, at
farthest, next day, the breaches will be reported
practicable. The enemy, however, are showing great
pluck and determination, for, strange to say, they

have managed to repair the ruinous Moree Bastion,
so as to admit of the firing of two guns from it.
Poor Captain Fagan was killed yesterday afternoon
in the Custom House Battery. He was shot through
the head. They say that he was in the habit of
exposing himself much too recklessly. He has left
a wife and seven children! Young Ward seems to
have quite taken up his abode in the batteries, for I
have seen nothing of him since he left. Best thanks
for yours of the 10th, which reached me yesterday
evening. I thought you would find Wilson's order
interesting. Yes, indeed, it is a blessing to think
that, however far separated from one another, we can
ever meet at the same throne of the heavenly grace,
pleading the same exceeding great and precious
promises. May we all be following the same path of
grace now, and meet around the endless joys of glory
hereafter. And all we ask is for Jesu's sake. Mr.
Rotton read and preached in the mess-tent of the
52nd to a congregation of, I suppose, about fifty. I
am glad you are to have prayers every morning
during the present time. Prayers will avail more
than all the pomp and circumstance of war and our
own arm of flesh to secure our ultimate success. I
shall be glad to leave this filthy camp, and breathe
uncontaminated air again. They say that the
Pandies will not let the residents leave Delhi, and
there is a report that 1,500 have been killed by the
fire from our mortars. The L.C. came in this morning. I wonder whether your puddings are nicer than
mine, but, to tell you the truth, I am getting sick of
chuppatties and puddings, but am grievously per-

L 2

plexed about a substitute for them. I quite longed
for a little jam this morning, to give a relish to my
dry chuppatties, but jam makes me very bilious if I
eat it for many days consecutively, which I would be
sure to do, if I once commenced.

September 14th.—The assault has been successful
as yet, 12.30. Martin and F. Grant have lost their
horses. Young Anson wounded in the hand. More
to-morrow.

In charge of reserve Cavalry protecting the camp.

MIDDLE OF CAMP. ON DUTY.
September, 15th, 8.30 a.m.

I am sitting writing on my knees in the open air
under a tree and do not expect to be relieved till the
whole of Delhi has fallen. The 200 men of the
regiment (two squadrons of 100 each) behaved
nobly. They were purposely (to save the Infantry
inside) exposed to a murderous fire outside the walls
for a long time, and their loss has been severe—between forty and fifty have been wounded, strange to
say none killed outright, but some are very dangerously wounded. The G Troop suffered most.
Our men are either very badly wounded or very
slightly, there is no *happy* medium. Eight officers'
horses were hit—two Grants, Jones', Hamilton's,
Martin's, Blair's, Drysdale's, and somebody else's.
Poor Rosser, 6th D.G., is mortally wounded. Our
officers breakfasted inside Delhi. We have taken
all the wall from the Water Gate to the Lahore ;
what else I cannot positively say. Rumour has it

that the magazine and treasury and Jumna Musjid are ours. We are firing at Selim Ghur now, and will soon effect a breach in its old crumbling walls. Tombs and Olpherts had seven guns out with the Cavalry and lost out of seventy men thirty-one killed and wounded, and forty-eight horses. Jacobs, of the 1st Fusiliers, is dead. Fitzgerald 75th, killed. Herbert slightly wounded. Brigadier-General Nicholson dangerously wounded. Young Nicholson, his brother, has lost his right arm. Cuppage, late 6th Cavalry, it is said, will lose an arm. Owen, 1st Fusiliers, wounded in the head. Major Read, of the Ghoorkhas, badly wounded, and many others. The 8th suffered a good deal. The 1st Fusiliers are almost annihilated. The 75th, indeed all the regiments, have a heavy list of casualties. Numbers of Europeans got drunk inside off champagne, claret, and brandy, purposely put in their way by the enemy. A cry of poison was raised, which did some little good. It will, I daresay, take two or three days to drive the enemy effectually out and seize all the strong places. The Cashmere force lost their four guns yesterday in the Kishna-gunge *contretemps*. The enemy were found too strong there, and effectually repulsed their attack, aided by some of our troops. It was most unfortunate, for it has served to give them some little heart, but it may in the end, by inducing them to hold out here, conduce to their extermination. It is too windy to write. The black ants are teasing me. I am sitting in the sun, too, which hinders my writing comfortably.

CAMP DELHI,
September 16th.

It would be hard for you to imagine the grievous, heartbreaking toil that our poor Artillery, Lancers, and Infantry have had to undergo during the last week of this awful war—awful because of the dreadful climate. Officers leave the batteries quite shrivelled up and as black as your shoe. Our Lancers are of the greatest possible use in working the guns, and noble indeed has been their behaviour throughout. The finest and handsomest man in the regiment, the man to whom Hope spoke in such familiar style at the last Christmas dinner, had both his legs carried off by a rocket in No. 4 Battery, and Couch had his arm taken off this morning. I am sorry to say that the regular Delhi intermittent fever seems to have taken hold of me. I have it regularly every other day. While on me yesterday I was obliged to get up shivering from my bed and stand for about an hour and a half, from 4 to 5.30 p.m., in a very hot sun, ready to oppose the enemy, who showed a disposition to attack us. To-day, barring that I have no appetite and feel weak, I am quite well. I am, however, going to take some quinine to-day, which I hope may keep the fever from coming on to-morrow. It is regular ague and fever, and, while on, totally incapacitates me from taking the least pleasure in duty work. Were I in Cantonments I would lie up for it, but this is such an awkward time to get ill that I am doing my best to hold out against it. I had a bathe this morning, the first for forty-eight hours. A squadron has just come back to the lines from Delhi, leaving one there. We are preparing batteries to break down the interior defences of the city. The enemy have secured their line of retreat, which I suppose will be Agra ways, with heavy guns. We shall have plenty to do, even after Delhi is completely in our hands. It is doubtful whether the Lahore Gate will fall into our hands to-day. It is an important one, commanding as it does the Kishnagunge suburb, &c. Keep up your spirits. We are in the hands of a merciful God· Whatever happens you may be sure will be for the best.

CAMP DELHI,
Thursday, September 17th, 1857.

We are, I am glad to say, going most solidly and cautiously to work, employing our Artillery to knock down the walls and houses of the town and make thereby paths to the points we want to attack, namely, the Jumna Musjid and the Lahore Gate, the Palace and Selimghur. It will, I daresay, take three or four days more to drive the enemy out of the city. They still keep up a dropping and sometimes galling fire on the troops from the houses in their possession. We changed our ground yesterday evening, and are very nearly on our old ground again. This was necessary in order to make the camp compact, and consequently more easy to defend. I am sorry to say that, in spite of all precautions, there has been disgraceful drunkenness amongst the troops, who happened to fall in with an immense wine godown, belonging to one of the richest natives in

Delhi. A party was obliged to be detailed to smash
the bottles up to prevent further mischief. There is
a report that General Wilson has issued a proclamation, stating his willingness to receive any mutineer
Sepoys that may choose to surrender, but I can
hardly believe it. I began the day with taking ten
grains of quinine, having taken ten yesterday. I
hope by this means to have but a very slight attack
this afternoon. It doesn't do to give in. Martin is
in the same predicament as I am, viz., fever every
third day, and he has been dosing himself strongly,
and feels weaker than I do in consequence. I find if
I can keep down one hearty meal a day my strength,
except during the fit, is not much reduced. The day
before yesterday the crying hysterical frenzy (the
grief that lasts not long) of a woman wailing for her
husband, a Golundanzee, who had just been killed at
Kishnagunge, sounded in my ears all day, varied by
the crying of her babe, whom, in the intensity of her
grief, she had neglected. While thinking about her,
a much more distressing object passed under my
eyes, a dhoolie with an unfortunate 60th Rifleman,
mortally wounded through the stomach, intestines
protruding. He had doubled himself up, thinking
it was the most comfortable position for him, but,
feeling pain, he stopped the dhoolie, and moaning
and groaning, and exclaiming "O my God!" he
asked to have his position changed, and stretched
himself on his back. Some forty-six officers were
killed and wounded on the memorable 14th. Pogson
has lost his leg. Drysdale had a very narrow escape,
a bullet scoring his pugree over his forehead for him.

F. Grant was doubled up with a spent ball in his stomach, which luckily did him no harm. It is supposed that if the rebels keep together they may make a dour on Agra, with the view of joining the Gwalior rascals. My communications to you seem to be copied by all the ladies in the place. Mrs. Tytler is making herself useful in nursing the sick.

September 18*th*.

Directly the campaign is over I must try and get a year's sick leave to the hills to recruit, for I never felt so completely done and good for nothing as I do now. The quinine stopped the fever from coming on strong, but I was (and am now) in a state of low fever all night. I have not the least spirit for anything, getting up only to lie down again. I drink large jorums of lemonade, but they only take away the little appetite that I may have. I require a thorough change home, for I am quite knocked up. I went to the hospital this morning with Hope, Wilkinson, and Drysdale, and saw all the wounded men, who, with one or two exceptions, are doing very well. We have taken the Lahore Gate and breached the palace, and matters seem to be going on satisfactorily. Eight hundred and thirty were killed and wounded at the assault. I saw Baird Smith this morning, in a dhoolie, with his arm and leg bound up. He tumbled down a well the other day, poor fellow, and hurt himself very much.

CAMP DELHI,
Saturday, September 19*th*, 1857.

I am feeling 20 per cent. better to-day, though I

had a fearful night-sweat. If the fever does not come on to-day I shall think myself quite well again to-morrow. This morning there was a reconnaissance in force by the Cavalry. We paraded at 4.30 and left camp about 5.30, to see where the enemy had gone. We went all through the fatal Subzi Mundi, and about a mile beyond, and saw that they were still in force, encamped on the other side of Delhi, waiting for the turn of events; for still having possession of the Lahore Gate, they have an idea that their chance of holding the city is not yet quite over. I am sorry to say that we failed in an attack on the Lahore Gate, through some unaccountable backwardness of our 8th and 75th, who could not be persuaded to advance, though Lieutenant Briscoe, of the 75th, sacrificed himself (being killed by a shower of grape) in a vain endeavour to rouse them. Nicholson's Europeans showed a similar recreancy on the 14th, when ordered to storm the Burn Bastion. He called upon them repeatedly to advance, and finding they did not, turned round to harangue them, and had got as far as " I never should have thought that Europeans would have quailed before niggers," or words to that effect, when he, poor, gallant fellow, fell mortally wounded, for the doctors have but very slight hopes of his recovery, the ball having smashed his ribs, and sent the bones right into his lungs, causing fearful inflammation. The 60th and 52nd appear to be the best and bravest regiments. The King, they say, has left the city and gone to the Koo-tub. Wilson came into camp last night to have a good sleep, being completely worn out for want of one and leaving Chamberlain in command in the city. I had nothing to do with the assault on the 14th, having been ordered to command the reserve Cavalry (about 400 of all sorts) and protect the camp. The 200 men of ours engaged were exposed to a very heavy fire in the performance of a most important duty, viz., drawing the fire off the Infantry while they were storming, and preventing the enemy from taking them in the rear. They say that they have removed the post-office into the town, which, if true, will prove a great bore for us remaining in camp. Here is a list of the wounded in my troop : On the 14th, Corporal Parker, Privates W. Clarke, Daly, Harrison, Moon, Talkington, Hing, Dyson ; on 15th, Walters, seven horses wounded and killed, and four missing. Some shopkeepers, soon after the assault, came and gave themselves up; they were passed by our people inside, but shot outside. During the assault I was on duty, all buckled up, and remained so for forty-eight hours, sleeping two nights on the ground, so you may imagine I could not write much, especially when I was floored by fever half the time. The church (Skinner's) is frightfully knocked about, and looks anything but like a church now.

CAMP DELHI,
Sunday, September 20th, 1857.

My fever did not come on yesterday, so I hope I have done with it. I am sure I shan't be sorry if it should have left me altogether, for anything more depressing and sickening cannot well be imagined. I shall, however, go on taking quinine for some days,

for I do not feel quite myself yet, and got up this
morning to go the same round we did yesterday with
a feeling of great languor and lassitude, the effect of a
sleepless night and profuse perspiration. I felt so
lively after my soup yesterday afternoon that about
4 p.m. I ordered my horse and rode down to Delhi,
entering it by the Cashmere Gate. I came at once
upon the church, which presented a terribly battered
aspect, and then meeting Young, I went on to the
magazine, where I saw no end of piles of shot and
guns. I got a peep at the wall of the palace, which
was undergoing a process of shelling, and then, re-
tracing my steps to the Cashmere Gate, turned sharp
round, to the left and went along inside the wall to
the renowned Moree Bastion, which I mounted, and
from which I had a superb view of our position on
the ridge and the advanced batteries. I met Lt.-
Captain Heath, of the Artillery, in command there.
Evans of ours was there assisting him and looking
very ill. The Cashmere Gate compound was filled
with rezais, lotas, and other brass utensils, old clothes,
and all the native rubbish you can imagine taken by
the sentries from those camp-followers who had been
enjoying the dangerous pastime of looting. I have
now been half round the city ; the river side is still a
mystery to me, but won't be for long, for yesterday
afternoon the Lahore Bastion was taken with very
little loss. The Ajmere followed, and now we only
want the palace and the Jumna Musjid to make the
city quite untenable ; in fact, soldiers and people are
now deserting it as fast as they can, and by this
evening, or to-morrow morning at furthest, it will be

wholly in our possession, and the "siege of Delhi in 1857" will be a thing of the past. What trouble and toil it cost us, with the thermometer seldom under ninety degrees, let future historians tell. It made me quite sad as I rode through the ruinous Subzi Mundi this morning, to think that 2,500 of our best warriors had been killed and wounded there alone. We may now have one or two general actions, but they will be comparatively easy work to what we have gone through. The 9th Lancers have fought well, and worked nobly for their country during this campaign. Poor Greathed, the Commissioner, expired last night from a bad attack of cholera. Metcalfe was also seized, but is recovering. The 75th are suffering greatly from it. How glad I shall be when we move from this pestilential camp. This morning the air on the ridge about three miles from camp was deliciously pure, and in two or three places only were our nostrils disagreeably assailed. I had taken the precaution of saturating my pocket-handkerchief with eau-de-cologne, and nearly brought on a fit by holding my breath too long. On the 14th I made the acquaintance of three Irregular Cavalry officers, Best, Gough, and Corfield. The first is no relation of our Bests. He is a gentlemanly and very talkative person. Drysdale's chin, Martin's lips, and my nose have all broken out terribly, proving the poisonous atmosphere we are breathing. Poor Jacob's, Mr. Barnett's, and Speke's (all of the 1st B.E.F.) things were put up for sale last night ; a railway blanket sold for sixteen rupees (full price) and a single-pole tent for seventy rupees. Drysdale's horse reared up and came over

with him on parade yesterday morning, but most
fortunately he escaped unhurt, for it was a very ugly
fall the brute, a trooper from the ranks, gave him.
He is so fond of his grey that he spares him as much
as he can.

DELHI,
21st September.

As I foretold yesterday, Delhi was wholly and
completely ours by the evening.   The Cavalry
Brigade went round the walls to the enemy's camp
yesterday afternoon.   Some poor wounded men were
put out of their pain, and lots of loot taken, Hodson
recovering sundry carriages and the mess-plate of
the 61st by a close pursuit of the enemy, who took
their final departure, with about eight guns, yesterday
morning with the intention of fraternising with their
Gwalior brethren.   I went nearly through the palace
this morning and picked up a small drawer full of
playthings for the children, things that I might
innocently take away as a kind of memorial of
Delhi.   Amongst them is a mother-o'-pearl lid of a
box with a Persian inscription upon it which might
do for you to wind a ball of thread on.   I met
Hope and Showers and many others looting innocently.   Hope had picked up a sandal-wood necklace.
Showers was deep in the mysteries of Persian books.
I feel much better to-day, and am in great hopes that
the fever has left me.   I should not like to leave
camp just now.   If we are successful at Lucknow
the Goojur and village massacres will be all that will
be required to be done.   Very few Pandies have been
killed.   We must trust to ulterior measures when

our power has been firmly re-established to take a bloody revenge on them. Best thanks for yours of 18th. I suppose I walked three miles inside Delhi this morning, and such a miserable, dirty-smelling place as it is. I drove down in the buggy, and foolishly forgot to send a horse to ride, so nearly killed myself with walking in the sun. One of the first things that met my eyes on entering the palace was a splendid engraving of a most beautiful English woman. Then I went into the Zenana, where I was nearly suffocated with atta, but where I packed up all the children's playthings.

DELHI,
Tuesday, 22nd.

Here I am writing, in the open, under difficulties again. My regular correspondence must, I fear, cease from to-day, for we have marched down here, six miles, to the Ajmere Gate, preparatory to a dour on Muttra after the enemy to-morrow. The moveable column is under Greathed, and consists of ourselves and Hodson's Horse, the 8th and 61st, and 1st and 2nd Punjab Infantry (Coke's and Green's), and Bourchier's battery and two troops Horse Artillery, Turner's and Delamain's. We shall, I suppose, march at least fifteen miles a day, and have no way of sending our letters by post till we get to Muttra or Agra. I am on a court-martial at 11 o'clock. Hope is not going with us. I hardly expect to return ; but think it probable that we shall remain at Agra or Cawnpore, most probably the latter, where there must be greater accommodation for us. You will be very glad to hear that we have got the King. Hodson brought him in yesterday. I went all over the Jumna Musjid yesterday, and to the top of one of the minarets, where I had a splendid bird's-eye view of all Delhi. I tiffed with Showers, who gave us champagne, and went with him. I pity the poor women and children drawn from their homes, and thronging all the roads leading to camp.

CAMP DELHI,
Wednesday, 23rd, 1857.

We did not march this morning, in consequence of the 61st having reported themselves unfit for active service from sickness, &c., and the 75th having to take their place. We are, I hear, to march this afternoon as far as the Kootub. We shall have, I expect, to march all over the country to Muttra, Agra, Gwalior, and Oude. You cannot imagine how completely this city has been plundered. You know what a native city is, how full of small pigeon-holes of shops. Well, the various contents of all these in every street have been thrown into the streets. The Punjabees are only to be surpassed by our Europeans, who have helped themselves plentifully. I went again into the city this morning, and took a walk with Drysdale and Wilkinson all through the palace gardens, which are anything but pretty. In the middle of the Chandnee Choke there were lying exposed, with only pyjamas on, the bodies of three of the King's sons, who were killed by Hodson's people. The centre one—a large, fat man—was the one who imbrued his own hands in the blood of our people. They gave themselves up, and denounced an European sergeant-major of the — N.I., who had been converted to Mahommedanism. He declares himself innocent, and that he was forcibly converted ; but I would not give much for his life. The King is located in a small house near the palace, and has lost all reverence and respect. It now only remains for the Sepoys to be decimated, and our revenge will be complete, particularly if Havelock's operations, which commence, as it were, to-day, turn out successful, of which, I should think, there could be no doubt. Colonel Burn is Governor of Delhi, and Colonel Jones commands at the palace. There will shortly be a proclamation, inviting people to return to the place and open their shops again, and in a month's time there will hardly be a trace left of our visit. Ouvry commands the Cavalry.

CAMP DELHI,
September 23rd.

You will be glad to hear that I have had no fever for the last four or five days, and that I am nearly myself again. The march, with constant change of air, will do me good. We shall all be glad to leave this disagreeable place. Harris, of the 2nd Fusiliers, having found some rupees in the city, was bringing them away with the intention of making them over to a Prize Agent, when three Sikhs, belonging to one of our new levies, met him, and, presenting their muskets at him, bade him " stand and deliver," which he found himself compelled to do. That will

M

give you a notion of the dangerous character of our
auxiliaries, who bid fair to become soon as bad
as the Pandies, of whom a nest was found in the
city this morning, and more than two hundred killed.
They were up a long lane, where they had killed and
wounded five or six of our Sappers. Did you observe
the eclipse on the 18th? I did not. Have you ever
seen Delhi? The Jumna Musjid is certainly a magnificent mass of architecture. Tritton has kept well
enough to get through an immense amount of work.
He is sure to get a C.Bship. Mactur I frequently
see. He is highly spoken of.

CAMP GHAZEE-OOD-DEEN NUGGUR,
LEFT BANK OF HINDON,
Friday, September 25th, 1857.

We marched from Delhi at three o'clock yesterday
morning, and did not reach this till nine. I had to
put my head inside a morah and protect myself as
well as I could from the sun till one o'clock, when
the buggy arrived, and afforded me its friendly
shelter. My tent was not up till six, and my bed
not till 9 p.m. This state of discomfort and exposure
applied more or less to us all, and was caused by the
breaking of the bridge of boats, which let an elephant
through into the water, load and all. The bridge
took some time mending, and the baggage was of
course delayed. Moreover, the camels are all more
or less weak and sickly, and unable to carry their
loads. I have now taken an expensive hackery
into my service. I am so bothered with the servants' wives and children. It is they who have com-

pelled me to ruin myself with a four-bullock hackery, which will cost me thirty-two rupees a month, and more. We have been obliged to halt to-day in consequence of the delay of the baggage, and never was halt more acceptable. To-morrow we hope to make a fair start for Bolondshuhur, and thence on to Muttra and Agra. I got yours of the 21st, while lying under the buggy, about three o'clock yesterday, and it was a great treat to me. Had I been going to remain at Delhi, I would certainly have done all I could to get a month's leave ; but you will allow the utter impracticability of my doing so now. Besides, the change to this has done me a world of good, and I feel quite a different man for breathing some pure air. The air at Delhi was loaded with poisonous malaria. One's flesh would have rolled away had we remained there much longer. The strongest began to succumb under its pernicious influence. Here the air is fresh and sweet, giving instant tone to the constitution.

CAMP DADRU,
Saturday, 26th, 1857.

Here we are ten miles further on our way to Agra. Never on any march before have I been so bothered about carriage. I find that my remaining three camels are utterly useless, and that in order to get on at all I must hire another hackery. My traps were among the very last up this morning. We got under the shade of a nice clump of trees and had (all of us) a kind of picnic breakfast consisting of cold

M 2

meat, bread and butter, and tea, which they all cried out was water bewitched. On the first evening we dined out in the open by moonlight, so that we take enough air. Dear old Drysdale is very poorly with ague and fever. He can hardly sit his horse, he is so weak, yet he won't give in, but sticks to his duty like a man. French is much better. Norman was dining with Ouvry last night, as merry and talkative as usual. He is certainly a very pleasant and agreeable little fellow. To-morrow we march to Secunderabad. The Meerut force are very busy coercing a villain near Mozuffurnugger. He has some 15,000 men about him.

CAMP SECUNDERABAD,
Sunday, September 27th, 1857.

We arrived here in good time, about 6.30, this morning, having started at 1.30 to march ten miles. We are going to march again this evening to Bolondshuhur, nine miles, so as, if possible, to cut off the retreat of a villain, said to be at Malaghur with 7,000 troops and ten guns. Three villages were burnt at Dadru, and in one some bonnets and gowns were found. Greathed says he intends burning every village along his track. He had ordered the Cavalry and Artillery to proceed alone to Bolondshuhur, but Turner protested against the measure as placing the Infantry in great danger, so we are all going to start at 7 p.m. This is a very large place, and it has been ruinously plundered by the Goojurs, who got seven lacs out of it. Those Goojurs must be very numerous to be able to burn and plunder such a considerable place as this. Poor Drysdale is no better. How he managed to sit his horse through the march this morning is a riddle to me. Thank God, I am quite well again. The fine fresh country air has done wonders for me. So Hope is at Kussowlee, and will tell you all about our eventful three months at Delhi.

BOLONDSHUHUR,
Monday, 28th.

It seems very doubtful whether my letters ever reach you now that the Goojurs are in our rear, plundering all they can lay their hands on. We had to fight our way here this morning. We found the enemy very strongly posted here under that rogue Nana, and we had to drive them out, which we did after three hours' (from six to nine) fighting. We charged through the town ; indeed, the brunt of the action fell on the Artillery and the Cavalry, the Infantry being scarcely engaged. I am sorry to say that three of our officers have been wounded. Sarel, right hand shattered and left arm wounded ; Blair, very severe sabre-cut on left shoulder, severing the joint, and down the back ; Thonger, shot in the left arm ; two or three men killed, and four or five wounded. I am not sure of these numbers ; two, I know, have been killed. While we were fighting, some sowars attacked our baggage, but were handsomely beaten back by our baggage-guards and Probyn's Irregulars. Poor Drysdale's horse was shot, and, falling on him, has hurt his chest and collar-bone very much, so the command devolves temporarily upon me. Two guns have been taken,

some say five; and we purpose renewing the fight
to-morrow at Malaghur. The officers of Irregulars,
Probyn, Younghusband, and Best, have distinguished
themselves greatly. Best is wounded. The Cavalry
and Horse Artillery found themselves in the main
street of Bolondshuhur enfiladed by the enemy's
musketry fire. We are to be joined by the Meerut
force to-day or to-morrow, and halt here to-morrow.
I am writing under the buggy with considerable
difficulty.

2.15.—Having just received yours of the 24th, I
will at once acknowledge it. Your feelings are most
natural, and it distressed me much to think how
deeply you would feel my going further away from
you. May God give us both grace and strength to
bear with due submission and resignation His will,
whatever seemeth best to Him in the way of trials.
How merciful He was again to me this morning.
While I saw others killed and wounded quite close
to me, He chose to guard me from all harm. Let
Him do what seemeth Him best. Though He slay
me, yet will I put my trust in Him. Keep up your
spirits, and think of me only as doing my duty to
my God—for this is a war in which we are pre-
eminently serving Him and smiting down idolatry
—my Queen and my country. What a blessed
thing it is to have faith in these times. Having
given us His Son, will He not also freely give us
all things? Whatever happens to our flesh, all the
goodliness whereof is as the flower of the field, we
have the rich consolation of knowing that the ever-
lasting God the Lord, the Creator of the ends of the

earth, has called us His sons and daughters. Poor
Drysdale has broken his collar-bone, and will be
laid up for a month at least. We rushed into battle
this morning quite blindfolded ; we were engaged in
pitching our camp, when the quartermasters were
disturbed by the enemy's round shot, and off we
went to fight them. My horse carried me splendidly,
and made a most beautiful jump from the top of a
high bank, which had a deep ditch in front of it.
I picked up a regular pair of tooth-drawing pincers
in the palace at Delhi. I took a fancy to them as
a family man. Hope will be still more annoyed at
his separation from us when he hears of our battle
this morning.

Tuesday, 29th.—Here we are still. Malaghur is
in our possession. It was abandoned with its guns.
I am ignorant of our next move. Blair's arm was
taken out of its socket, a bit cut off, and then put
in again. The operation, a very severe one, was performed under chloroform. The arm must be always
stiff and useless at the shoulder-joint, and shorter
than the other, but he will have the use of it from
his elbow downwards. Sarel's fore-finger (right
hand) has been cut off below the knuckle. Drysdale's collar-bone has been set, and he will not go
on the sick list for it. He was going at full speed
when his horse was shot under him, so you may
conceive what a burster he must have come down.
There is the sound of guns in the distance, as if the
Meerut force were fighting their way on. Bolondshuhur stands for ever linked to the name of our
regiment and to the B.H.A. How necessary the

prayer, Strengthen the hearts and hands of those
who are fighting our battles. My hackery broke
down yesterday, and I am at present without
another. Moreover, most stringent orders have been
issued regarding the reduction of our truly immense
line of baggage, which affords such facilities for
attack to the truculent Goojurs and sowars. I shall
be quite glad when I am reduced to soap and a
towel, à la Napier. I shall then begin to think
myself a veritable soldier. Fancy quiet, peaceful
Bolondshuhur, a place I have passed through so
often, being the scene of such a war spectacle as
we witnessed yesterday. Artillery banging down
its main street, and dying men and horses rolling in
agony on the ground. Two men of Blunt's troop
showed themselves perfect heroes, serving the gun
most nobly under a hot fire. One was Sergeant
Deane, or Dane, the other a young Irishman. I was
within seven or eight yards of them the whole time,
and witnessed most fully their admirable gallantry.
Money will be pleased to hear of this. I lost one
of the best dragoons in my troop, a man of the
name of Clayton, who was shot right through the
throat. Our loss was three men killed, Clayton,
Farrensking, and Stillman, and seven wounded.

CAMP BOLONDSHUHUR,
29th September, 1857.

Shortly after sending off my letter, I had the
pleasure of receiving yours of the 23rd and 25th. I
am so glad to think that you have some little measure
of enjoyment at Kussowlee. I saw Blunt after the

battle yesterday morning, and we had a few minutes'
conversation together. I am glad you had such a
satisfactory answer from Hope. I am now, thank
God, feeling quite myself again, and was compli-
mented at mess last night on my personal appearance. If we get sixpence each prize-money we shall
be fortunate. The property consists chiefly in brass
pots and pans, and dirty clothes and rezais. We have
not heard a word of Havelock's doings. We are very
anxious to do so. The Nana being nearly caught
here looks as if Havelock had been successful. We
have a post-office in camp, and our letters will go
safe enough if the Goojurs, amongst whom we are,
will let them. Your letter to Showers would have
probably found him on his way to Muttra. His
operations there may keep us in this neighbourhood
for some time.

  30th September.—Here we are still engaged in the
operation of blowing up the fort of Malaghur, while
the greater portion of the enemy are quietly ferry-
ing themselves across the Ganges at a place called
Anoopshuhur, about twenty-four miles from this.
Hope, I see from F. Grant's letter, was still at Delhi
two days ago. Drysdale was an hour with me this
morning. He will be all right again in three weeks,
and is now able to walk about camp and do all his
dismounted duties. They talk of sending the wounded
to Meerut. This long halt is a very great blessing
for them. The Sikhs looted a quantity of Shahjehanpore loaf-sugar, and Drysdale, Goldie, and Wilkinson
were lucky enough to get a whole loaf for two rupees
eight annas. I sent for some, but was too late, for a

Mahajun, having bought it wholesale, was retailing it
at one rupee a seer. I got, however, five and a half
seers for four rupees eight annas. There was an
auction in the camp of the Irregulars yesterday, and
a native officer gave 180 rupees for a splendid scarf.
Amongst the loot there was a magnificent diamond
brooch found, said to have belonged to Mrs. Sapte,
the wife of the civilian here. Some very handsome
sword-blades have been found. Young Plowden
paid me a visit yesterday, and asked to be made an
honorary member of our mess, which he now is. All
we have heard about Havelock is that he purposed
to attack the enemy's entrenchments on the other
side of the river, where they were very strongly posted
with a good many guns, and that he expected to be
at Lucknow on the 22nd. There is a great deal of
sickness amongst the natives, from fever and ague
principally.

CAMP BOLONDSHUHUR,

Thursday, 1st *October,* 1857.

Here we are still waiting for dhoolies from Meerut
and ammunition from Delhi. We may remain here,
I daresay, two or three days longer. We are quite in
the dark as to the whereabouts of the enemy, and
may start him like a hare any day. There was a
good deal of loot found in Malaghur. I was sitting
next young Watson at dinner last night, and he
amused me much with an account of the vain efforts
he made to secure something worth having. His
attention was fixed on a beautiful gold and blue
vase, of the value of four or five guineas, and he was
handing it over to his orderly to take care of for

him, when Mr. Sapte claimed it as his own. He next
picked up a very pretty gold-mounted riding-whip,
and meeting Mr. Sagrin, was addressed with, " Oh!
where did you find this? It is my wife's." So he
made it over to him. Soon after Greathed comes in,
and seeing the whip in Sapte's hand, immediately
claims it as his sister-in-law's (Mrs. H. H. Greathed).
Sapte, however, retained possession, Greathed con-
tenting himself with observing that it was the very
counterpart of Mrs. Greathed's, and Watson waiving
his right to it in spite of the rival claimants. Young
Anson found a bottle of rose-water, and while he
was examining it a Sikh comes up abruptly, knocks
its neck off, and bathing his hands and face with the
liquid, naïvely observed, " Bote atcha, Sahib."

Some of Watson's men looted a tattoo, which,
among other things, was carrying away a box of
superb medical instruments, and a ruby brooch worth
about £20. Watson is a fine young fellow, brought
up in the school of Chamberlain and Nicholson, both
of whom he looks upon as wonderful heroes. Poor
Nicholson died the day we left Delhi, and a great
loss indeed he is to the army. The following appeared in orders last night: " Lieutenant-Colonel
Greathed, commanding moveable column, begs to express his best thanks to every officer and soldier of
the force under his command for the manner in
which, after a march and during an engagement,
altogether a period of eleven hours, they forgot
fatigue in chastising the rebels who ventured to hold
their ground against them yesterday." Captain Gordon, of the 75th, has been appointed Prize Agent to

the force.   Private Jordan, the man who so gallantly
stepped forward to Drysdale's assistance, has lost
the middle finger of one of his hands.   Did I tell
you of young Anson's sending one of our lances
through the head of a hackeryman who would per-
sist in placing his cart across the road to stop the
way?   He also was of good service to Drysdale,
shot with his pistol a Sepoy who was firing a pistol
at Drysdale on the ground.   Ouvry has mentioned
in his despatch "the conspicuous gallantry" of Captain Drysdale, and certainly most richly does he deserve the compliment, for never was there a man
placed in apparently more real danger on the ground
surrounded by the enemy.

CAMP BOLONDSHUHUR,
Friday, October 2nd, 1857.

We marched only three miles this morning to the
Allyghur side of the town, and yet, owing to the
narrow passages and streets, our traps were a long
time coming up, past 10 a.m.   We halt here a day or
two longer, for reinforcements from Delhi, consisting
of two 18-pounders, the Kumaon Battalion, and about
100 more Europeans, and then we march on Allyghur, which is about fifty miles off, and occupied by a
number of fanatical Mahommedans, who rose upon
the Hindoos and the Jāts sent from Agra with three
heavy guns to defend Allyghur, and obtained possession of the place and fort.   Showers's column, I hear,
has taken a vast deal of the enemy's plunder and
treasure, which it seems they could not carry further
than the Kootuab.   My bearer is crying away and in a

dreadful state of mind, because I have been forced to give him a peremptory order to part with his wife and children, either to leave them here or send them to Meerut, at both which prospects he looks in blank despair. I never in my life saw such a number of women and children as there are with this moveable column. We are quite encumbered by them, lengthening the line of baggage and tempting the Goojurs as they do. The order separating them from us is a most necessary and imperative one, and must be rigidly enforced for the good of the service. I wish to goodness Hope was with us, instead of in that horrible hole Delhi, which, since all the quartermasters have left, has become so stinking as to be quite beyond endurance. —— gave orders last night for a village seven miles from this to be surrounded by Irregular Cavalry, and every man in it killed· This indiscriminate sort of massacre does no good— simply goads the villagers on to commit atrocities on our defenceless people.

CAMP KORJAH,
Saturday, October 3rd, 1857.

We marched here some ten miles this morning and learn that Allyghur is unoccupied, and that there is no enemy worth mentioning in this Dooab. Two marches more will take us to Allyghur, but I fear we cannot leave any troops behind to take care of Mr. G. Campbell, who is marching with us and will probably accompany us to Agra. I am writing under the buggy, at 8.30, with considerable difficulty. I do not expect my carts up for two hours. We are in the middle of a ploughed field and exceedingly rich culti-

vation all round. You will be very sorry to hear that
poor young Home, the Engineer, blew himself up
with the fort at Malaghur. A conductor, too, was
very much injured—both legs broken. We hear that
in a village about five miles from this there is a
Miss J—— immured. Two Irregular Cavalry regiments have been sent to liberate her, with orders to
kill the inhabitants and burn the village if she has
been subjected to any indignity. She is a girl of
fourteen, and F. Grant says that he knows many
young girls who, rather than see their friends after
such a catastrophe, would sooner immur themselves
in a convent, which would be foolish, I think. Much
better plunge into the bosom of their family. The
enemy are assembling at Muttra, I hear—some
3,000 with guns are already there. We expect to
receive orders from Sir Colin Campbell at Allyghur.
He is dreadfully in want of Cavalry and H.A. guns,
so it is probable that we may have to join him by the
shortest route and leave European Infantry at Agra.
I was introduced to Campbell, the civilian, this morning, and had half an hour's conversation with him on
the march by moonlight. He is all for leaving Rohilcund alone just now, and securing our communications with the down country. The air is very pleasant,
and has quite an exhilarating effect upon us all.
How I wish Hope was here to enjoy it. Both the
bearer and Baluk sent away their wives yesterday
evening with the sick, under Colonel Farquhar's
escort, to Meerut. The parting was a most affecting
one. No two English gentlemen could have more
tenderly supported their wives to the hackery.

CAMP SOMNA,
Sunday, October 4th, 1857.

We arrived here this morning (twelve miles) about six, breakfasted about seven, under a tree, after which I went to lie down under the buggy till 9.30, when the tent was reported ready. We enjoy our picnic breakfasts amazingly, and dreadful is the quantity of bread and butter that we consume. We had coffee this morning in addition to tea. There is always lots of cold meat. Drysdale ate ravenously this morning, and is better now in his general health than he was before his fall. We have some very fine young fellows in command of the Irregular Cavalry with us. Probyn is about the handsomest and best-made man in India. He had such a race on the 28th ult., with one of his native officers, after a Pandy sowar. To his great chagrin, the native officer beat him, because he happened to be better mounted, and speared the man first. Watson is another young hero. Younghusband is very good. Best thanks for yours of the 28th, with all the good prayers and wishes you have expressed. What with fresh air and regular exercise, my spirits and appetite are wonderfully improved. There has also been good news from Lucknow, which has been relieved by Havelock, and the mortality amongst the officers found to be much less than was expected. No particulars given. To-morrow, at Allyghur, we expect to hear a good deal of news. Ouvry, hearing that there was a good deal of English plunder in Korjah, turned out a large force yesterday evening to coerce the place and make the people give it up. All he got, besides some rotten old carbines, was a good English double-barrel gun which was made over to the Prize Agent. The civilians, Campbell and Sapte, would not let him sack and burn the city, which is a large, strong place, and they were quite right, for though there were probably a hundred or so bad characters in it, why rob and kill and spoil thousands for the budmashes? The last three or four days have been very hot from eleven to three. The mornings are delightful, and the nights getting quite cool. The men wore their tunics to-day for the first time, and I found my stable-jacket comfortable enough. My carts get along much faster now that they are free from the living freights.

CAMP ALLYGHUR,
Monday, October 5th.

After a ride of from twenty-six to thirty miles, I am not much in the humour for writing. Some horribly impertinent fanatics of Mussulmen attempted to hold this place against us with telegraph iron stumps for guns and wire for ammunition. They had the impudence, too, to spike these curious guns. They ran away, and we pursued them about five miles along the trunk road, killing in all about a hundred of them between us all, but frightening the poor wretched inhabitants and villagers out of their wits. Had we been a day later we should have found the Bareilly Brigade, with sixteen good guns, snugly ensconced here, and great indeed would have been the trouble and loss of dislodging them, for the strong, woody, jungly compounds in which the place abounds. Everything has turned out for the best. I am very sorry that while we were going in skirmishing order through the Kates, and the men were firing their pistols in the most reckless manner, one of them managed to wound my " Delhi " (charger) in the hindquarter rather badly. I was so annoyed at this being done by one of our own men, but they were firing their pistols in the most dangerous, reckless way.

CAMP OCKBARABAD,
Tuesday, October 6th, 1857.

You must expect to see me return without a heart or feelings of any soft humanising tendency if I am destined to witness, day after day, such harrowing scenes of revolting brutality as have been perpetrated during the last two days, and are at the present moment enacting in this place, which has a very bad name, and which is being treated with corresponding severity. Fathers are shot with all their womenkind clinging to them, and begging for their lives, but content the next moment to lie down in their blood, howling with despair. Yesterday in the Kates there was a sowar with three women on the top of him, trying to conceal him. One woman got shot in the arm by accident ; the sowar got up and ran away, twelve pistols being fired at him without effect (this was the time when my horse was wounded) ; he was finally, but with much difficulty, lanced. Unarmed cowherds were mercilessly pistolled, together with about twenty armed men. What the poor women and children in this place are to do without their men, who are being killed in every house, I cannot

N

say. You will be glad to hear that the Headman, a notorious villain, Mungal Sing, and his brother were completely surprised by the Irregulars, and, with others, killed by them in the villain's own compound. It was a bright thought of Ouvry's sending on the Irregulars before the column at a rapid pace. The surprise was the most complete thing in the world, and Greathed is in very high spirits. We are bound for Agra now direct, and expect to be there on or about the 12th. The Sikhs are such desperate plunderers that to keep them out of the city we are going to encamp on this side of the river. George Campbell killed three men this morning, and that awful little snob B. boasts of having killed six, but I do not believe him. Just before leaving our picnic breakfast this morning, I saw him nearly put out the eye of his hardworking syce for some trifling offence by a severe blow with his fist. The only real wonder to me in this land is that *all* do not at once rise upon us and exterminate the hated Feringhees who so grievously oppress them. I felt so angry with my servants this morning, my carts were the last to leave the ground, and of course the last up. There was no reason for this, but their own laziness. Others keep their servants in order by perpetual kicking and thrashing. I do not like doing this, so the brutes take advantage of me. That awful snob H., who is one of the lowest of the bad sort of selfish Irishmen, treats his servants like beasts—even worse. A bullet has just come whistling over the tent from the town, where the work of destruction is going on so ruthlessly. Good-bye. You must expect to see me a fiend! if I witness many more of these horrors of war.

CAMP OCKBARABAD,
Wednesday, October 7th, 1857.

We are halting here to-day. We were to have gone six miles on our way to Hatrass, but at 9 p.m. we received an order to halt, and may perhaps return to Allyghur to-morrow, to meet there the reinforcements that are coming out to us from Delhi. Young Anson shot a man at Allyghur, just in time, for he was on the point of dealing a blow at him. Anson had lost his sword, but luckily had his pistol. His bridle-hand, you know, was wounded at Delhi, and he will probably lose the use of the middle finger of it, so he finds it rather difficult to manage his runaway horse. Yesterday afternoon two squadrons turned out under my command and had another hunt through the Kates of high, up-standing jowar for any stray Mussulmen. We thought we saw some mounted in the distance, and off we started in full pursuit over very rough ground. They turned out to be poor Hindoo villagers flying for their lives. We were suddenly brought to a halt by one of our men tumbling headlong, horse and all, into a blind well, some fourteen feet and more. Fortunately the horse went down hind-legs foremost, or else the rider must have been killed or suffocated. As it was, there he was sitting on his poor animal and entreating to be rescued from his perilous position. We got some ropes, and in about a quarter of an hour lifted him up. The man's name was Evans, of G Troop, and he

N 2

was not hurt in the least. How he will talk about it for the rest of his life! I lamed my Cape horse, and mounting a trooper who would carry his head very high, was very nearly coming to grief at a small deep ditch which the beast regularly tumbled over. Hurford says I may ride Delhi again now, but, poor beast, he cannot make out what has happened to his hind-quarters, which are still achingly sore. Fancy one of those horrible brutes of the 8th yesterday breaking with a stick the skull of a poor wretched Hindoo, who was ministering to the wants of the last hour of an equally wretched Bunga who had been mortally wounded by another of the devils, and was lying in agony on a charpoy. The Sikhs cried shame, and appealed to Evans, who was near, to put a stop to such atrocities. Evans said that they did not belong to him, but he was heartily ashamed of them. "You do not see our Lancers behave so, do you?" said he. "Oh no," they replied, "you are fine fellows, but these men have filled us with disgust" (pointing to many bodies of poor unarmed Bengalees and Hindoos), "that we cannot remain in the town any longer." These are the men too who behaved so badly at Bolondshuhur, that could not be got to look round a corner, or to advance in any way. Evans brought this to the brute's recollection, and called him an arrant coward. The Agra people are exceedingly anxious to see our faces, for there a gathering of rebels at Dholpore, which they do not like.

CAMP OCKBARABAD, FOURTEEN MILES FROM
ALLYGHUR DOWN THE TRUNK ROAD,
4 p.m., Wednesday, October 7th, 1857.

We may have to go as far as Dholpore after reaching Agra. Greathed himself is very much averse to doing so, but he must obey orders. Mrs. H. H. Greathed was frightfully overcome by the news of her husband's death, and proceeded at once to Mussoorie under the escort of her wounded brother-in-law, of the Engineers. The hopes of the family now depend on him. Should he not be blessed with a son, the name of Greathed will become extinct. There is no chance of our name becoming so. God grant of His infinite goodness and mercy that all our children may be brought up in His fear and love. Sarel was not quite so well yesterday; he gets very tired and feverish sometimes, and I wish for his sake that we were at Agra, where he would have a few days' rest. House has been voted Prize Agent to this force. He will have lots of trouble, and but little reward for it. At present we have got about eight annas for every man. The Delhi prize-money, they say, is looking up, and the agents fully expect to make a good thing of it.

October 8th.—Under buggy Camp Gunge, seven miles from Ockbarabad, on the Kutcha road to Hatrass, where we march to-morrow. The Kutcha road being narrow and bad for hackeries, they came up very late this morning. It is now nearly ten, and my tent not nearly pitched. I should be horribly dependent without my buggy to lie under. We had a little rain last night, and to-day it is uncommonly cool and pleasant. There is no particular news.

AGRA,
Sunday, October 11th, 1857.

We have been so busy since 10 p.m. of the 8th that I have had no time for, nor indeed has there been a possibility of, writing to you. At 11 p.m. on the 8th we marched from Gunge, in consequence of most urgent expresses arriving from Agra requiring our assistance, the enemy, 6,000 strong, being within a few miles of the place, with many guns, and talking of laying siege to the fort itself. At 8 a.m. on the 9th we found ourselves at Sydabad, twenty-six miles, having passed about midway through Hatrass. At 2 p.m. an express came out from Agra to the effect that the enemy were within three miles, and urging us on, so we marched nine miles more to a place called Kundowlie. It being the general impression that we should have to go on to Agra, and Roberts, the D.A.Q.M.G., having told me that there was so great a chance of it that he had ordered the camp not to be pitched for half an hour or so, by which time he expected another express from Ouvry, who had gone on by mail-cart to Agra, I asked leave of Turner (whom Ouvry had left in temporary command—H.A. and Cavalry only having pushed on to Kundowlie) and of Drysdale to precede the regiment, and pick it up again as it passed the fort. They gave me leave, and off I started, in company with Patton and Mr. Campbell, C.S. We had just got to the bridge of boats when we meet Ouvry

coming out again on the mail-cart. He asked who
had given me leave; I told him.   He repudiated their
authority, and ordered me back to camp, which he
said, as C.O., I had no business to leave.   I remon-
strated, told him that my horse had marched forty-two
miles, so had my syce, and that I was much fatigued.
Would he give me a seat in the mail-cart? He
repeated the order in the harshest terms, and drove
off at full speed.   I dismounted, sent my horse and
syce on to the fort, and proceeded in search of a
tattoo.   It was now quite dark, and we had been
murdering Mussulmen by wholesale not fifteen miles
off. I could not get a tat, and had to walk the
weary long eight miles back to camp.   I got back
to camp about 10 p.m., dead tired, having ridden
forty-two and walked eight miles, flung myself under
the buggy, and was soon asleep, but awoke shortly
with a frightful fit of ague.   I drank a scalding
hot cup of tea, and went to sleep again, but woke
with my teeth chattering again ; nor was I comfortable till 3 o'clock, when the *reveillé* sounded, and I
got up and drank three cups of tea running, and,
mounting my horse, marched with the regiment to
Agra, when the whole fort turned out to greet and
welcome us as their deliverers.   I saw the Muirs and
Dr. Farquhar *en passant*, and shook hands with the
former.   When the regiment got to its grounds, I obtained leave to go into the fort, about a mile off, and
breakfast with the Muirs.   They were as usual very
late at breakfast.   The scene in the fort, the crowds
of men, women, and children, the narrow space, the
heaps of good furniture, is perfectly indescribable.

The Muirs, with their five children, have only one room, about as large as our dining-room at Umballa, which they can call their own, though they have some two or three rooms belonging to others to roam over. Mr. Reid, Mr. C. Thornhill, Mr. Lowe, Dr. Farquhar, and Dr. Brown formed the breakfast-party. Just after breakfast we heard guns firing. The enemy were attacking our camp! I got into a palka gharee, then into a buggy, then upon the first horse I came across, and rode up to the regiment, drawn up in battle array. I was just in time to charge with them.* A large body of Pandy Cavalry, 1st L.C., mutineers of Probyn's, made a sweep round upon the camp and cantonments. They were met and repulsed by us. My brute turned out a run-away, and it was all I could do to hold him. Poor French was killed, and Jones is, I fear, mortally wounded. Well, we gained a complete victory, pursued them to the Kala Nudder, about ten miles off, took every gun (thirteen) that they had crossed and from 300 to 400 hackeries. I was out with a squadron seven miles on the pursuing road this morning, burning and destroying everything I could find—powder, shot, hackeries, and innumerable clothes and rubbish of all sorts. We are to remain here three or four days till Hope comes with reinforcements, and then off to join Havelock.

* The attack on Agra was a time of great confusion, and in some published works credit is not given to my father for leading the charge which dispersed the enemy. The following is an extract from the official report of the battle : " A most spirited and decisive charge, in which his regiment, led by Captain Anson, broke and dispersed the enemy's cavalry."

CAMP AGRA,
Monday, October 12th, 1857.

I stayed in camp yesterday till 3 p.m., having, with Wilkinson's assistance, arranged and lotted off all French's things. I then drove down to the fort, saw the Muirs and their children, and walked with B. to the Moter Musjid, which has been turned into a hospital, and had a look at poor young Jones, who is, indeed, desperately wounded, having been shot in both arms, cut about both eyes, having further been cut down the back and across the stomach, and received a dangerous cut on the back of his head. In spite of all, he retains his senses, and is doing as well as a man can do in his circumstances. B. and others are looking after him in the matter of soups and jellies, and there is, I hear, a good chance of his ultimate recovery, though he lost nearly every drop of blood in his body. French was shot right through the body, and some large artery must have been touched. He had only time to ride about 100 yards when he fell off his horse and died. These two officers appear to have been struck down in advance of their men. They were in support of guns, and had to charge in defence of the guns, which were nearly lost. Directly the Pandies saw us bearing down at full speed on them, they one and all exclaimed, "Wah, wah, Delhi ke Bullum regiment, barghera, barghera," and off they ran faster than they came, with the exception of a few, whose horses carried them on to destruction. All we had to do was to show an imposing front. Turner, to whom I was speaking this morning, says that he had

twenty-seven casualties amongst his Artillery, which
is more than his share out of the total number, viz.,
sixty killed and wounded. B. says she never was
so frightened in her life when the battle commenced,
and when she went afterwards to the hospital to
make herself useful, the sight of the wounded turned
her so sick that she was obliged to leave. I spent
an hour in the fort walking about most unconcernedly
with her, through dining-rooms and sleeping apart-
ments, the Macphersons and the Gwalior widows
(three) treating us with great courtesy, till we reached
the Marble Hall again, where I had told Sarel to
meet me, and I would drive him down to camp in
time for French's funeral. We were just in time,
and after the funeral there was a church parade, so
that, considering I was out for five hours in the
morning destroying the enemy's ammunition and
burning their hackeries, &c., &c., on the Gwalior
road, by which they fled so precipitately, the day
was a busy one for me, and I was glad to get
to bed. This morning I was on a Commissariat
Committee, and made the acquaintance of Captain
Dickens, who seems to be an amiable and gentlemanly man. A quantity of rum had been lost,
owing to the camels throwing off the kegs when
the firing and consequent confusion commenced,
and such a scene of confusion as the road between
the camp and fort presented beats all description.
Had the Pandy Cavalry succeeded in gaining our
rear, what a lark they would have had. There was
an Agra volunteer chased by a loose horse (horses
on these occasions invariably have their own bit of

fun), which finally laid hold of his horse's tail.   A
trumpeter of ours happening to kill a 1st L.C. man
with three medals on his breast, an Agra volunteer
immediately tore the medals off and showed them
as the trophies of a man whom he had killed.
Another volunteer asked Ouvry for a certificate
that he had been under fire, with a view to prize-
money, I suppose. There were many personal con-
tests during the pursuit, in which two squadrons only
of our regiment were engaged, the Headquarters,
under my command, with Blunt's troop H.A.,
remaining to protect the camp, which had been
so seriously menaced. Norman killed three men.
Colonel Cotton one or two. The Sikhs were very
active, and, as usual, got an enormous deal of
plunder. One of our men got some gold mohurs
in a bag five inches long. Turner says that the
three brass 24-pounders alone are worth ten to twelve
thousand rupees. Young Anson and Evans got bad
falls during the pursuit. We are, I hear, to march
on Wednesday towards Gwalior, to meet the Gwalior
rebels, who are somewhere near Dholpore, with between forty and fifty guns. When they have been
encountered and defeated, Agra will be quite safe,
and we shall be at liberty to join Havelock and the
main army, but not till then. I am going to dine
with the Muirs in the fort at 6.30 this evening. Mr.
Harrington* enquired very kindly after you and the
children. I saw the ladies looking at us the morning
we marched in. I do not know what we shall do
for officers, having only six for regimental duty,

* Sir Henry Harrington.

exclusive of Wilkinson and Grant. Sarel is going
to remain behind here for a few days with Chalmers.

CAMP AGRA,
Tuesday, October 13th, 1857.

I went down to the fort about 4 p.m. yesterday,
and found B—— hard at work copying letters for
her husband, who was scribbling away despatches as
hard as he could. Meanwhile the children got all
round me. They had paid me a visit in the morning,
and were regaled with some cold tea and the sight of
the inside of my tent. About 5.30 I set out with
B—— on a peregrination through the fort, saw the
quarters of the Protestants and Roman Catholics
face to face, for they are occupying what were the
bullock sheds, and went to the top of the fort, where
I saw no end of double-pole tents, and which I con-
sidered by far the healthiest spot in the fort, from its
very superior elevation and the delicious airy walk
always at hand round the ramparts. At last we
alighted upon the Harringtons and all the big wigs
sitting upon a sort of Chiboutra, outside a very respect-
able-looking barrack-room. Mrs. Phillips was there.
Her husband is very strongly built, and a very fresh,
good-looking man. The enemy in this immediate
neighbourhood have dispersed, and there is now none
worth mentioning between this and Gwalior, which
latter place, however, will always keep Agra in apprehension from being able to present itself before
Agra in a week or ten days with a regular siege-train
and huge shells, which, in the present crowded state
of the fort, are indeed frightful to contemplate. They

cannot spare a man from Delhi, and poor Havelock, terribly beset and surrounded by enemies, is
clamorous for our assistance. His force is quite
inadequate to the conquest and retention of the vast
city of Lucknow, and is going to fall back on Cawnpore, with all the women and children, leaving a
garrison strongly entrenched at Lucknow. At Mynpoorie and Futtyghur there are refractory Nawaubs,
with small forts. It would be far better to leave
these alone for the present, and join Havelock at
once, form one grand army, and demolish their places
on our way to Rohilcund. If proceeded against
separately by moveable columns, great loss of life
will ensue somewhere, and the result be anything but
satisfactory. I read such a charming letter yesterday
from Herbert Benjamin Edwardes to Dr. Farquhar.
He describes the wonderful way in which they have
been preserved at Peshawur to the successful establishment of the mission there ; lauds the Lawrences
to the skies, " There were giants in those days " ; is
highly in favour of strong places in India. What
would the Agra people have done without their fort ?
Suggests the advisability of each Cantonment having
its entrenched Dum Dumer. Talks of the nonsense
and folly of those who are for hiding Christianity in
India, and looks upon this horrible storm as the
means of opening everybody's eyes to the necessity
of an open and unflinching profession of Christianity.
That respectable body, the Agra Militia, having
challenged us to play cricket, we have been obliged
to muster up an eleven to fight them. B——'s
account of how for some days they were entirely

without servants, and had to cook and do everything
for themselves, is worth hearing. The ladies, too, in
the absence of servants, were most assiduous and
unremitting in their attentions to the sick. The
doctors would have been nonplussed without them.
The sanitary and ventilatory arrangements in the
fort are now of course admirable; but they were at
first anything but so, and cholera and fever of the
most deadly kind presented themselves.

CAMP FIVE MILES FROM AGRA,
LEFT BANK OF JUMNA,
ON MYNPOORIE ROAD,
Wednesday, October 14th, 1857.

Here we are again marching, and it is now reported
that we shall probably fall in with Havelock at
Futtyghur, which is to be made an example of, harbouring as it does the greatest villains in the North-
West. The moveable column is much offended with
the cold and shabby treatment they received from
the Agra people in the fort, who made not a single
effort to please them, or show their sense of the great
service we had rendered them, dispersing in a few
hours a force which they themselves would never
have got rid of. A cold collation or breakfast at the
Taj for the men, and a dinner to the officers in the
fort, would have sufficed to keep us in good humour
with them. I drove down to B—— about four,
intending to stop to dinner, but on our return from
half an hour's saunter about the Taj we heard that
about one hundred sowars were disturbing the peace
of the neighbourhood, and this sufficed to drive me

back to camp at once, though the report turned out untrue.   Showers's column has been doing good service.   The Tooleram rajah yielded up his fort, with thirteen guns all ready loaded, and everything ready to resist us.   A combined movement is now to be made against the Nijjur rajah from Dadres, the authorities having complete documentary evidence of his complicity in the rebellion.   We shall probably settle affairs in Rohilcund, and then revert to Oude.

CAMP ETAH MADHPOOR,
Thursday, October 15th, 1857.

I trust Hope will succeed in his endeavours to join us.   Our hard, harassing work is but just only commencing.   I wish I could see any end to it, for being no longer young and elastic in body or mind, I am beginning to feel very weary of marching for hours during the night.   On the 10th a superb diamond and ruby necklace was found in one of the hackeries, and sold by the Sikh who plundered it for 1,000 rupees.   It is worth 40,000 rupees, and has been redeemed as prize-money, a great catch for House, who, as Prize Agent, gets 5 per cent. on all obtained.   There is no chance of our meeting Havelock before we get to Cawnpore.   His presence at Lucknow cannot be dispensed with.

CAMP FEROZEBAD,
Friday, October 16th, 1857.

It is said that the diamond necklace found in the Agra pursuit is worth one and a quarter lacs, though we are not to get more than 40,000 for it.   House, however, pockets £200 by this lucky hit alone.   I cannot tell you how completely the enemy surprised our camp. The orderly-room-clerk of the Artillery was killed in his tent, hit by a round shot. House, while bathing, had three round shots within three or four paces of him, and says that he never put on his trousers faster in his life. His syce was grazed by one. Our advanced guard were caught unarmed and in their shirt-sleeves, eating their breakfast, and it is wonderful how they escaped so well. A merciful Providence ordered it all for the best. The camp was not nearly pitched, and our artillery were at work in less than five minutes, and most signal was the discomfiture of the enemy. Did you hear of young Plowden's narrow escape on the 10th? A bullet grazed his left cheek ear, and took a bit out of his hat. Havelock seems to be in a difficult position at Lucknow. He has it all his own way with the exception of being able to leave the place, which, surrounded as he is by numbers, he does not choose to do at present. Hodson's Horse have been left behind at Agra, where they seem to be anything but easy in their minds.

CAMP SHAKOABAD,
THIRTY MILES FROM MYNPOORIE,
Saturday, October 17th, 1857.

We came nearly fifteen miles this morning, and are bent on hurrying down to Cawnpore, and thence to Lucknow, as fast as we can, leaving Futtyghur alone for the present. Havelock is very much in want of us, and the main point now is to form a junction with him. When we, therefore, pass Futtyghur our communication with Allyghur and the North-West will be precarious indeed, as the Futty-ghur man is a notorious villain, and has cut off the hands and killed more of our kossids than any other scoundrel. We shall return to him when we clear Havelock and all the women and children, &c., from Lucknow, where, by the way, the Gwalior force, to the great joy of the Agra denizens, are at last bending their way, so in a despatch from Muir to Greathed received last night. Mr. Harrington is with us, intending to reach Cawnpore under our protection· He was very nearly bringing his wife, but thought it a little too risky for her. He is going to dine with young Grant this evening, and were not my mess bills so high I would ask him too. Mr. George Campbell accompanies us in an official capacity, and is about to organise an intelligence department of his own. We find it extremely difficult to gain any accurate information of the enemy's movements, and may come upon a large body of them any day, strongly posted in some one or two of the numerous villages we pass through every march. We hope to be at Cawnpore on or about the 27th. It is being scientifically entrenched, and is now in the hands of a portion of the Naval Brigade. How intimately associated with my Indian career has Cawnpore been. What a melancholy place it will in future hold in the annals of India, as the scene of the most horrible massacre of modern times. How passing strange the circumstances under which I am about paying it another visit. Two thousand camels for Havelock have been placed under our charge.

O

CAMP EIGHTEEN MILES FROM MYNPOORIE,
Sunday, October 18th, 1857.

Here we are, having marched only six and a half miles this morning. We are to make Mynpoorie in two marches, so we are not going on very fast, but we are hampered by a terrible amount of baggage, our own and what we are taking down to Havelock. It is very doubtful whether the Mynpoorie man will resist us or not. I do not think he will, but I am not quite so sure that we shall pass by Futtyghur, off the road as it is, unmolested by those villains, the Nawaub and Hydur Allee. What a surprise we had at early breakfast this morning—only fancy, Hope and Hamilton popping in upon us in a Government bullock-cart drawn by coolies. Hope commands us all now; Greathed the Infantry, and Ouvry retains his position as Commandant of Cavalry. Mr. Harrington dined at mess yesterday evening with young Grant. It was a noisier night than usual, and he seemed to be somewhat astonished. We have a son and nephew of his in camp.

CAMP MYNPOORIE,
Monday, October, 19th, 1857.

We marched twenty-four miles in here this morning, and were expecting resistance to the last hour; but the Rajah, thinking better of it, fled, and the city and fort were surrendered to us without firing a shot, and Cocks is now in the fort dismantling it, and sending messages to the Rajah that since he had protected some of our people and had committed no diabolical acts of atrocity, his life would be spared. We are taking over some two or three lacs on account of Government, and there is a chance of our halting here to-morrow, but it all depends upon the news and information brought in to-day by the intelligence department. This is eight marches from Cawnpore, where we still hope to be on the 27th. Our next march is to Bewar, a place you know well; it is about seventeen miles from this. Hope was sitting writing in my tent nearly all yesterday afternoon. He holds a very responsible command now and will, I hope, retain it even when he joins Havelock. F. Grant was quite knocked up by the sun this morning.

CAMP MYNPOORIE,
Tuesday, October 20th, 1857.

I feel just now absolutely good for nothing, and yet I have just taken over the command of the regiment from Drysdale, and been detailed as captain of the day for the Cavalry Brigade, which will oblige me to be up from 10 to 12 at night visiting the picquets, and we march at 2 a.m. This Mynpoorie seems to have been in perfect order before the mutineers broke in upon its shady and serene tranquillity. It does great credit to the civilians who have had charge of it during the last twenty years. The trees along the road have been so well cared for, so have the public buildings and town. The young Rajah was foolish enough to run away, though we should have treated him kindly, because he saved some Europeans and sided only with the ruffians when he could not help himself. He was, I suppose, blinded by terror and made himself scarce, so another man has been made

Rajah in his room. The gate of the fort, as well as a strong house inside, are to be blown up. The news from the front is that the rebels have all decamped from Bewar, where they had partly entrenched themselves, and the chances are now that we shall reach Cawnpore without firing a shot.

CAMP BEWAR,
Wednesday, October 21st, 1857.

We marched eleven or twelve miles this morning and the Pandies had left so lately that their fires were here and there smouldering. Two days ago they occupied the place in force, and some 3,000, with ten guns, marched on Cawnpore. Our force there met them at Poorie, and it is said defeated them, inflicting a loss of five guns and 1,000 killed and wounded on them. This is not yet authenticated, but I daresay we shall hear something about this battle in the course of to-day or to-morrow. It is now reported that the remnant have made Futtyghur their place of refuge. Another report is that the enemy are leaving Futtyghur as fast as they can. I started at 10 p.m. last night to visit my picquets, and, as I fully anticipated, got completely bewildered amongst the fields, kates, and villages. After pottering about for about an hour, I stumbled upon the picquet that I had intended visiting last. It took me two hours and three-quarters finding the four picquets out, and it was 12.45 when I got back. At one, the *reveillé* sounded, so you may say that I was marching from 10 p.m. to 8 a.m. The country round Mynpoorie happens to be particularly difficult just at this time, before the crops are cut. We

propose marching to-morrow in regular battle array,
so as to be prepared for any sudden movement that
the enemy may make. There was an auction yesterday in camp, under the Prize Agent's orders, of the
property taken in the Mynpoorie fort, consisting
chiefly of the contents of the shops of the Mynpoorie
boxwallas and some curious silver things (plates,
baskets, and hookah bottoms) and matchlocks and
ivory and carved marble, the property of the Rajah
himself. About 2,400 rupees House realised. He
ought to have got much more, but the guard he set
over some valuable shawls, silver goblets, &c., plundered the property instead of guarding it. There
was a quantity of tea and sago and sundry of our dâk
wallets destined for our people in Rohilcund. You
will hardly believe that the thermometer is $90\frac{1}{4}$ now
(1.40) in my tent. This will give you an idea of the
power the sun has still in these southern regions.

CAMP GOOSAYEGUNGE,
Thursday, October 22nd, 1857.

We marched in here this morning, twenty-nine
miles, our orders being to hurry down to Lucknow as
fast as possible, and avoid, if possible, any detention
by the way. Now Futtyghur would probably have
fallen an easy prey to us, but would have entailed a
halt of one or two days, and it will fall just as easily
three weeks hence. We are now within sixty-eight
miles of Cawnpore, and, I daresay, you know the
place very well. We thought we were going to have
a fight this morning on arriving at our ground, for
Ouvry came galloping in for Watson's Horse, in order

to cut up some two or three hundred men that he had seen running away, and who were supposed to be the advance guard of the enemy retreating from Futty-ghur, fancying that we were in their rear instead of parallel to them. They made sure that we would go to Futtyghur, but as this did not suit our convenience, we came here instead, and sorely puzzled them. We caught an Irregular Cavalry sowar yesterday, and he was shot. Two have been caught to-day, and are sure to meet the same fate. We are twenty-five miles from Futtyghur. We marched at 8 p.m. last night, and it was past nine this morning before we reached this, and the baggage was much delayed. We slept for two hours on the side of the road, and without this sleep I do not know how I should or could have got to the end of the march, for I was nearly tumbling off my horse from downright want of it. The sun down here is uncommonly fierce, and everyone feels it very much.

CAMP KUNAOJ,
Friday, 23rd, 1857.

Just a few lines on the bare chance of this reaching you. There was a small affair here this morning, under Ouvry, who commanded the advance guard. On coming here he learnt that the enemy (500 Infantry and four guns) had not left the place more than two hours. On that he pursued, overtook, and captured the four guns, the Irregulars cutting up about 150 of them, supported by the 1st Squadron, under Fawcett, who came in for their leavings—five or six stragglers in the Kates. The enemy contrived

to cross their guns over an arm of the Ganges ; or,
at all events, a small fordable river, and opened them
on O. as he advanced. O. silenced their fire with
his own two guns, and then, crossing his Cavalry
over the ford, caught the flying enemy in a fine
open plain, where the Irregulars made fine havoc
amongst them. We are now within fifty miles of
Cawnpore. This is, as you know, a very curious
old place.

CAMP POONA,

Saturday, October 24th, 1857.

It is unsatisfactory work writing now, because I
feel sure that my letters never go beyond that awful
savage, the Nawaub of Futtyghur.   However, one
line a day, on the mere venture, you shall have. We
made another forced march this morning, twenty-
three miles to this, and are now within two easy
marches of Cawnpore, into which we propose walking on Monday morning ; and how changed the
scene will be from 1850 ! There was no skirmish
or affair this morning, barring Ouvry's dour (raid)
with thirty of poor Probyn's tired Irregulars (three
of his horses died from fatigue yesterday), after a
budmash six miles off, said to have money and arms
concealed in his place. We got here this morning
at 8.30, having started at 12, so that we are improving in our marching. This column will soon
be able to conquer all India. Our men are longing
for a charge against the " Neemuk arams," and how
they would delight in serving Nana Sahib out if
they could but catch him. Havelock and we will
make a tremendous example (D.V.) of the Lucknow

rebels, who are at present hemming him in in the most inconvenient manner.

CAMP CHOWBEPORE,
Sunday, October 25th, 1857.

Here we are at this, to you, well-beknown place, eleven miles from Cawnpore. We marched at three, and were in by seven, having passed, about five miles from this, the place where the Cawnpore garrison, or part of it, went out with six guns to meet the rebels with twenty-two, and forced them to retire. Young Anson, or little Anson, as the natives call him, and Roberts are on their way to Cawnpore to cheer them with the news of our near approach. There are 1,500 Europeans in garrison there, and the bridge of boats is very nearly ready for heavy Artillery. They are very badly off for carriage, and have begged us to bring them as many camels and hackeries as we possibly can. We are to encamp on what was, years ago, the Cavalry parade ground, and every preparation has been made for our comfortable reception. The chances are that directly after relieving Havelock we shall hark back to Futtyghur, and clear the road effectually thereabouts. The rascal has occupied it, since we passed, with guns. Hope regretted very much being obliged to leave him unpunished. The Gwalior contingent are marching in two columns on Jhansi, the ruler of which has engaged their services. With the second column is the siege-train. Jhansi, therefore, bids fair to become a second Delhi or Lucknow, and must soon be visited in force, Bundelcund being one of our richest dis-

tricts, and a formidable country to war in. What
an anxious time this is for all wives! Hope is very
angry with —— and —— for being absent now that
the regiment is fighting nearly every day and is very
short of officers. We scarcely expect to meet Little
and Co. to-morrow, but hope we may, with all our·
hearts. What pleasure it was to me hearing that
the children were the admiration of all Kussowlee,
and what infinite credit it does you that they should
be so. I saw MacPherson's brother at Agra, and
a fine, gallant old fellow he seemed. He is resident
at Gwalior. Our sick officers are doing very well,
and Drysdale has taken a wonderful turn for the
better.

SUBAHDAR'S TANK, CAWNPORE,

Monday, October 26th, 1857.

Here we are close by the Tank you know so well.
I am going out at 4.30 to spy out the nakedness of
the land. The blood, hair, and garments of our poor
unfortunate murdered women and children are still
to be seen at the assembly-rooms and about the
compound. Ouvry brought away the frock of a
baby that could hardly have been a month old, and
in Wheeler's entrenchment he laid his hands on a
page of what must have been a Church Bible, from
the large size of the page and print. It contained
part of the Sermon on the Mount. Drysdale has
had a few lines from Little, from Allahabad, where
he, Powys, Coles, and Rich are waiting for the first
favourable opportunity of joining us. Steele and
Johnson are behind with the military-train. We halt

here to-morrow, and Hope is very anxious to push
on the next day, and release his friends, the Inglises,
from their awkward predicament. The authorities
here are very anxious to keep us for a few days, in
order that we may advance in force on Lucknow.
We can have now 1,000 Infantry, but in a week
would certainly have more than 2,000 fresh European
Infantry. Three hundred are expected in to-morrow,
and every day after will bring its quota. The
Infantry are worth waiting for, but Hope is one of
the most obstinate of mortals, and will probably
have his own way. We have a firm bridge of boats
to cross over. It is fully commanded by the entrenchment, which is somewhere up by the Artillery
lines, at the very end of Cantonment. I can see from
here even how the church in which I have been twice
married has been desecrated by those awful savages.
It is hardly safe to go and see the old houses at
Nawaubgunge.

CAMP CAWNPORE,
October 27th, 1857.

Yesterday I went to see the house where so many
of our unfortunate women and children were murdered.
It is a low, flat-roofed house, about 100 yards to
the left front of the assembly-rooms, close to the
northern gateway of the general's house. It is a
villainous-looking place, and will be more famous in
history than the Black Hole of Calcutta. We saw
lots of remnants of gowns, shoes, and garments dyed
in blood, and blood upon the walls in different places.
Outside in the compound there was the skull of a
woman, and hair about on the bushes. Oh! wha⁺

pain, and grief, and fear must have reigned there!
Oh! what tearful eyes and aching breasts must there
have throbbed! From there I went to see Sir H.
Wheeler's entrenchment, and found it to be our old
hospital surrounded by a trench. Such despicable
cowards, however, were the awful savages, that what
would have taken us a couple of days to level with
the ground, they in twenty-two days damaged only
the exterior walls of, very few of their shot penetrat-
ing the outside wall. Our fire from the entrenchment
seems to have kept them completely at bay, and had
not provisions and ammunition failed, they would
have held out till H.'s arrival. This morning I
walked to see the Spiers' house, and a most melancholy sight it presented. The trees all round scorched
and killed by the tremendous blaze of the bungalow,
which, with its fine verandah, pillars still standing,
looked noble in its very desolation. From there I
went to your old house, to the gate of it, for I did
not venture in, being all alone, walking with only a
stick in my hand. It was in an admirable state of
preservation, and lots of people were cutting the
grass in the compound. Further than this I did not
go, much as I wished to see the Wemyss's house; it
was hardly safe for a lone European, unarmed, to go
so far. My dreams—and I dream most vividly—are
all about war and war's alarms. In my sleep I fancy
I hear the roar of artillery, and see its damaging
results. The other night I dreamt that the camp
was attacked, and rare was the scene of confusion.
Colonel Campbell and Major Halyburton have been
severely wounded at Lucknow. Between the 25th

September and 15th October we have lost sixty-two
officers, killed and wounded.   Sir Colin Campbell
joins us at Lucknow on the 2nd or 3rd.

Wednesday, 28th.—I should like you to see the
assembly-rooms and compound.   In the latter are
carriages and buggies of every sort, and howdahs and
palanquins, and broken-up furniture.   In the former
there is every conceivable description of household
property and clothing, from the magnificent pier-
glass to a mouse-trap.   We are now to halt here, or
just on the other side of the river, till the arrival of
Sir Colin Campbell on the 1st or 2nd prox.   Nearly
400 of the 93rd Highlanders arrived yesterday.   It
is an uncommonly fine-looking regiment, in splendid
discipline.

CAMP CAWNPORE,

Thursday, October 29th, 1857.

Little, Powys, Coles, and Rich joined yesterday.
Steele is a few days behind.   Two or three cornets
are on their way out.   I walked through the Gwal-
tolah bazaar this morning to the magazine, and
found the bazaar in good order, except here and there
where a house had been looted.   It is the nicest,
most shady, and respectable bazaar in Cawnpore.
The magazine presented a most ruinous spectacle,
the buildings inside being all more or less tumbled
down, and the strong wall of the place itself in some
parts laid low.   The compound inside was filled with
the *débris* of magazine stores.   When I surveyed the
surroundings of the place I came to the conclusion
that Wheeler was quite right in not shutting himself
up in it.   Indeed, it would have been very difficult

for him to have chosen a better position than our old hospital, which is greatly isolated, and standing on a plain where he could see what the devils were about. We march at six to-morrow morning across the river. The report is that the rebels have abandoned Lucknow, and that we shall have only to walk into it. We must bring the brutes to bay somewhere or other. They fly before us so soon, that it will be very difficult to catch them in a *cul-de-sac*, the only way we can make a terrible example of them. In taking up a position, the first thing they look to is a secure retreat. By patience and perseverance and good commissariat arrangements we may eventually starve them into submission.

CAMP BUNNEE,
FOURTEEN MILES FROM LUCKNOW,
Sunday, November 1st, 1857.

Here we are reduced to Cossid post. To-morrow we march to Alum Bagh, four miles from Lucknow, and there wait a day or two for Sir Colin, and then proceed to the operation of relieving O. and H. It will be something like Delhi, without its stink I hope. We hear the heavy guns going from this. Hope will command all the Cavalry, Little the 9th, and Ouvry the Irregulars. Colonel Grey commands the Infantry. We are all well. Cole's squadron (the 3rd) is at Cawnpore waiting for Sir Colin, who may be with us to-morrow. The want of carriage below and above Benares is very much felt. Nothing but hackeries, and but very few of them, their owners having destroyed them.

CAMP NEAR ALUM BAGH
(ABOUT FIVE MILES),
Monday, November 9th, 1857.

We are waiting here till we have made all our preparations for driving the enemy from Lucknow. We shall, I expect, now in four or five days be hard at work, and have some precious tough work to do. What a blessing and comfort to think that nothing happens to us by chance in this world, that our times are in God's hands. How much more grievous must separation be to the ungodly, I mean to those who don't believe in revelation. We have bought a nice new double-pole tent at Cawnpore, and are, as far as mess arrangements are concerned, very comfortable. I see a good deal of Martin, who is at present doing duty in my squadron, which goes on picquet every third day. He is very strong and hearty just now. Not a line have I had from you since the 21st. It is cruel, heartrending work not hearing how you are all getting on, and takes away half the pleasure of my existence.

CAMP NEAR ALUM BAGH, LUCKNOW,
Wednesday, November 11th, 1857.

There is a general parade this afternoon for the Commander-in-Chief. In two days, I fancy, we move onward to conquer (D.V.). Captain Peel has arrived with the remainder of the Naval Brigade and four heavy guns. The Commander-in-Chief was very nearly falling into the enemy's hands near Futtehpore. He escaped only by the merest chance. Some 3,000 mutineers surrounded 500 of our soldiers on their way up between Allahabad and Cawnpore, and the 500 had to fight desperately before they drove them off. Colonel Powell was killed, and 100 of ours killed and wounded. Colonel Cotton has had a fight at Futtypore Sikree, near Agra ; twelve of the enemy were killed and we had seven wounded.

CAMP ALUM BAGH,
November 13th, 1857.

We pitched our camp here yesterday, not without a skirmish, however, on both sides of the road. On the right, where Sir Colin was in person, two small guns where taken by Gough's Irregulars. Gough himself got slightly wounded ; about twenty of the enemy were killed. On the left a large force of Infantry and Cavalry suddenly showed themselves, and Brigadier Hope marched against them with Infantry and Artillery and Cavalry. Happening to be the senior officer present, I commanded the Cavalry, and it very nearly had a good deal to do, for at one time we were not more than 200 yards from the flying enemy. Being wholly unsupported, and two miles away from the column, and seeing bad ground in front, and the enemy making for an entrenched position in a tope close by, from which they opened guns upon us, I deemed it prudent to retire upon the guns I had sent word to support me. I had about fifty of the military-train with me, besides one squadron of the 9th, and we were within an ace of getting into great difficulties, and having more than half of us used up. A force is now attacking Jellallabad, and the enemy are firing round shot into our left front picquet.

CAMP ALUM BAGH,
Wednesday, November 25th, 1857.

The very great work of relieving the garrison of Lucknow is so far complete. Both yesterday and to-day have been very busy days. The labour of removing 428 women and children, besides some 1,000 sick and wounded, has been immense, and attended with no little risk. We had not evacuated the Martiniére fifteen minutes to-day before it was swarming with Pandies like a nest of ants. The same with the Dilkooshah. The Commander-in-Chief's column arrived here yesterday ; Outram's to-day. I arrived in camp here yesterday at 7 p.m., having been the whole day out, and at 1 a.m. this morning I returned to the Dilkooshah on escort duty, and formed, with others, the rear guard of Outram's column. The Pandies followed us up for about half a mile, and then ceased to molest our formidable array of British troops. Poor General Havelock died about eleven o'clock yesterday, at the Dilkooshah, and was buried here this morning. He died of an acute attack of dysentery, brought on, I verily believe, by running nearly three-quarters of a mile, under fire, from the residency, to meet the Commander-in-Chief, and greet him as his deliverer. His son, poor fellow, is terribly cut up by the blow. His loss is indeed a great blow to the Havelock family. We march to-morrow *en route* to Cawnpore with the ladies, &c., &c., and sick and wounded. There was such a quantity of spoil left at the residency, I mean good furniture and things pertaining to ladies' wardrobes.

CAWNPORE,
December 14th, 1857.

We are to halt here for three or four days, and then proceed up country to Futtyghur and Rohilcund. Our plans, however, are not quite settled yet. I have a young cavalry cadet, of the name of Sitwell, attached to my troop. He has a brother on Outram's staff, lying wounded in the entrenchment. Sitwell is a gentlemanly young fellow, of good principles. I cannot keep the Highlanders and other troops of sorts out of my buggy in the line of march. They fall out, pillage some mess or officer's hackery, get drunk, and then tumble into the first conveyance they find on the road. So great and shocking have been the irregularities committed that the Commander-in-Chief has ordered a roll-call every two hours, and two parades a day, and enjoined the provost-marshals to the rigid performance of their duty. Willis is expected every hour from Allahabad.

NAWAUB GUNGE, CAWNPORE,
Tuesday, December 15th, 1857.

We shifted our camp here yesterday morning. We are close to Mr. Perkins's, and sad, most sad, it is to behold the ruinous state all his fine missionary buildings are in. I took the Rev. Mr. Mackay over them, to give him some idea of the grandeur of missionary enterprise in India. He was quite astonished at the size and convenience of the different buildings. Mr. M. is quite new to the country, and he arrived at Cawnpore on the 26th ult., was forced to take refuge in the entrenchment with the rest of the inhabitants,

P

and saw scenes of blood, and wounds, and death, and encountered personal dangers, and heard the most horrid blasphemous oaths, such as falls to the lot of few reverend divines to experience. I went all over the dear old Wemyss's house this morning, cut two or three walking-sticks in the garden, and picked up sundry bits of octrified glass in the different rooms of the house; in one room a timid hare was sitting, and scuttled off through the house when she saw me. It is a noble bungalow. Every bit of the roof is burnt off.

NAWAUB GUNGE, CAWNPORE,
Wednesday, December 16*th*, 1857.

Just a few lines on their usual venture, before going to play the Artillery at cricket. We all seem to have much enjoyed these few days' halt. That was good news that came yesterday, that Jung Bahadoor was on the point of invading Oude with 10,000 men and three batteries, we paying all his expenses. I should not be surprised now if the insurrection were thoroughly subdued by April next, and we at liberty to go to our homes. How thankful I ought to feel to a good and merciful God for having so wonderfully preserved me hitherto in health and safety.

NAWAUB GUNGE, CAWNPORE,
Thursday, December 17*th*, 1857.

I am dreadfully stiff to-day from my cricket efforts of yesterday. I happened to have a good innings, forty-five, and enjoyed the game exceedingly, but there is no pleasure without pain, for I got two severe blows on my right leg, and suffered horribly from cramps in both legs nearly all night. I was obliged to call the bearer in to shampoo them. We had only one innings, and the 9th Lancers have scored 190 to the Artillery's 140.

NAWAUB GUNGE, CAWNPORE,

Saturday, December 19th, 1857.

Here we are still, the Headquarters, I mean, for three squadrons, under Steele, Coles, and Johnson, marched hence yesterday forenoon for Etawah, to try and prevent an enemy's force from occupying the place. We shall be all together again, I expect, in ten days. I went to your old house yesterday morning, and bore away from the walls four hand-somely-carved Fenoose-holders and three or four punkah ornaments. Since they were the wretch Nana's property I had the less scruple in taking them. In the little corner bottle khana on the left as you enter, there had been a grand smash of bottles, and of a cabinet holding them. I was very nearly meeting with the reward of looting, for, just as I was about knocking off another Fenoose-holder, I discovered that a lot of bees had made their nest behind it, so I let it alone. I went into every room of the house so familiar to you, and found it in better order than I expected. I have taken three or four pleasant walks in the Company's garden, which, as you may imagine, is fast becoming a wilderness, though it has been so well cared for that it is still most attractive in its adversity. The Tank, with its pretty trees all around and within, looks still like a spot that fairies would choose for a moonlight dance in.

Willis, Thursby, Murragh, and Chadwick joined us last Thursday, the 17th, and have all gone on with the three squadrons.   Fawcett, Martin, Sitwell, and myself are left with the Headquarters.   Grant is well, but very anxious about Mrs. Grant.   Bourchier and Blunt have gone on with the advance party. That dreadful rogue must be stopping our dâks, for no letter from you has reached me since the one of the 27th ult.

CAMP NAWAUB GUNGE,
Monday, December 21st, 1857.

We shall most probably spend Christmas here, for the commissariat arrangements for 30,000 men take some time perfecting.   Meanwhile we have two effective moveable columns, Showers's and Walpole's, driving the foe into our net.   There are, I hear, 820 Cavalry at Allyghur, consisting of Hodson's Horse and a squadron of the Carabineers.   Our friend Sir M. Barlow has been appointed to do duty with the 2nd Dragoon Guards. You have seen, I suppose, that we Delhi-ites are to have six months' batta " forthwith distributed" amongst us.   It should have been twelve properly, but we shall have that eventually. Nothing has as yet been found in the well at Bithoor, but they are still continuing the search.   After digging for some time they came to water, then they touched on brick and mortar, and after that, on wood, which has given them some hope of their labour being finally rewarded.   Mr. Mackay gave us two excellent sermons yesterday.   He is a most popular man and effective preacher.   I saw Turner and Grant there.

NAWAUB GUNGE,
Tuesday, December 22nd, 1857.

I was walking up and down the noble verandah at " the Gunge," for half an hour this morning, and indulging in all sorts of sad and glad reminiscences. We shift camp to-morrow, and will probably march again about the 26th. There is an officer of the 93rd Highlanders to be tried for drunkenness by G.C.M. to-day, and a poor colonel of the 82nd has been pronounced by special court of inquiry incompetent to hold the command of his regiment. Clouds are gathering, and we may expect some rain now in a few days. We want it, for it is getting very hot and sultry. We sit down ten and twelve to dinner, and eat no end of vegetables—peas, cauliflowers, turnips, and young potatoes. The fish here, too, is very nice. I go out very little, and generally remain in my tent all day long. I hope you are looking after my books, &c., at Umballa. I am getting very badly off here for all sorts of things.

NAWAUB GUNGE,
Wednesday, December 23rd, 1857.

A merry Christmas to you, thus early, lest ought may prevent my giving you a line on the 25th. This will be the third Christmas I have passed in this unfortunate place, viz., 1844, 1850, and 1857. I was talking to Wilkinson last night about the batta, and he thinks that it would be most advisable to wait till the men get back into quarters before they get it, inasmuch as their kits are in a wretched state, and thirty-eight rupees would go far to mend them. My

young sub, Sitwell, draws very nicely. He has made
a very spirited sketch of the affair at Serai Ghat, and
he is going to send it to the *Illustrated News*, so that
you may perhaps light upon it some day. We hope
to be somewhere near Agra about the 15th prox., and
then what a batch of letters overland and every sort
we shall get, for I suppose all our letters have been
detained there. I see very little of Hope now that
he is a general and lives altogether at the Commander-
in-Chief's expense. He is, however, the same good
kind, unaffected man he ever was. No promotion
will ever spoil him, he is such a thorough gentleman. Little is at the head of our mess, and behaves
himself in a very pleasing, gentlemanly way, spinning
long yarns of the happy days he spent at Norwich.
Hamilton is now quite a distinguished gentleman,
with little or nothing to do, being D.A.A.G. of the
Queen's Army. I shouldn't wonder if some day he
were Adjutant-General.

CAMP CHOWBEPORE,
Thursday, December 24th, 1857.

Here we are at last, out of Cawnpore, and well on
our way to Futtyghur to punish well and most
severely, I hope, that frightful old villain who has
been stopping all our dâks. We had, as usual, on
the line of march our breakfast lying seated on the
ground under the shade of a pretty little grove.
Mine consisted of some very good veal-pie, the wing
of a duck, and bread and butter, with two cups of
coffee and one of tea. Just as we had done, Hope
and his staff appeared, and set to work right hand-

somely, but I must say that lying down is a most uncomfortable posture to eat in. Every day now brings me nearer you and gives me more chance of hearing from you. Of thirty letters in November written by Mrs. Norman, her husband has received only two. Norman says that we stand a chance of picking up some letters as we go along, since some wallets, for safety's sake, were thrown down some dry wells in places known to the individuals carrying them. I hope this may be true. There are a number of pretty jewels in camp belonging to the unfortunate ladies and people who were killed and looted at Cawnpore and other places. The native jewellers have evidently done their best to become, by hook or by crook, the receivers of stolen property.

CAMP CHOWBEPORE,

Christmas Day, 1857.

As merry a Christmas as circumstances can possibly let you have. I am glad we halted here, inasmuch as it has given Mr. Mackay such a good opportunity of doing us good. He preached one of the best sermons imaginable this morning from Rev. iii. 20. He has a good voice and a good expression of countenance, and an excellent delivery, and is, I should think, one of the very best preachers in the country. The road will, I trust, be open now in the course of two or three days, and we shall have some chance of hearing pretty regularly ; what a comfort that will be. I hear that all the notes that I have been writing to you for a month past are in a hackery in camp. You will be glad to hear that Outram has gained a victory at Alum Bagh and taken four guns, field ones, which they can very ill spare. It is a subject of deep congratulation and thankfulness that he has been able to inflict such a blow upon the enemy, and will render our conquest of Oude much easier. Hope and staff are coming to dine with us this evening. This was the place where, in November, 1850, I struck off for Bithoor. The Commander-in-Chief sent over there yesterday. The Commander-in-Chief's camp is full of small hill-tents, all pitched in two long lines, and every tent has a small blackboard posted up with the owner's official designation, such as A.D.C. to General Grant, &c.

CAMP AROUL,
December 27th, 1857.

We came here this morning. I could not write yesterday, being on rear guard all day. Futtyghur is evacuated. The budmashes have flown to Bareilly. You will be glad to hear that £5,000 worth of property (family plate, &c., &c.) has been already fished up from wells at Bithoor, and that we expect to get about twelve lacs altogether. I hope to see you again (D.V.) in April next. We have now been separated more than seven months. Little did I dream such a heavy trial was before me.

CAMP MERUN KE SERAI, NEAR KANOUJ,
Monday, December 28th, 1857.

I was much surprised this morning by Hope putting into my hand yours of 17th inst. House is very jealous of my superior means of communication, since he has had only three letters for the last three months. Frank Grant met with a very bad accident going down country. The tyre of one of the wheels of his gharee came off as it was rapidly descending a hill. He put his head out to see what was the matter and it caught him right across the face, cutting his nose and inflicting a deep gash on the forehead. Seaton's victory is very satisfactory. It seems that he killed 1,500 of the enemy, and took fifteen guns, of which nine were our own. Three officers of Carabineers were killed, and some 48 men of all corps. We lost all our mess-silver this morning, some horrible thief having coolly stolen it. A brigade under General Windham* was despatched this morning to blow up the Rajah of Futteeah's place, about eight miles from this. So Mrs. Grant and her sister are going home. Hope told me this morning that he had strongly advised their all doing so.

CAMP MERUN KE SERAI,
Tuesday, December 29th, 1857.

We are halting here for to-day, and perhaps we shall do so to-morrow too. Hope's brigade from Bithoor joins us this afternoon, and Windham's from Futteeah to-morrow. In six weeks or so some 1,600 more Punjab Cavalry will have arrived, besides the Cavalry from England. There is no occasion for our hurrying up country now that Futtyghur is evacuated. Our presence hereabouts does more good. We must just bide our time, get all our forces together or in combination, and then, driving the

* General Sir C. Windham, K.C.B.

brutes into some corner or another without a chance of escape, try and annihilate them all at once. Oude will furnish the corner. We have now some 16,000 troops between Allahabad and Umballa. In six weeks we shall probably have 30,000. May the Lord avenge His people and be gracious unto His servants. Mr. Mackay, Little, and myself and others are going to see Kanouj this afternoon.

CAMP MERUN KE SERAI, NEAR KANOUJ,
Wednesday, December 30th, 1857.

They must be blowing up Futteeah most effectually, for we have heard numerous explosions. Mr. Mackay and I went exploring into Kanouj yesterday evening, and were much pleased with our trip. It is an uncommonly curious place, full of the oldest tombs and ruins. Mr. M. took many notes. A large party have gone there to-day. Brigadier Hope's brigade from Bithoor joined us to-day. We hear that Head was severely wounded in Colonel Seaton's action, but that he is doing very well. How strange that I should have borne a part in the relief of Delhi, Agra, Lucknow, and Cawnpore. All well in camp.

CAMP GOOSERAIGUNGE,
December 31st, 1857.

Here we arrived this morning, and on the march Hope got a cossid from Bessie, and handed over to me yours of the 24th inst. and two of the 22nd. You may imagine how pleased I was to get these late letters, and how much shorter the reading of them on horseback made the march appear. No sooner however, did we arrive upon the ground, than my troop was ordered out on picquet, a surprise rather, for we have lately been having picquets of only a sergeant and twelve men, but it seems necessary to increase them, now that we are approaching the Furruckabad villain, so here I am, about a mile from camp, sitting under a tree in a delightfully shady tope, scribbling away, seated on a morah, and commanding two guns, two companies of Infantry, and my troop of Cavalry. At this place, the road to Futtyghur branches off from the Grand Trunk road, which for the present we have left. The brute, they say, is at this moment in Futtyghur, but, deserted by most of his tag-rag and bobtail, not knowing whether to make a stand or not. Meanwhile, he has done all he can to delay us, by breaking down the suspension bridge on the Kalee Nudder, and others *en route,* so that we may perhaps have a halt or two before reaching his den. My opinion is that he will not make much of a stand, thanks to Colonel Seaton's column, which seems to have cleared the way handsomely for us. Our Simla friend Murray, of the H.A., is lying down by my side reading one of my books, and Captain Gore, 53rd, has charge of the Infantry. We are putting up the tele- graph as we proceed. I have been schooling young C—— this morning into a proper style of dress and riding, and begging him not to look so much like a " cad " if he can help it. He took all I said in very good part. I saw Turner this morning. He came up to confab with Hope after receiving his cossid. Martin and thirty men remained behind this morn- ing and will join us to-morrow again. We are marching through a beautifully-wooded and well-cultivated country. We are three marches, or about forty miles, from Futtyghur. The officers of the Carabineers killed are Wardlaw, Wise or Vyse, and somebody else. The former rushed a long way in front of his men, into the middle of the enemy, who shot him down at once. Another was shot while going through a field of jowar.

CAMP GOOSERAIGUNGE,

January 1st, 1858.

A happy New Year to you all, and many of them. May God of His bountiful grace and mercy keep and preserve our lives, so that we may be able to bring up our children in His fear and love. What a wonderful year the past one has been, and how many dangers, both seen and unseen, hath it pleased Him to lead me safely through, and how good He has been to you in strengthening your heart, mind, and spirit to bear all that sickening load of care and anxiety which has fallen to your lot. " How will the present great tribulation augment the bliss of a world at once sinless and sorrowless. How will earth's woe-worn cheek and sin-stricken spirit and tear-dimmed eye enhance the glories of that perfect state, where there is not the type or symbol of sadness, not the solitary trace of one lingering tear-drop."

I made two mistakes in my yesterday's letter. Captain Gore, of the 53rd, turned out to be something less than a month senior to me, and took command of the picquet, and the place is only twenty-eight miles from Futtyghur, not forty. I had precious little sound sleep last night, the 53rd were so very noisy. They relieved sentries at the odd hours, while we relieved at the even, so that there was constant moving and noise in the camp, all night long. We are on again to-day, there being no relief for us, so that I expect to be quite knocked up after to-morrow's march. Sitwell and I had a nice little dinner together, and he told me all about his family, which is one of the oldest and richest in England. Colonel Seaton's column is at Bewar, and will join us at Futtyghur. He has, I hear, brought down an immense convoy of supplies for us. I saw our Cawnpore cricket match in the *Bengal Hurkara*," of the 23rd December. It will, I fear, be long before we have another, as every day now we shall be busier and busier, till the end of March. Mr. Hoossain Bux is terribly put out by my cutting him two rupees last month towards paying for the stolen mess-silver.

CAMP THREE MILES FROM SUSPENSION BRIDGE,
    AND THIRTEEN MILES FROM FUTTYGHUR,
        Sunday, January 3rd, 1858.

Yesterday, you know, we were about five miles on the other side of the bridge at Gooseraigunge. Well, I had just been relieved off picquet and had time to have a comfortable breakfast, to which I was sent by hearing guns in the distance, when Little came galloping in and ordered us all to turn out, as the enemy were attacking Hope's brigade at the bridge. We turned out sharp, trotted down about five miles to the bridge, and found both sides pounding away at each other. We got under a cover, behind a village, till we were wanted. While waiting there, some 24-pounder shot came unpleasantly near, and the top joint of the second finger of one of the Irregulars' hands was taken off by a Minié ball. Younghusband had breakfast up, and there we were all under a tree exceedingly comfortable, with the exception of seeing the poor wounded coming in, till about three, when we were ordered to mount and pursue the enemy. After a three miles' canter, we came up with them in very great numbers. Then commenced the work of cutting and pointing, and sights the most bloody that you can conceive. I knocked over three, young Anson seven, Martin some three or four, Fawcett the same, and even that young, gentle lad Sitwell pistolled one. Some 200 and more were sabred. Unfortunately, we had no light artillery up with us, or their casualties would have been much more numerous. Our march back into camp was quite an ovation in its way, for we had, somehow or other, got hold of the exceedingly elegant colours of the 10th Oude Irregular Infantry, the Queen's colour of which is beautifully embroidered in the centre. Large silk colours they are, about two and a half yards square. We also had a gay red and green embroidered Mahommedan colour, so you may imagine what an imposing appearance the head of the column had, with these silks streaming before it. As we passed the Commander-in-Chief, the men gave him three cheers, and the whole camp turned out and gave us three cheers—such a row as you never heard. Moses of my troop is slightly wounded; West rather badly. Leonard and Fuller are all right. I had three horses killed (the sergeant-major had his killed), four wounded, and one missing. "Alma" carried me beautifully. He is a blessing and protection to me indeed. Poor Younghusband is, I fear, mortally wounded. He went up to a Pandy with a musket on his shoulder to cut him down, but before he could manage it, the man discharged his piece, and the ball went right through poor Y.'s chest. There were no end of these men carrying muskets, and this it was that so enhanced the danger of the pursuit. Maxwell, of the B.A., is badly wounded in the leg. We march at 11 a.m. to-day, and it is nearly 10, so I must finish.

CAMP FUTTYGHUR,
Monday, January 4th, 1858.

How pleasant it is being able to write at large to you as usual. Here we arrived about 3.30. p.m. yesterday, and I am glad to say that the battle of the 2nd has had its proper effect, in causing the brutes to fly from this in the utmost consternation, leaving a beautifully-placed new 18-pounder, beside other guns, in the fort, now to be for ever occupied by us. There is a tope (clump of trees) of considerable extent lining the parade ground (where we are pitched), and this tope was made use of as a convenient shelter for innumerable workshops in wood and iron connected with the gun-carriage agency. All these workshops were made of temporary materials, wood and thatch, and underneath the tope all sorts of buggies, carriages, boxes, and loot of every description, including ladies' dresses and crochet-work, were heaped up in a mass of confusion. The brutes set fire to the tope, and it, and everything under it, blazed and crackled away sky high. On our arrival there were mountainous heaps all smouldering away, and a blaze here and there. Our people, however, set to, and brought away half-burnt buggies, palkee gharees, chairs, portmanteaux, dresses, boxes, &c., &c.; everything, in fact, you can imagine. We are two miles from the native town. Walpole's brigade and our three squadrons join us again to-day. We shall probably halt here three or four days. Hope has presented Sir Colin Campbell, in the name of the regiment, with the beautiful Queen's colour that belonged to the 10th Oude Irregular Infantry. The other three squadrons will be dreadfully jealous of our fight. It was certainly a very plucky pursuit, considering the numbers of the enemy. I want my shirts very badly, and spyglass and spurs. I wish I was as well off for clothes as the invalids. You give a most comfortable account of their wardrobe. It is a very good and graceful plan making the dear children mindful of me in their daily prayers. —— has got more leave (H. tells me), and is living up in the hills. If he but knew what bad odour he is in with Grant and the regiment, how shocked he would be. H., who was much worse than ever —— was, managed to join and get himself nearly killed. I told Sergeant-Major Rush all the regimental news in yours of the 26th, giving an account of the Christmas dinner. I was very sorry to hear of poor Dyson's death. I had not heard it before ; and now I hear that

Goldsmith and King, two more of my troop, were also killed.

CAMP FUTTYGHUR,
Monday, January 4th, 1858.

I had just finished my letter to you, when who should drop in but our friend Kinleside, whom I was delighted to see looking so well and hearty. He has been fighting his way down here with Seaton's column, and all the reward he gets for this display of zeal is an order to return to Meerut and command the 1st Brigade, instead of the 3rd here, to which he was posted.

Poor Younghusband is dead, and he is a great loss. An Irregular Commandant, like he was, cannot be made in a hurry. He was a tried man, a very good soldier. Probyn and Watson, than whom there could not be finer fellows, will grieve over Younghusband's death as they would over that of one of their own loved brothers. I am thinking of buying one of his horses, for my poor old Cape is on his last legs. I should very much like to have a glimpse of Walter, whom I knew as a child during his happy Bithoor days. I intended going to Younghusband's funeral at 3.30 yesterday afternoon, but instead of that I had to patrol with my squadron and two guns up to the city gate, about three miles. To-day Brigadier Hope's brigade goes to the city fort to blow it up and bring away the six guns that are planted there. Under penalty of destroying the whole city, that puckha (thorough) scoundrel Nazir Khan was brought into camp bound hand and foot upon a charpoy. No wild beast could have attracted more attention. He

Q

was for ever being surrounded with soldiers, who
were stuffing him with pork and covering him with
insults. He was well flogged and his person exposed,
which he fought against manfully, and then hung,
but as usual the rope was too weak and down he fell
and broke his nose ; before he recovered his senses he
was strung up again and made an end of. He died
game, menacing a soldier who rubbed up his nose
with, " If I had a tulwar in my hand you wouldn't
dare do so." He it was who wouldn't spare our
women, and treated them with every possible indignity. Some 30,000 maunds of grain have been found
in this place. We shall, probably, now go and clear
out·Calpee, where there are some 3,000 or 4,000 with
six or seven guns ; then Bareilly, and then Oude.

CAMP FUTTYGHUR,
Wednesday, 6th January, 1858.

My squadron is off with Brigadier Hope's brigade
to burn a place called Mhow, about fourteen miles
from this. We are likely to be away some days.

CAMP SHUMSHABAD,
7th January, 1858.

Just one line to say that we arrived here quite
unmolested this morning. It and Mhow are the two
places we have been ordered to chastise for cruelty
and insolence during the last six months. A party
of Sappers and Miners have gone into the town to
blow up all the puckha (brick) kotees belonging to
Mussulmen. What a good thing for some of us that
the Pandies did not hold Furruckabad, which is an

enormously strong place. The Commander-in-Chief is going to destroy some of the principal gateways. Our force consists of two of Remington's guns under Traill, some Royal Artillery under Captain Smythe, two heavy guns, 93rd and 42nd Highlanders, Greene's Sikhs, 300 of Hodson's Horse, and ourselves. I have just seen Hodson. He is quite well, and is the perfect model of an Irregular Cavalryman in his get-up. Mhow is six miles from this. We may halt here to-morrow to blow up Shumshabad, then march to Mhow, do the same there, and be back in camp at Futtyghur about the 13th or 14th. I am afraid that I shall not hear from you during the dour.

Sergeant-Major Rush got 113 rupees off the Sepoy he shot on the 2nd.

CAMP MHOW,
Friday, January 8th, 1858.

Here we arrived this morning, meeting with no resistance, nor are we likely to meet with any. I don't believe that there is any force of the enemy within 100 miles of us this side of the river. Across the river, the villages are full of armed Sepoys. On visiting my picquet of a sergeant and twelve yester-day evening, I found the sergeant and five men drunk ; too disgraceful, was it not? They not only ran imminent risk of having their own throats cut, but might have also endangered us all by their bad watching. I have ordered Sergeant S. to be tried to-morrow, and mean to punish the other five as severely as I can. Those systematic burglars —— and —— were rather put out by the court-martial, as it put

a stop to their looting for the nonce ; however, they
were at it directly they came in this morning, and
found in the Nawaub's small fort some photographs
of different ladies, &c. Sitwell, who accompanied
them, got no end of pretty photograph picture-frames,
white enamel with black borders, all ready for pictures, and the " Landscape Manual " for 1832 with
every picture in it. Mr. Bradford is the civilian in
authority over us, and had it not been for him yesterday all the best houses in Shumshabad would have
been blown up. There was a piano and all sorts of
furniture and babies' clothes found in the Nawaub's
place. This is a very pretty place. No end to the
topes about it, and in the large town itself beautiful
trees rear their heads in every direction. Numerous
are the old Moslem tombs about the place, signifying
its importance years ago.

CAMP MHOW,
Saturday, January 9th, 1858.

We are halting here to-day to admit of the more
effectual destruction of the puckha kotees in the
place and of the boats seen at various ghats along
the river Ganges, from which we are distant about
six miles. Fawcett and Martin are off again this
morning to see what they can pick up. They were
in no little danger yesterday, as well as that gentle
and gentlemanly little fellow Sitwell, who accompanied them, for they broke into a court-yard where
they found a number of sowars, with their wives and
families, and five horses picketed close to them.
Quite unmindful of the sowars, who bolted, they

forthwith proceeded to appropriate their horses and ponies, and returned scatheless to camp. Hodson went through great risk the other day on his ride back from Gooseraigunge to Mynpoorie. One of the villages at which he left twenty of his men to secure his ride back contained a lot of Pandies, who rose upon his men, and killing two, forced the others to fly. On his way back this was reported to him, and he was strongly advised to make a detour and not to go through the place. However, he chose the latter, and going through at a walk unmolested clapped spurs into his horse when on the other side and soon distanced his pursuers, if he had any. Poor Dyson had his arm shot off by a round shot, and was soon after killed on the spot by a discharge of grape.

CAMP MHOW,
Sunday, January 10*th*, 1858.

It is hot even now in a tent in the middle of the day. What will it be six weeks hence! I had Sitwell's looted horse well tried this morning by Sergeant-Major Rush, to ascertain his character. He was found to be most exceedingly rampageous, and would not therefore answer for me. There were fourteen men hung, or rather tortured to death (some of them), in the town here yesterday afternoon. One fat Patan was pinioned and taken to rather a low branch of a fine tree and lifted up like a stuffed dummy to the noose, into which he himself was very anxious to put his own head. However, it was just out of reach, so the people hanging him got two small morahs, and putting one on the top of the other, stood, with the

doomed on the topmost one ; but the morah slipping
down, they all came a heavy fall, especially for the
pinioned Patan. Well, they put a piece of wood
between the morahs, but this proved also a failure,
so at last they got an elephant, hoisted the doomed
man on upon him, adjusted the rope, and the elephant
walked away, leaving the man to slip into eternity.
He must have died a most painful death, for there
was no proper knot on the rope, and he had nothing
of a drop to help break his neck. Only fancy, fourteen hanging at the same time close to one another,
some dead, and some living, and it being very difficult
to distinguish between the two. Sitwell has drawn
a spirited sketch of the affair on the 2nd, showing
the Lancers pursuing the Pandies. He gets five
pounds for every sketch he sends home to the
Illustrated. A particularly pleasant and agreeable
young major of the 42nd Highlanders dined with
Fawcett yesterday evening. His name is Wilkinson,
and I never met a more pertinacious talker in my
life. Priestly, the senior Major, has just been calling
upon me. We were at Sandhurst some three years
together, so I asked him to dine with me this evening.
I have ordered my men to parade for Divine Service
at 5 p.m. The Highlanders have Presbyterian clergy-
men with them. We are to be back at Futtyghur
on the 12th. Do not be surprised at not hearing
from me on that day, as we shall have a long march.
Bareilly, Shahjehanpore, both reported to be strongly
occupied by the enemy, will be our next destination.

CAMP UMBEEAH,
Monday, January 11th, 1858.

Here we are half-way back to Futtyghur whence, however, we expect to march on Wednesday, a brigade, we hear, having already crossed into Rohilcund. We marched at seven this morning, and, going through the village, I saw one of the most remarkable sights I ever in my life beheld ; no less than twenty men all hanging naked to one tree, besides three or four others hanging to different trees close by. I thought for a moment that I was in Madame Tussaud's wax exhibition in Baker Street. I cannot describe to you what a queer sight it was, seeing twenty fat and lean fellows all hanging pendulous on one tree. War certainly familiarises one with horrors. We marched about thirteen miles this morning over a cutcha and very sandy road, and I thanked my good judgment in leaving the hackery behind. Traill, of the H.A., messes with us. The 42nd Highlanders have challenged us to play at cricket, and as there are some first-rate players amongst them, we expect to have an excellent match.

CAMP FUTTYGHUR,
January 13th, 1858.

We have been parading all the morning (having a Brigade Field Day) on the other side of the river, and are only just in, and it is late. I will write at length to-morrow. A strong brigade under Walpole* crossed the bridge this morning into Oude.

* Lieutenant-General Sir Robert Walpole, K.C.B.

CAMP FUTTYGHUR,
Wednesday, January 13th, 1858.

I am quite sorry to come back to this dirty encamping ground, after the beautiful country and fine, fresh air we have been enjoying. We are, however, going to shift camp to-morrow, certainly not before a very sensible necessity for doing so. We were out this morning, for three hours, at brigade exercise, under Hope Grant. The day was most unfavourable for it, for a strong wind was blowing up clouds of blinding sand. A trumpeter's horse broke his leg; how he managed it I cannot tell, for the ground was soft enough. "Alma" carried me nobly. He is by far the handsomest horse in camp; Hodson says so, and I certainly have not seen a handsomer. It was a curious sight seeing thirty or forty elephants—all loaded—swimming over the Ganges, which is about 300 yards wide here. The stream was flowing at a great pace, much ruffled by the wind, and from the centre of the bridge the view up and down was uncommonly fine. The bridge is in capital order; but coming back we fell in with all Walpole's brigade's loaded camels, and were obliged to march over by single file. It was rather ticklish work, especially where a camel had fallen, and obstructed the narrow way so as to oblige us to halt. The sight altogether was a most picturesque one. There is a general whisper that Hope has been made a Major-General, which, if true, makes me senior Captain, and places me in an excellent position, because Steele will not then purchase over me; if he did, he would be junior Major, and obliged to go on half-

pay, one major alone being allowed at home. Our
friend, the Hon. Randolph Stewart, dined with us
yesterday evening, and thoroughly appreciated our
good dinner. They live in the most uncomfortable
way, having no mess, and thinking wild pigeons a
great luxury. When he saw our nice beefsteak-pie
at breakfast, and our superb mutton at dinner, he
was quite astonished, and said he hadn't tasted such
things for months. I hear firing across the river, and
am inclined to believe that Walpole has already
lighted upon a nest of Pandies. Futtyghur is one of
the finest old towns in India, and the view from its
old fort is wonderfully fine. Captain Bruce, with
fifty sowars, has gone to see whether he cannot
pounce upon the Nana, whose days, it is thought, are
now nearly numbered. General Windham and others
have left for Cawnpore under an "escort of Irregulars."
You will soon see him at Umballa. You will be surprised to see Hope and young Anson within a day
or two of receiving this. Hope starts this evening
(14th) and Anson to-morrow. They are to be back
very soon ; indeed, they are going away under the
sound of cannon, for Walpole is again engaged with
the enemy this morning. We hear the firing of his
heavy guns distinctly enough.

CAMP FUTTYGHUR,
Friday, January 15th, 1858.

How surprised you will be to see Grant, Turner,
Norman, and young Anson, and how they will make
you long to get some such glimpse of me ; but your
good sense will tell you that I could not possibly

afford to take such a run up to Umballa. We shall probably be delayed here about ten days, in consequence of the bridge over the river Rām Gunga having been destroyed by the enemy, who occupy the opposite bank in force. This *contretemps* has rather perplexed us, for there are no boats on the river itself, and if we want a bridge of boats, we must wait till, by some means or other, boats can be procured, or any other sort of good, strong bridge can be made. The river is now about 150 yards wide, and deep, a formidable obstacle, you must acknowledge, and which may perhaps prove the cause of our having a hot-weather campaign in Rohilcund. At present affairs at the river stand like this. We occupy a village on this side, and they two on the other, enabling them from their position to obtain a cross fire. There was a good deal of firing yesterday, but only two bullocks killed on our side. A strong party of Rifles went up the river to reconnoitre. They had not gone very far before they came upon a village strongly fortified, and the enemy throwing out a thousand skirmishers on the sandy plain in front of it. The Rifles had to retire in good order. This shows that the Pandies are determined to have a fight for it in Rohilcund and Oude. Report says that the inhabitants of Lucknow have bought them out of the city itself, that the Moderates have dispersed, but that the desperadoes have gone to Fyzabad. Meanwhile Outram, furnished from the town of Lucknow with everything that he can possibly require, is living in clover. Walpole is firing away now—12 o'clock noon—and it sounds a little more distant than it did yesterday. Whom should I see this morning but Robertson, looking pale certainly, but otherwise well. He has been appointed Deputy Judge Advocate to our division. I saw Bishop, too, this morning, with the finest beard I ever saw man wear. That quiet little Presbyterian cemetery near the unfortunate church has been made the receptacle of all sorts of dirt, &c. The church compound holds the field hospital.

CAMP FUTTYGHUR,
Saturday, January 16th, 1858.

I feel rather tired this morning, having been up since 5 o'clock. I was captain of the day yesterday, and had to visit picquets that took me six miles and two hours poking away in the dark. Of all camp duties this is perhaps the most disagreeable. I visited our own picquet a short mile down the Cawnpore road soon after 10 p.m., after which I turned in, and got up again at five to visit the two Irregular picquets, which I had some difficulty in finding, even in the day time. On the road I saw five bodies of natives shot by order of Power, the magistrate. The Commander-in-Chief, escorted by a troop of Lancers, has gone this morning to take a look at Walpole. The bridge will be ready in a day or two, boats having been procured ; planks are being laid down. There has been no firing as yet to-day. George Hervey dined with Little at mess last night. Futtyghur is in his district, and he has taken advantage of this to take a peep at the camp. He says that one can buy in this country as many uncut diamonds as one chooses ; that amethysts, esteemed so highly at home, are despised out here. A good many people have been taken in by the soldiers of the 32nd, who have been selling large diamonds, full of flaws and defects, for large sums, much more than they are really worth. It appears that the 32nd broke into some room where there was a kind of throne studded with gems of every hue and size and sort, and that they still have a number of precious stones amongst them. Provided you can pay them in sovereigns, you can get them cheap enough. They find rupees heavy, and drafts trouble-some. One of the Nawaub's tigers (he used to keep two in wooden cages) got loose two days ago, and killed a native in the town before he was shot by some officer with a revolver. I hear firing now in Walpole's direction. The Pandies are probably saluting the Chief. How very interesting Norman's account of the mutiny is in the *Friend* of the 7th.

CAMP FUTTYGHUR,

Monday, January 18th, 1858.

I saw Robertson this morning, and he told me that his wife had heard the firing of guns some twenty miles from Roorkee. This must have been, I sup-pose, the affair that Mrs. Hutchinson told you of. R. did not think that Roorkee was in any danger, but yet he did not at all like the idea of his wife's being alarmed with the sound of guns, and talked of moving her, if the district became at all disturbed again. I cannot get poor Mrs. Lysaght out of my head. What a great fight of affliction she had to endure, seeing her husband shot before her eyes, and then being bayonetted herself. Like Stephen, however, when he was being stoned, she was breathing the atmosphere of Heaven, in prayer, on her bended knees, and bearing with calm equanimity the heaviest cross, in the prospect of an endless, sinless, and sorrowless immortality. What a hot furnace she had to pass through.

> " O, who could bear life's stormy doom,
>   Did not the Word of Love
> Come brightly bearing through the gloom
>   A palm branch from above ?
> Then sorrow touched by thee grows bright
>   With more than rapture's ray ;
> As darkness shows us worlds of light
>   We never saw by day."

I do so love to think of the stars in connection " with the galaxy of promises " shining brightest and clearest in the midnight of trial. There has been some heavy firing this morning in Walpole's direction. I am going to the city to see the Nawaub's brother, who has been caught, so good-bye.

CAMP FUTTYGHUR,

Tuesday, January 19*th,* 1858.

No post in yet, and past noon, so I had better begin my letter to you. Nearly all the officers have gone to see the Nawaub's brother hung, also three or four other miscreants. I was very busy yesterday afternoon. I started about 2.30 p.m., and got home just in time for dinner at 6.30. We went first of all to the Nawaub's palace in the city, about four miles from our camp. There is a most magnificent pros-

pect of the surrounding country from what was once
a beautiful terrace, but what is now an elevated, shape-
less mound of earth and brick and mortar, the effect
of our engineering. We poked about into all the
little sinks of iniquity, and were gratified to see how
completely the work of destruction was going on.
Stalwart and picturesque Royal Highlanders were
holding watch and ward over the waste, and preventing all further looting. Great digging was going on
in the centre for hidden treasure, and Churchill picked
up a calcined and conglomerated mass of pearls and
precious stones. Amongst the rubbish I particularly
observed a regular man-trap, huge barrels of musical
boxes, fragments of most beautiful china, porcelain
vases, and scent-bottles. I picked up two or three
valueless things as a memento of the place, and then
drove in the buggy to the Cantonment fort, about
three miles off, and close to where Dhuleep used to
live. I saw the bastion where Tudor Tucker was
killed, and all the desecrated tombs in the picturesque
old churchyard. Mountain's is being put to rights
again. Colonel Hickman's is quite a little mauso-
leum in its way. He must have been a popular
character here some thirty years ago, for the society
of Futtyghur raised the gorgeous tomb to his memory.
There is supposed to be about a million's worth of
property in wood and iron, &c., in the fort, and,
strange to say, the fiends made no attempt to burn
the piles on piles of the former. Never was a little
battle like that of the 2nd attended with more important results. The engine-room and workshops re-
minded me much of Roorkee   We walked nearly

all round the ramparts, saw the spot where the brutes had sprung their mine, met the Commander-in-Chief superintending the provisioning of the never-again-to-be Pandy fort, and drove home. Did I tell you that by the mail of the end of December Sir Colin had written to the Duke of Cambridge to do something extraordinary for Hope, whose services during all the campaign have been so great? The Duke has written to Sir Colin to be quick in sending in the names of those he wishes to have honours, in order that he may give them at once. I saw the extract of my letter of the 3rd to you in the *Lahore Chronicle* to-day, and had no idea that I had written it so well.

CAMP FUTTYGHUR,
Tuesday, January 19th, 1858.

I have just received yours of December 6th, kindly forwarded to me in an envelope by " J. W. Power, Cawnpore, 17th January, 1858," and yours of the 15th January. No, I did not write often between the 13th November and the 13th December. There was such uncertainty about the dâk. On the 17th November the enemy attacked our rear, and were made to run, beaten off by my squadron and two R.A. 9-pounders. They burnt some hackeries and killed and wounded three or four unfortunate natives before we came upon them ; one of them was a lad of twelve or fourteen, whose head they cut off. On or about the 20th November they attacked the rear once more, and came running up so close that they fired three balls into my shuldaree : again were they driven off by Infantry, Blunt's guns, and my squadron. On the 24th my squadron was the last to see the Dilkoosha, having been placed under Outram's orders for the nonce, and thus forming part of the force that retreated last from the Dilkoosha. The month you speak of was one of great and intense excitement. One never knew what an hour might not bring forth. On the 15th November my squadron formed part of the rear guard under Ewart, who had immense responsibility on that day and the following, till we reached the Martinière about 3 p.m. While sitting down in the compound, two of the enemy's rifle balls struck the ground quite close to me. I am sorry to say that noble-looking fellow Probyn is very dangerously ill of lung disease. How much I should like to see dear little C. in her new brown straw bonnet. How my heart yearns after you all. This separation from you all for so long is, to a man of my temperament, who cares so little for anybody else but his own immediate family, relatives, and particular friends, a very sore calamity. My deep knowledge of human nature renders me, I am sorry to say, rather misanthropical, and I find I cannot play the part of a gay deceiver, and be hail fellow well met with everyone. Don't fash yourself about soap for me; I bought some at Cawnpore, and have enough to last me for six weeks. My beard is about seven inches long, and very thick. It is like a ruffle, and keeps my throat nice and warm.

CAMP FUTTYGHUR,
Thursday, January 21st, 1858.

This is such a disagreeable, dusty, windy day that most of us have taken refuge in the comfortable double kunauted mess-tent. Yesterday evening I rode (for a wonder) to the Naval Brigade band, where I saw Blunt, who now commands what was Bourchier's battery. It was quite refreshing to me seeing him, half afraid as I was of his having flitted to Umballa. Since you say nothing more about Mr. Thornhill's ugly reports of the state of the country round Saharunpore, you have, I hope, received better news, and have your minds more at ease. You may, I think, be looking out for a move to Meerut ; at least there is a strong rumour about our depôts being ordered there, and House has to-day written to his people there to have everything ready for a move if ordered. The Pandies appear to be doing what we want ; that is, collecting in our front on the other side of the Ram Gunga. When it suits our convenience we shall dart across, give them a good licking, and then follow them into Lucknow, where there will be a final smash of them we hope. Powys commanded the Headquarters of the regiment on the 2nd, I the only squadron remaining at Headquarters. The leader of the Pandy force that last attacked Outram, and met with such a grievous repulse, was dressed up as a monkey.

CAMP FUTTYGHUR,
Friday, January 22nd, 1858.

I think I wrote to you from Bithoor a day or two

R

after the Suraj Ghat affair, which is by far the greatest feather in Hope's cap. I went round my picquets at five this morning. At dinner Mr. Mackay sits next me, and young Sitwell opposite, and we get on famously together. I enjoyed the hotch-potch soup and the fish very much yesterday. Lieutenant F. A. Weatherly, of the Carabineers, sat next me on the right. Major Bickerstaff, and he and the other two, marched this morning to join their squadron with Walpole, who has been using his riflemen with advantage in rifle pits, and astonishing the Pandies with their deadly distant shots. Showers and Sawyer are, I see, members of the court-martial that is going to try the King of Delhi. I was surprised to hear that you had seen Head, who seems to have made a wonderfully rapid recovery from his bad wound. My kind regards to the Montgomeries ; I am so glad that that nice girl of theirs is going to marry a good young fellow of Engineers ; you have only to look at her once to see that she will make the best of wives.

CAMP FUTTYGHUR,
Saturday, January 23rd, 1858.

It is kind of Hope bringing me a small parcel, for I know well how much he dislikes being troubled with anything of the kind. All the materials for constructing a bridge are ready, but the bridge itself is not to be made till it is wanted. There has been this morning the sound of guns from Walpole's direction. He is simply watching the foe and line of river just now, and using his riflemen as occasion offers.

Outram, it appears, has gained another victory over the Oudites, slaying 1,000, and reoccupying the Dilkoosha and Martiniére. Some heavy guns and ammunition have been ordered from Agra, and are expected here about the 28th, and we shall, I suppose, march on the 29th, if not before. I went with Mr. Mackay and Dr. Dalzell to the Suddur Bazar this morning, and came home by the church and racquet-court, which stand next to each other. The former is a perfect ruin inside. By a marble tablet, the only one in the church, we learnt that the church was consecrated on the 7th January, 1837, by Daniel Wilson. This tablet had been much shot at, but, strange to say, was not cracked. We are hourly expecting rain ; this has been the most cloudy day we have had. Mr. Mackay has lent me a very interesting book to read, called " Prophetic Land-marks," by H. Bonar, who is a great millenarianist. It is beautifully written, and very strongly argued is the subject. I have lent him "Pantika," which he says must have been written by a clever boy of seventeen, with an unnaturally fervent and vivid imagination. Sarel and two or three others at mess took such a playful rise out of Dr. Dalzell two nights ago. He retired rather early from mess, and, when in his first sound sleep, was awoke by his bearer with a note which professed to be official, and ran thus : " Dr. Dalzell will hold himself in readiness to accompany the Detachment Carabineers *en route* to join Brigadier Walpole to-morrow morning, and since they have reason to expect an attack by the way, he will take care and provide the necessary

R 2

medical comforts, and mind and keep the dhoolies close up." Up he sprung, dressed himself, and went over to the mess to enquire particulars, where they were almost bursting with suppressed laughter. At last they had it out, and he consoled himself with some whisky-punch.

CAMP FUTTYGHUR,
Sunday, January 24th, 1858.

As I shall probably (if the rain doesn't prevent me) be going to church in the staff-tent at twelve noon, I may as well write you a few lines *en avant.* I have not long returned from Divine Service in the Artillery lines, where the Naval Brigade chaplain performed the service, leaving out the " Te Deum," and all the Psalms and Lessons, and again reading the Prayer for the Church Militant, by way of sermon. Certainly the weather was against him this morning, it being gloomy, cold, windy, and dusty. Powys was snug in bed, so that the command of the regiment devolved upon me. Who should call upon me yesterday and seem so glad to see me but Dr. Farquhar, of Agra, the Muirs' great friend. He has just come over for a few days to take a peep at the camp, and is going back again to-morrow. Dr. Farquhar gave me a flourishing account of the Muirs, and how happy they were to be able to live in the Kotee in their compound, especially for the children's sake. To-morrow there are sky races, and goodness knows what, to amuse all the youngsters in camp. Mrs. Grant's departure makes me feel for you very much. She is a friend indeed. They say that seventy pieces of heavy ordnance will

open on Lucknow when we really set to work. A
party went out fishing and otter-shooting on the
river yesterday, and caught some fine large fish, and
saw lots of otters.

CAMP FUTTYGHUR,
Monday, January 25th, 1858.

Young Anson has just been here, giving me a
flourishing account of you. He said that he called
twice, and you were out, but that he met you out
twice. They met with no adventures on the road,
which was lined with Sepoys going to their homes.
I am going to see the sports at 2 o'clock. The
sailors' race will be worth seeing. I am now writing
on my knees, young Sitwell being at the table trying
to trace rather a good likeness that he took of me on
my white slate. He did not succeed to his liking;
such as it is (as also his abortive attempts on foolscap,
all giving you an idea of his style), I enclose them
all. Little thought the likeness on the slate very
good. I told him that I thought the traced one very
like Sir Henry Lawrence, so he wrote his name above
it. Hope has just been here, and I have had the
happiness of eating your delicious sponge-cakes, and
distributing them to my friends. I was reading
about them in your letter, when in they came. I
gave Anson, Wilkinson, Little, Sitwell, and Norman
some, and they all declared them, those, I mean, who
ate them in my tent, exceedingly nice. Warmest
thanks for all the much-coveted contents of the
parcel. Hope says had he known that it contained
any sponge-cakes, he would have eaten them up on

the road. They all seem to be the better for their
trip. Mr. Mackay preached such a good sermon
yesterday from Titus ii. 11, 12, 13, 14 verses—about
the most comprehensive text in Scripture. Young
Tritton came out with Mr. Mackay, and won the
hearts of all on board by his singing and constant
cheerfulness and amiability of disposition. Mr.
M. says that he was a remarkably clever boy, and
so full of spirits. Mr. M. felt quite a pang when he
heard of his death at Calcutta.

CAMP FUTTYGHUR,
Wednesday, January 27th, 1858.

I have not much time to write, being on the court-
martial again to-day. The mutineers have had the
impudence to approach within fourteen miles of our
camp on this side of the river. They are at Shumshabad (where we were the other day), with eight
guns and some thousands strong, so Brigadier Hope's
brigade of Highlanders, with twelve or fourteen guns
and Johnson and Steele's squadrons, started from this
at 10 o'clock last night, with the intention of sur-
prising them. The atmosphere is so thick and damp
that we could not well hear guns such a distance off.
The chances are, however, that the brutes made off
directly they heard of the march of the brigade from
some of their friends in Futtyghur. I am not sure,
but I think I hear now (9.30 a.m.) guns in the
distance. I saw Hope this morning in our lines,
very busy in pushing forward supplies on to the
Shumshabad brigade. Fancy a German philanthro-
pist at Bristol, of the name of Müller, having collected

£120,000, and more simply by prayer, and making his designs known without asking anyone for a sou, and supporting a great number of orphans of both sexes. Robertson is rather a slow Judge Advocate ; he is at present young at the business. Having a clear head, and being fond of writing, he will soon make an excellent one. I went to the races for about an hour, and used the spy-glass. Officers were racing their ponies and horses, and the fun, I thought, was rather stupid. Sir Colin was there, and his horse was almost too fresh for him.

CAMP FUTTYGHUR,
January 29th, 1858.

Hope's brigade came in about 6 o'clock yesterday evening. McDowall is dead. Do you not recollect his acting in the charades at Umballa ? Steele had a very narrow escape of his life ; he was attacked by a man on foot with a tulwar ; his sword-arm, just above the wrist, was cut in the first instance, then his reins, and while he was fumbling away for his chain rein his horse kept spinning round, and he seems to have been completely at the mercy of the wretch, who, aiming a blow at his head, missed it, but inflicted a long, deep wound on his thigh, and ran off. The wound was stitched up at the time, but had to be unripped again last evening, for it had bled much internally, and the leg was much swollen. When opened, the wound was probed, the blood-vessels tied, and he is now progressing satisfactorily. McDowall's leg was carried off by a round

shot below the knee, and he seems never to have recovered from the shock. Johnson was commanding
the Cavalry, and Steele the regiment, and Goldie and
Willis the squadrons. Goldie's squadron was the
only one that charged right home amongst 1,500
runaways, of whom they killed more than 300. A
lamentable accident occurred next morning. A
private of the 53rd fired his musket into what he
supposed was a lot of straw, giving cover perhaps to
a Pandy or two. It turned out to be powder, and
thirteen men were blown up, and seven or eight so
badly hurt that they are not likely to recover. I
saw Turner yesterday evening. He has been appointed gun-carriage agent here ; staff salary alone
1,000 rupees a month. He takes up the appointment,
which, by the way, he does not at all like, directly this
business of Oude is settled, in about six weeks or
two months. When at Umballa he dined at the
B——'s, and he seemed to think that they and their
friends with their Turkey carpets and beautiful
dresses, and height of luxury altogether, had but
ittle idea of the storm and tempest we had gone
through to enable them to live so. Of you and the
children, especially the baby whom he took in his
arms, &c., &c., he gave a most flourishing account. I
have just seen Steele, who is doing very well. I have
just been warned for the general court-martial again
at eleven to-day. Waite, of H Troop, is the name of
the man who had his head carried off by a round
shot. Blunt and Remington's guns were out, and
the captains distinguished themselves greatly, blowing up three tumbrils in a very short time.

CAMP FUTTYGHUR,
Saturday, January 30th, 1858.

Again am I circumscribed as to time, having to go to the grand court-martial at eleven ; but this, I trust, will be our last day. We shall, I fancy, be leaving this on the 2nd or 3rd, but no one knows exactly where we are going—whether Rohilcund or Lucknowwards. The ownership of fighting dogs is rather apt to lead one into scrapes. There was quite a tiff this morning between two officers, whose dogs were trying to bite and shake each other's heads off. *Young Anson, contrary to all expectation,* won the horse race yesterday, which had created quite a stir in camp. He had backed a fast young Arab of his against one of Captain Trench's. So you have got my hair at last, and I am proud to think that you wear it round your neck, and that you are so fond of it. May God be gracious unto us, and grant us a happy meeting soon. There are members of the G.C.M. whose father I might well be—this makes me feel very old. There is a young MacPherson of Clunie, one of the nicest-looking young fellows I have seen for many a day. Sitwell sends you the enclosed, with his kind compliments. He is sorry that he has not been able to make it more like, though he took great pains to do so. Walpole has been firing away a good deal the last two days.

CAMP AROUL,
Tuesday, February 2nd, 1858.

Here I am lying under the lee of a tree, for the wind is disagreeably high, trying to write you a few lines. I was so busy yesterday that I could not write. After a march of twenty-five miles to Jellalabad, I had seven miles of picquets to visit by day and night ; in all fourteen miles. I dined at five, off hash and a bottle of excellent beer, just arrived, and then turned in till 10.30, when I got up and had a four-mile drive (there and back) to the rear picquet. We have come twenty miles to-day, and two more twenties take us into Cawnpore. We found the Lahore Light Horse here on their way to join Franks at Benares. Turner's troop is with us, and Probyn's cavalry. It will take some days organising 25,000 troops at Cawnpore for the Lucknow business. I was very glad to leave Futtyghur, and breathe fine, pure air again. At Gooseraigunge we picked up twelve hackeries laden with brandy and beer, and we have sixty dozen of the latter waiting our arrival at Cawnpore, so that our mess supplies are again looking up. Johnson is a famous mess president, devoting much time and attention to the mess. Mr. Mackay is with us.

CAMP CHOWBEPORE,
Wednesday, February 3rd, 1858.

We marched twenty-four miles this morning, and have sixteen more to Cawnpore. Lord Canning is at Allahabad, and Sir Colin goes down to meet him. Young Scott has joined. Half the 54th have been shipwrecked—a sad episode.

CAMP CAWNPORE,
February 4th, 1858.

Having got my court-martial over sooner than I expected, you may have a few more lines from me.

Mr. Mackay admires my decision of character for writing to you under the difficulties he has seen me contending with ; for instance, yesterday in the open under the tree, the wind was very high, and blowing the paper up and down in the most irrepressible manner. He seems himself a good correspondent, but yields the palm to me—*al fresco.* My morah and I are, he says, inseparable. I am, indeed, always carrying it about, finding it most useful in many ways —as a seat, as a support to my back, as a writing-table, as a breakfast-table, &c., &c. Chadwick, who is a very nice gentlemanly fellow, was amusing himself with throwing bits of bread and pie-crust up into the air for the kites to pounce upon in the air. One succeeded to our perfect admiration. M. commanded the advanced guard this morning, and was very angry with F. for telling him that he had exceeded his powers in giving one of his (F.'s) men three days' drill. They had quite an unpleasant tiff about it, but in a quarter of an hour were the best of friends again. Our new doctor (Macrae) has joined. I sat opposite to him at mess yesterday, and took rather a fancy to him. Colonel Campbell has got the cavalry division, and Little will keep his brigade command. Sir Colin has gone to Allahabad.

CAMP CAWNPORE,
Friday, February 5th, 1858.

Large stores have come in for us to-day from Allahabad, and the mess is now well supplied with everything but champagne. The "Bays" had a small fight at Secundra on their way up. They were

in the saddle from 9.30 a.m. one day to 5 p.m. the
next, without once feeding their horses. The 7th
Hussars are over the water. Balmain was in command of the Lahore Light Horse, but I did not see
him. I took a walk this morning to view the second
desolation of the Cantonment. You have no idea
what a waste the poor unfortunate station is—compounds eaten up, trees all cut down, walls all broken
down—it is quite difficult to find one's way about
so utterly changed is the whole aspect of the place.
The spirit of judgment and the spirit of burning
has passed over it. Familiar as I was with every turn,
I was constantly thinking what turn to take. The
assembly-room is roofless, and one vast mass of
bricks and rubbish inside, with huge beams, charred
all over, lying about. Huge shot-holes are visible in
nearly every large house. There are wooden benches
in the church and a Seirkee roof over it. Mr. ——
astonished the congregation the other day by preaching an English charity sermon to them instead of
something appropriate to the times. He had not the
brains to stop, but went on rattling away, asking them
to give their money to some coal and blanket association at home. The large trees in the church compound have been well peppered with round shot, and
the bridge over the nullah is in a terribly dilapidated
state. The canal is dry just now. What splendid
cover the brutes had. The well containing the remains of the poor massacred women and children
has been puckahed over with a view to some large
monument being placed there. Meanwhile the 32nd
have raised a small one, with a very pretty Greek

cross on it, to the memory of their own women and children. I saw Brigadier Inglis yesterday evening, and he told me that Nana was over the water, about twenty-five miles off, leading a wretched existence, head all shaved and suspicious of everyone, seldom sleeping two nights in the same place, and contemplating crossing the river again as a Faquir. Our policy is to keep him were he is, and where he is almost sure to be taken, one of his friends even now engaging to hand him over to us. We are to have prize-money after all, not so much perhaps as we expected. I have seen young Burroughs, of the Highlanders, the smallest man in the British Army. Soldiers are digging away for money and jewels in Wheeler's entrenchment. One found 300 rupees buried there the other day.

CAMP OONAO, TEN MILES ON ROAD TO
LUCKNOW.
Saturday, February 6th, 1858.

To our surprise we came here this morning, for we thought there was every chance of our staying a week at Cawnpore. The 79th and 7th Hussars are to march on ahead. We are assembling our army on this side by degrees. I am sitting under a tree with the mess-dhoolie six paces off, and a high wind blowing. We had a little rain this morning.

Sunday, 7th.—Here I am on escort duty, and have no time to write but these few lines. I am going half way only to Cawnpore, but the convoy is large and the duty will take more than half the day.

CAMP OONAO,
1 *p.m. Sunday, February 7th,* 1858.

I have returned in time to send you a few more
lines. We had to escort in 800 hackeries, and 2,000
camels laden with grain, &c., &c. In a few days
there will be a thundering ammunition convoy; in
fact, there will be no end to this sort of duty for some
days. Young Anson is to be recommended for the
Victoria Cross, and Blair and Jones are to get it;
Probyn and Watson also. Dr. Fuller has been per-
manently appointed to us, and Dr. Macrae has received medical charge of the regiment from Clifford,
who is trying to effect an exchange with Franklin.
Hope has been appointed to the command of the
Cavalry Division, with Campbell and Little as brigadiers under him. No one has got the Infantry Division, but Brigadier Hope stands a good chance of it.
A Captain Evans, one of the Lucknow heroes, called
upon me yesterday afternoon. His wife and family
were massacred at Cawnpore. I have asked him to
dine with me to-morrow. A battalion (or part of
one) of the Rifle Brigade are entrenched here in a
tope close to us, and little mud entrenchments have
been built here and there along the road for any hard-
pressed party to run into. The bearer has been
behavin very well, and so have the other servants.

CAMP OONAO,
Monday, February 8th, 1858.

It was quite a chance my getting yours of the 4th,
which was a great treat to me. Yes, indeed, we shall
have heaps to do shortly, but (D.V.) I fully expect

to see you again and rejoice with you and the children again by the 10th April. If we return to Umballa, and I believe it is almost settled that we do, we shall leave all our heavy baggage behind and march from Cawnpore to Umballa in one month, but it is early days yet to enjoy visions of you and the sweet pets. Hope arrived this morning and assumed command of the Cavalry Division. Brigaded with us are the military-train, Watson, Probyn, and Wale. Under Campbell are the 7th Hussars, 2nd Dragoon Guards, Volunteer Cavalry, 12th Irregulars and Hodson's Horse. We hear the heavy guns firing at Alum Bagh, which is thirty miles off at least. To-day two fat and most military-looking subahdars, more than sixty years old, with more than forty years' service, were caught. They were miserable to look at. Their story may be true. They say they are not mutineers—on the contrary, have been robbed of every pice and shamefully ill-treated by the Sepoys. I am half inclined to believe them; but then visions of wailing, bleeding women and children rise up and stifle all feeling. Yesterday did not seem to me a bit like Sunday, what with my escort duty in the morning and the violent flogging of seven grass-cutters and a chowdree of John Scott's troop, for bringing in liquor for the troop instead of grass for the horses, in the afternoon. Then in the evening all the brutes of dogs were let loose, and no end to the barking, biting, and fighting. John Scott amuses me much, and I like him much, and am always glad when he is near me at dinner.

CAMP OONAO,
Tuesday, February 9th, 1858.

I had a visit from Hope this morning. He has the command of all the force—Artillery, Cavalry, and Infantry—between this and Bunnee, and is off to-morrow morning to Busserut Gunge to inspect the 7th Hussars, &c. Captain Evans came and we talked away about Indore and E., and his wife, and Robert Hamilton.* Young Brown asked me to dinner yesterday and enquired kindly after you and the children. He is coming to dine with me to-day. I am either getting bigger every day or everybody else smaller, for everybody seems so small to me nowadays. They tried another well at Bithoor, but after going down a certain depth they found the water gain on them so rapidly and copiously that they were obliged to desist for the present, but mean to try it on again at a more convenient season. My grass-cutters have got such a lot of loot that they are all disposed to run away, and I am thinking of keeping them two months in arrears.

CAMP OONAO,
February 11th, 1858.

One line more to tell you that the 2nd and 3rd Squadrons march to-morrow under my command to Bunnee, some twenty-three miles, and that the chances are I shall not have an opportunity of writing to-morrow. We shall, I daresay, be detached seven or eight days from the Headquarters. Goldie is to get the "Victoria Cross" for valorous conduct at Shumshabad. I was calling on Hope this morning,

* Sir R. N. C. Hamilton, Bart., K.C.B.

and he begged me to send you and Mrs. Martin his
love. He had heard of Mrs. Grant's safe arrival at
Mooltan.

CAMP OONAO,
Thursday, February 11th, 1858.

On coming home from the Fusilier mess last night
I was surprised to find yours of the 7th lying on my
table. It is indeed delightful to see how rapid and
regular the dâk is becoming. I was not so comfortable last night as at my own mess, for I was
squeezed up in the middle of the table without room
to move my elbows. I sat opposite a man of the
name of Hall, and got to know the faces of Dr.
Charles and Messrs. Watson, Magniac, Cunliffe,
Maxwell, Chapman, Money, and Warner. I left
about eight o'clock. We shall probably march six or
seven miles further on to-morrow, for the 7th Hussars,
&c., &c., have gone to-day six miles on to Nawaub
Gunge. The 7th are well-mounted, and Hope was
much pleased with their general appearance. Do hurry
off ——. He is getting into a terrible scrape. H——
tells me, and I was greatly astonished to hear it, that
he is still at Umballa, and does not intend leaving till
the 16th. Setting honour and all fine feeling
aside, his pay is being cut all this time. He must
join Headquarters before he can draw pay from the
1st inst. We are assembling our force by degrees.
We furnish an escort every day for miles of
hackeries, and the largest convoy, that of shot and
shell, &c., has yet to pass. The Highlanders are now
over the river, and a regiment has just marched in
here. In less than a week we expect to be at them
tooth and nail. Meanwhile they have been strengthen-

S

ing themselves in every way, by means of stockades, entrenchments, and loopholing and mining in all directions, so that we must be careful how we tackle them at first. It will be a fine sight seeing them take to their scrapers, with the Cavalry scuttling after them. We shall have about 30,000 troops, European and Native, to persuade them to show us their heels. The Highlanders (what a splendid sight they are!) are marching in. I am glad you got at last all my despatches. I send you a memo. of troops in garrison.

INFANTRY.	CAVALRY.
42nd Highlanders	9th Lancers
78th Highlanders	7th Hussars
79th Highlanders	2nd Dragoon Guards
93rd Highlanders	Military-Train
1st and 2nd Battalion Rifles	Volunteer Cavalry
5th Fusiliers	Hodson's Horse
23rd Fusiliers	Probyn's Horse
1st Madras Fusiliers	Watson's Horse
1st Bengal Fusiliers	Bruce's Horse
10th Foot	Wale's Horse
20th Foot	Detachments 1st and 12th
38th Foot	Irregulars, besides other
90th Foot	detachments, making up
84th Foot	perhaps one regiment.
95th Foot	
97th Foot	

68 Siege Guns.
50 Field Pieces.

CAMP BUNNEE,
Saturday, February 13th, 1858.

I have only time for a very few lines. We arrived here about 1 p.m. yesterday, after a long and tedious march of twenty-one miles and more. The force at present here consists of Anderson's troop of H.A. (Royal), two heavy guns with detachment of Naval

Brigade, three squadrons Hussars, two squadrons Lancers, 79th, 38th, and 34th and Watson's Irregulars. We form at present the advance guard of Sir Colin's army. We have just received orders to shift camp. Sir Colin, they say, joins us on Monday, the 15th. He is very much vexed at Nana's escape across the water. I should not wonder now if Hamilton caught him. Oh, the dust and hackeries on the road yesterday! The mere fighting in war is nothing—the means to the end something stupendous. Hope and staff are here, living with the 79th Highlanders. Bunnee itself is carefully entrenched—made a little fort of. We hear the Alum Bagh guns booming away very distinctly. Martin is my acting-adjutant.

CAMP BUSSERETGUNGE,
Monday, February 15th, 1858.

Just one line to say that we received orders about 9 p.m. last night to march back here, fourteen miles, this morning—two squadrons Hussars and ourselves, troop of R.H.A., and H.M. 38th, with Watson's Irregulars. We are going somewhere on a dour, for we have ten days' provisions, and no wheel-carriages of any sort are allowed to be taken. Don't expect to hear from me for a day or two.

CAMP FUTTEHPORE, CHOWRASSEE,
Wednesday, February 17th, 1858.

Our last two marches have been through the heart of the country, through crops of green-wheat, grain, and cotton, and groves of ancestral trees to this, one of the favourite haunts of the Nana. Such was the winding, tortuous way we came yester-

S 2

day, that we went over eighteen miles and had not our tents pitched much before sunset, though the distance in a straight line could not have been much more than nine. We just came upon the tail of the enemy here to-day, and Cole's troop had a six-mile gallop and skirmish with the brutes, killing about thirteen or fourteen of them armed with matchlocks and tulwars. They brought in, too, a sort of Moonshee as prisoner. Two small guns were also taken. Secrecy is so much the order of the day that there is no knowing where we are going. We may make another march to-morrow, and if we do not come upon the enemy, we shall most probably make the best of our way back again, to assist in the taking of Lucknow. Poor Turner got such a ducking this morning in a tank—swell H.A. uniform and all. His naughty horse would lie down and roll with him in the water. Martin has been appointed B.M. in addition to his acting-adjutancy.

CAMP BAJAREE, MHOW,
Saturday, February 20th, 1858.

What would you, or Mrs. Turner, or Mrs. Blunt, or Mrs. Martin do if you were in the predicament of the women in the large populous villages our greedy, ruthless Sikhs and camp-followers have been looting contrary to orders and in spite of all that Hope can do to prevent them?

I can fancy you singing to your baby as you were nursing it : " Hush, hush, my sweety, the Feringhees are coming, but it is not the Feringhees I fear. In their train are the robbers of the widow and the fatherless, and soon shall your pretty bangles be torn from your fat little limbs, and your mother be forced to endure all things. O! Nana, Nana, how couldst thou have brought this day of visitation upon us, this desolation which cometh from afar? To whom shall I flee for help—O where shall I leave my glory? The rod of the Feringhees' anger is justly upon us, they are accounting for their slain. Woe, woe unto me and mine. The Sikhs and the looters are down on me, and visions of fire and the bloody sword and spear make me faint." Human nature, you know, in spite of colour, race, and creed, is pretty much the same all over the world. We are halting here to-day, to blow up the strong places, and secure the great quantity of powder and other military stores found in the place, which could have been vacated not twenty-four hours before our arrival. To the last they were strengthening it and loopholing every available corner. So rapacious were our looting scoundrels yesterday, that Hope was obliged to have recourse to a ruse to get them out of the place. He put in Division Orders at 3 p.m : " The force will march at 6 o'clock this evening," and out they all came streaming to their legitimate work of preparation. Doubtless, too, the order had the effect of forcing the Nana, in terror of a night march upon him, some twenty miles further off. We are becoming acquainted by degrees with the officers of the 7th Hussars. Slade was dining with us yesterday. His father was the old Peninsular general, and a great friend of my father.

CAMP TEKEEAH,
Monday, February 22nd, 1858.

So you are not pleased with Sitwell's representations of me. He copied them both from the felicitous one on the slate. It seems a wretched sort of dream altogether, our long separation. Sir Colin's plans, however, must now be nearly formed, and by this time next week Lucknow will be coming to grief. Sir Colin's rear is threatened from Calpee certainly, if not from Bareilly, and he wants Sir Hugh Rose to clear Calpee at least before he advances on Lucknow. He has, I believe, certain information that the brutes are meditating another descent on Cawnpore if they can possibly manage it. Again, troops have been coming up but slowly. There is a hitch at Bombay and Kurrachee, where they have been kept too long. We shall not, I fear, be at Umballa before the end of May. I feel the want of maps, &c., so much that will you kindly do this for me? Rout out my Bengal and Agra Guide and Gazetteer, and tear out the maps and letterpress concerning Oude, Rohilcund, Gwalior, Futtyghur, all the country, in fact, round about this; and if you could send me a tolerable map of India—the postal one that used to hang up in my room will do—I should feel much obliged. That will be turning the book to some good account. We were at a place called Sultan Gunge yesterday. The Nana and family and followers are in a strong fort about thirty miles from this, but as he would inevitably run away to Lucknow, and our provisions are running short — this being the eighth day of the dour, and ten only having been provided for—it was deemed most advisable to leave him alone. There are a whole lot of budmashes and a few Sepoys with him, with nine or ten guns of sorts. I read prayers at 5 p.m. yesterday to my wing. How fast the weeks run by. We must be up and doing soon. We are now five short marches from Bunnee, where, or near which, we hope to be on the 26th or 27th.

CAMP MEEA GUNGE.
Wednesday, February 24th, 1858.

We did a good day's work yesterday, taking in a few hours, and according to rule, the fort of Meea Gunge. We heard at Tekeeah that the brutes had determined on making a stand at this strong place. When we got within two or three miles of it, the Cavalry and H.A. proceeded at a trot to reconnoitre and surround the place. We formed two lines, Hussars and Watson and troop of R.H.A. in first ; Lancers, Gough and Turner's troop in second, and about 400 yards from the first. We skirted the place all round, and finding it strongly occupied by the enemy, waited patiently for the heavy guns and Infantry to come up. About 1 p.m. the breach was reported practicable. It was a large hole made through the wall—three men abreast might have squeezed through it. The 53rd were told off as the column of assault, and, headed by Captain Jones, R.N. (an amateur), and young Anson, waded through the deep tullao, and pressed onwards about fifty yards to the breach ; Jones first, Anson second. No resistance was offered, and no sooner were the In-

fantry well into the place than the enemy came
pouring out in all directions, and then our fun commenced.   The Cavalry and Horse Artillery being
handled by a man wholly without experience, were
not as advantageously disposed as they might have
been.   The R.H.A., besides being dreadfully slow
and red-tapish, did not dash on to the front, where
the enemy were to be seen flying in numbers, with
the same zeal and gallantry that so greatly distinguish our friends of the B.H.A.   One or two
griffs of subs. allowed Fawcett's troop and Gough's
Irregulars, under my command, to pursue an enemy
six times our numbers without any support.   We
cantered about three-quarters of a mile, when, coming
within range of their muskets, we gave a shout and
charged with all our might.   In a minute we were
in the middle of them.   I nearly tumbled off my
horse in a vain attempt to cut down a man who
dodged me and then deliberately proceeded to shoot
me.   However, I went at another, but he dodged me,
too, and stood at bay with his drawn tulwar inviting
me to come on.   I was just preparing for a rush
when Gough* came charging down and felled him
with a powerful blow on his head.   Fawcett's horse
tumbled in consequence of a man running right between his legs.   F. got up, cut the man's head open,
and mounted again just in time to charge with me
and nine or ten of the men through a patch of about
five yards square of cotton-trees alive with the brutes
hiding in it.   There were fourteen men killed in it.
Just at this time we came up with Turner's troop,

* General Sir C. J. S. Gough, K.C.B., V.C.

and remained to protect it, Fawcett simply taking
four or five men to kill three or four of the enemy
whom he saw running across the plain.   Coles's
squadron had a good deal to do, and C.'s horse was
killed.   Evans, of his troop, started off with eight
men after some of the wretches, and killed about
sixty.   E. himself, armed with a lance, killing eleven,
and each of the men seven or eight.   Coles was also
armed with a lance, and being used to pig-sticking,
killed two men right and left with great skill just
before he lost his horse.   The 7th Hussars—a squadron of them—cut up about 200.   They had three
men wounded, and we had two privates, Gough and
O'Brien.   Our loss altogether was very trifling.
There were about twenty of the 53rd wounded, and
one officer badly through the stomach.   In the afternoon a house inside the fort was found full of armed
men, so the men there proceeded to smoke them out
by lighting a fire at the door and making a hole
through the roof.   One man, waiting till his face and
legs were well singed, bolted out, and had immediately five bullets through him.   The remainder—
about thirty — were content to be smothered and
burnt alive.   This is Hope's first fort, and he is
much pleased with the doings of his small force.
Martin was very nearly wounded in the foot, a ball
having just taken the edge of the sole of his boot
off.   We are halting here to-day.   I do not think
that we shall meet with any more opposition now on
our way to Headquarters at Alum Bagh.

CAMP MOHAN, TWELVE MILES FROM BUNNEE.
(Mohān is on left of road going to Lucknow, and
fifteen miles from Alum Bagh.)

Thursday, February 25th, 1858.

Here we arrived this morning, unmolested by the
Pandies, whose vedettes we saw well away to our left,
towards Lucknow, and some 3,000 of whom very
considerately bolted from a village last night about
four miles further on, thereby saving us the trouble
of ejecting them. Sitwell has made a very pretty
sketch of the breach in the wall of the fort at Meea
Gunge. Three elephants bathing in the tullao (tank,
reservoir) are done to admiration. I am sorry to say
that a number of women were killed while clinging to
and trying to hide their delinquent husbands, &c.,
&c., and many, too, were burnt in a house that they
could not be induced to leave. Their moans were
most pitiable. However, their fate was preferable to
that of two unfortunates, who were ravished to death.
What beasts men are when their passions are in a
blaze. We are, I hear, to remain here for some days,
and stop the enemy's supplies of green forage, &c.,
&c., from this beautifully cultivated district. We
got eggs this morning, for a wonder, and nothing
can exceed the civility and attentions of the poor
villagers. God grant this beautiful country may
soon feel the benefit of our rule. We have sent in
for some more supplies, having run short of nearly
everything. Evans, the Deputy-Commissioner, and
Wilkinson dined with our Evans and Thursby re-
spectively, and the battle of Meea Gunge was fought
over and over again. It is the first fort Hope has

taken, and he is much charmed with the business. May he never know what defeat is. Really, these Sikhs, and some of our Infantry, too, are shocking plunderers. Hope found some of our Infantry plundering at Bhajaree Mhou, and ordered fifteen to be flogged instanter, and harangued the regiment on full parade in the afternoon. Did not your father know all these places that we have visited very well? I think I have heard him talk of some of them. I cannot tell you how we have been smartening up the 7th Hussars. They have had the good sense to adopt all our neat ways, and look quite a different regiment now to what they did the first day they were with us. Their acting-adjutant said to me, " Well, I am so glad we have come this march with you, for you have been of the greatest use to us, and I am now trying all I can do to perfect our men according to your model." This man's name is Wilkins. He is a very gentlemanly man.

CAMP FOUR MILES FROM MOHĀN.
(Nearer Bunnee, and across the Bunnee river. A fine open Maidān, with beautiful topes and luxuriant cultivation).

Friday, February 26th, 1858.

We shifted camp here this morning, and here I am, under a tree, determined to lose no time in acknowledging the receipt of seven letters from you yesterday, brought by Johnson from Bunnee. His squadron came over as an escort to a quantity of rum, &c., for us, and went back again by moonlight. Upton joined three or four days ago, and has a tent of his own. Young Scott has been appointed D.A.Q.M.G.

to Lugard's division.   Steele talks of joining us again in a few days.   There is to be a grand review of all the troops, at Mangungee, in three or four days, preparatory to commencing operations on Lucknow. Another convoy is coming out to-day, so that I may, perhaps, get yours of the 20th.   More to-morrow. This written under difficulties.

CAMP NEWELGUNGE (TEN MILES FROM BUNNEE),
Saturday, February 27th, 1858.

The name of the place we shifted to yesterday is Newelgunge.   It is a large place, and evidently one of some importance, for it has a most expensive and elaborate Hindoo temple, and used to be the residence of one of the ministers of the King of Oude. I went this morning to see the pretty house and garden, redolent, oh! how sweetly redolent, of the aroma of the lime and jessamine.   I found the house gutted, and burning—Evans, the Commissioner, with some of his police, and accompanied by those prime looters, F. and E., having yesterday worked their will on it.   F. wanted to present me with a whole handful of little grotesque brass gods and goddesses, and I at first thought that inasmuch as they could not well be broken, they would be just the things for the children to play with, but on maturer consideration I returned the curiosities to him, because they might perchance give an idolatrous turn to the pets, when they saw the servants salaaming to them, and bringing them offerings of rice, &c., &c.   Don't you think I was ight?   They were, barring this, such capital playnings that I was sorely tempted to take them.   Some sixteen beautiful silk rezais were burnt in the house. Outram has been attacked again and has signally repulsed the brutes, who also had the impudence to attack one of our convoys near Alum Bagh. Fortunately the escort was a strong one, and beat them back handsomely. We may expect now hotter and hotter work every day; our duty here for the few days we are to remain will be to patrol in every direction, and cut off their supplies, &c. We have a strong main picquet on the Lucknow road, and innumerable small ones all round the camp, which looks compact and handsome on the glorious plain. Turner, on the twenty-third, did his best to save some half-dozen wretches, who had given up their arms, but F. said that they were his prisoners, and would not let him, so they were taken four or five yards away, and there shot one after the other, and really they are not subjects for pity—the more that are killed the better. We have heard an ugly rumour of a defeat sustained by our friend Scindia, who, it seems, has had sixteen splendid guns taken from him. This contretemps will give Rose plenty to do; and Gwalior will have to be taken after Lucknow. It is a strong place, I know it well, and cannot help thinking it a great misfortune its having fallen into the enemy's hands, and sincerely hope that the story may be untrue. Fuller and Leonard are very well; the former has proved himself a most useful N.C.O. Good-bye. May God bless and prosper you, and give you health and strength to go through your manifold duties. I am so glad to think you have such friends as Mrs. Turner, Mrs. Blunt, and Mrs. Martin.

CAMP NOELGUNGE,
Sunday, February 28th, 1858.

Gough is coming to dine with me this evening. I
do not usually ask people to dinner on a Sunday, but
it is well just now to take advantage of a quiet halt
day, and of the three or four days' supply of wine
and beer we had out yesterday from Bunnee.
Roberts and Gore are coming to dine with Fawcett,
so we are going to make the mess-man give us a
good dinner. Fawcett was patrolling this morning
with his troop, and caught two Nawaubs, thirty-five
women, and eighty Sepoys. There were 200 of the
latter, but the remainder bolted. He caught them
about 1½ miles from camp. We are beautifully
situated here for annoying the enemy in every way,
and to-morrow, they say, we are to go on about five
miles nearer Lucknow, which will bring our picquets
within four miles of the town itself, where there are
71,000 men and 162 guns ready to oppose us. The
enemy, too, are swarming at Calpee, and that, I
believe, is the reason of the Commander-in-Chief's
delay. Sir Colin is very desirous that Rose should
render a good account of the Gwalior force before
he commences operations against this place. Meanwhile the delay is strengthening us, and giving time
for our troops to assemble near us in all directions, so
that I trust that in ten days or so the smash of Lucknow will be complete. I do not think that there is
much chance of the 9th going up country. We are,
I fear, destined to form part of the large garrison
which must be left here. However, you may depend
upon my joining you if I can possibly manage it.

Sir Colin will have no difficulty in putting up 7,000 or 8,000 men in Lucknow for the hot weather. The Martiniére itself will probably be turned into a temporary barrack. I have just returned from Divine Service in the Artillery mess-tent. Turner read prayers, and a good sermon afterwards, and the congregation consisted of Anderson and his sub., R.H.A., Harrington and the doctor, B.H.A., Martin, Wilkinson and I, and a Sergeant Morrogh. I had a few lines from Macfarlane this morning, dated Kirkee, the 5th February. He wanted to know whether any of our captains would exchange at once with Sir W. Gordon, Bart., Captain 17th Lancers. None here feel disposed to do so. Hope is well. Turner is unhappy about his letters having gone astray.

CAMP DILKOOSHA,
Wednesday, March 3rd, 1858.

Under buggy, having just shifted camp. Wind cool, but high ; blowing up dust. Camp just out of range of the fire of enemy's heavy guns at La Martiniére. Siege-train and rest of army marched in this morning from Bunterah. Outram still watching Alum Bagh. Franks expected in to-morrow. We left Noelgunge at 3 p.m. on the 1st, and joined the Headquarters camp at 7.30 p.m. Marched at 4 a.m. on the 2nd, and fought our way to this, driving in a strong picquet and taking three guns from the enemy. When we got to the Dilkoosha we found that the enemy's batteries commanded the place all round. We were under fire all day. Little was wounded in the left arm, near the elbow, and we had two men wounded, Turner, of G Troop, losing half his jaw and tongue. One round shot killed two of the Naval Brigade, about fifty yards from us. We did not get into our lines till 7.30 p.m., having been fifteen hours in the saddle. No tents were pitched, but I slept very soundly on my bed, in the open, in my clothes.

CAMP DILKOOSHA,
Thursday, March 4th, 1858.

Here we are just keeping the brutes amused while we are preparing for a good bombardment from more than eighty pieces of heavy ordnance. They are very cheery, expecting to keep us as long here as they did at Delhi, but in four or five days they will see that it is no laughing matter, having brought down the wrath of Christian England on their doomed heads. They have been firing away into the Chief's camp and he has consequently been obliged to shift it. An 18-pounder went through Sir David Baird's tent. I had a short ride with Turner this morning. He has got all his letters. Walpole's brigade marched in this morning. Sir Hope said so innocently of Lady Grant, " She had, you know, no idea of ever being a lady." Is not that good! There was such a lively discussion last night at mess about whether it was right or wrong to kill one's wife, sooner than let her fall into the hands of the Sepoys. We came to the conclusion that it was wrong, but that if we happened to be jurymen in the case, we should let the delinquent off. A strong way of putting it is this : It is not justifiable to commit suicide under any circumstances, how much less to take the life of any other person.

I renewed Fitzgerald's acquaintance this morning and was agreeably surprised to hear that his wife and family were living close to you at Umballa. Were I you, I would be looking out for a nice house at Simla, or Kussowlee, for the hot weather. Never mind me, you may be sure of my joining you, wherever you are, as soon as the exigencies of the Service will allow me.

Sir Hope remarked this morning on my vigorous appearance, and strong, healthy constitution, and Lugard too was astonished to see me looking so well and powerful. I am sorry to say I ate too much breakfast this morning, and I cannot imagine why, for I was not particularly hungry. However, there is something very exciting in being so near the enemy, and hearing the roar of artillery going on all day. I paid Dickens a visit this morning. He is looking uncommonly fresh, very different from the poor, wretched, harassed creature he was here in November. The commissariat arrangements are all now splendid. In the fort of Jellallabad, close by, there are provisions stored for two months, and directly this business is over, the whole country will be open to us. I saw a cannon-shot go very near Norman the other day. He was out reconnoitring with two others, when the enemy fired at the party. Some of our men had a wonderful escape the other day, on the 2nd, an 18-pounder coming flop down amongst them without touching man or horse, and about ten yards from where I was standing.

T

CAMP DILKOOSHAH,
Friday, March 5th, 1858.

Here we are still, barring the 4th Squadron, which has just gone over the Goomtee to protect our Engineers at work on the bridge against the 4th Lancers; at least, they have got flags like ours and look amazingly like our old friends. The 7th Hussars and Tombs's troop H.A. left yesterday with fifteen days' provisions to protect our communications *vià* Alum Bagh and Jellallabad, the Pandies having succeeded in burning two hackeries laden with cheroots. The bridge over the Goomtee is nearly ready, and from the left bank manifestly will the town be bombarded; the assault will most probably be given from the right bank, because the river won't be in our way at all. Cawnpore is, I fancy, threatened again. What a thorn the old place has been in our side. It will be Monday, I think, before our batteries will be ready. Sir Hope is to inspect the Bays about 5 p.m. this evening, and I was thinking of taking a look at the regiment. There is a dreadful war going on between E—— and the 75th. I should not be surprised if it ended in E——'s being tried by G.C.M., for he won't retract; simply says that his letter was not intended for publication. Does Dr. Balfour remember me? He is one of the best doctors in India, and you are very fortunate in having him at Umballa.

CAMP LEFT REAR OF MARTINIÉRE,
Sunday, March 7th, 1858.

I am feeling so poorly that I can only write you a few lines. Yesterday's promenade and fight knocked me up entirely, and to-day the enemy attacked us in force, and for two hours we had to fight and beat them back. The Calvary were not called upon to act offensively, but protected the guns, which were banging away all down the line. The Bays made a vigorous charge yesterday and lost their major, Percy Smith, shot through the heart. We have turned the enèmy's left, and have now got a fine position. I had fever and ague last night, and a great pain on the right side of my chest, from holloaing, I suppose. We were twelve hours in the saddle yesterday, and had a gallop at speed of some two miles.

CAMP DILKOOSHAH,
March 10th, 1858.

I have received your telegram. I am better to-day. The work of the 6th strained me all over, and I feel something like a wreck. I am easier just now than I have ever been, having just had a hot flannel fomentation applied to all the aching parts. Up to within a few hours of this I had been having agonising spasms and griping pains. I am only half a man just now, and am writing this in bed on my back. I never was bled before, and twelve ounces is a good deal to lose. You will be glad to hear I am a major for Delhi, but honours are nothing when you cannot enjoy them. There is a talk of an assault to-night on the Martiniére. Outram took the racestand, &c. &c., this morning, under a very heavy cannonade.

CAMP DILKOOSHAH,
March 13th, 1858.

I am perhaps a little better to-day, but feel utterly

weak and good for nothing. We have the Secundera-
bagh, and Outram is now working his way up to the
Residency on the other side. All is progressing most
satisfactorily, thank God, and the crisis is approaching
fast. I have eaten nothing since the 7th evening, and
feel so uncommonly queer at times. The servants,
poor creatures, do their best, but I miss you horribly.
It was a skirmish when we took the Dilkooshah ;
but the affairs of the 6th and 7th were much more
serious.

DILKOOSHAH,
Sunday, 14th.

I have got a room in this place. I could not have
lived in camp. I am feeling better to-day. I cannot
get anything to eat. The ration bread chokes me.
Mr. Mackay read to me yesterday for some time out
of my little "Sacra Privata." I cannot read much.
There is very heavy firing going on.

CAMP DILKOOSHAH,
Monday, March, 15th, 1858.

I had a very bad night and am not feeling better
to-day. I am to remain here when the army moves.
I could not march about with the regiment, and then
the doctor talks of sending me to the Hills. I am to
occupy one of the rooms in the Dilkooshah. I
suffered such pain in my side when I got up this
morning that I was obliged to send for him. He
ordered seven more leeches, and they relieved me
much. I shall not be able to mount a horse for six
months and more. Begum's palace stormed last night,
Captain McDonald, 93rd, and some men blown up.
Hodson reported mortally wounded, and others.

DILKOOSHAH,
Monday, March 15th, 1858.

I am in no pain, but I have been hearing shouts of pain from those poor fellows who were blown up yesterday and frightfully burnt. The Kaiser Bagh fell yesterday. The enemy are now confined to the native city, some six miles in circumference. Two days at the most will suffice to drive them out thence, so that Sir Colin will be able to telegraph by the mail that leaves Bombay on the 17th the complete success of his operations. There promises to be a fine example made of these Lucknow ruffians. Dr. Clarke, who is attending me, is very attentive, and dear old Wilkie is very kind. I had a visit from Dr. McAndrew yesterday. The old gentleman seemed to be as hearty and robust as ever.

DILKOOSHAH,
March 17th, 1858.

I am not strong enough to travel yet, but directly I am, intend speeding my way to the Hills. Turner kindly wrote about me yesterday. He leaves to-morrow for Futtyghur and then on to Umballa to bring his wife down. This place is taken—completely at our mercy. Sir Colin wants a crore as ransom and the delivery of all the Sepoys. Failing this, he will destroy the native town itself. A strong column under Grant has gone Rohilcund ways, and the Commander-in-Chief will probably scour it with a division, and summer at Simla.

DILKOOSHAH,
March 20th, 1858.

I wish I could see my way up to Umballa, but I

am too weak and too ill at present to be able to stand
such a long journey there. How I wish you were
nearer. Had I only myself to think of I could run
down to Allahabad, slip by steam down to Calcutta,
and get to sea at once. I am sorely tempted to do
so, being utterly sick of the Hills and Upper
Provinces ; but this will never do, I must, when
returning strength allows me, make the best of my
way up to where you and the children are. Half the
regiment was seriously engaged yesterday afternoon
and found itself in a very considerable sort of a fix ;
in nullahs and entrenchments, crowded with Pandies,
who by whole regiments fired at them. Marvellous
was their escape. Hutchinson is, I fear, mortally
wounded, one man killed, five or six wounded, and
some twenty horses killed and wounded. H——
was wounded with an arrow through the eye into the
brain.

DILKOOSHAH,
March 21*st.*

I am feeling decidedly better and stronger to-day,
and wish very much I could see the chance of a move
towards you. I got yours of the 12th, 13th, and 16th
yesterday. What a time you seem to have been hearing of my illness. Don't, please, don't bother Hope,
or anyone about me, I shall obtain a medical certificate to the Hills, but the question is how to get there.
It seems to me, in my present weak state, an awfully
long journey—enough to kill me. All is quiet here
now. Poor Hutchinson is still lying in a very precarious state, more dead than alive. Fawcett cannot

move from rheumatic gout. Coles, who is very rickety, is the only captain fit for duty. Havelock has left Hope's staff and has reverted to his former command in the 12th Irregulars. Steele is going home. Franks is going home sick. I see Mr. Smith every day. Robert Hamilton has been slightly wounded. I wish that Sir Hugh were quicker in his movements. He is at Jhansi, I hear. God bless you. He has been very good and gracious to me, and I have sometimes had very sweet thoughts about heaven.

DILKOOSHAH,
March 22nd, 1858.

I am to leave this on the 25th, hope to start from Cawnpore on the 26th, and be with you on or about the 30th. I shall probably require a rest of one or two days before proceeding by dâk to Kussowlee. I am very weak, but I hope (D.V.) to accomplish the journey. The bearer accompanies me. I am in a very pleasant room here—with all my servants.

Poor Banks, of the Hussars, has lost his right arm and right leg.

LUCKNOW,
March 25th.

My papers will be made out in the course of the day and I hope to be <i>en route</i> to Cawnpore at seven to-morrow evening. I go in a dhoolie as far as Bunnee, and must drive the old buggy in the rest of the way. Once at Cawnpore, it will, I trust, be pretty plain sailing up country. I am feeling much better and stronger, but shall not feel quite happy till I reach Cawnpore. Grant has been successful again near

Seetapore, having taken fifteen guns and dispersed a large force of the enemy. Poor McDonald, of Probyn's Horse, was killed. There are seven of us going to-morrow evening—viz., Steele, Dalzell, Hopkins, 53rd, Thomson, Volunteer Cavalry, Dr. Greenhow, somebody else, and myself. I am afraid I cannot be up at Mussoorie before the 2nd or 3rd, if so soon. Keep your mind easy about me, for I am doing very well, thank God. May He be a tower of rength and comfort to you.

www.ingramcontent.com/pod-product-compliance
Lightning Source LLC
Chambersburg PA
CBHW030934150426
42812CB00064B/2870/J